GERMAN AMERICANS ON THE MIDDLE BORDER

GERMAN AMERICANS ON THE MIDDLE BORDER

FROM ANTISLAVERY TO RECONCILIATION, 1830–1877

ZACHARY STUART GARRISON

Southern Illinois University Press | *Carbondale*

Southern Illinois University Press
www.siupress.com

Printed in the United States of America

23 22 21 20 4 3 2 1

Cover illustration: *St. Louis Turnverein* (St. Louis German Turner shooting club), 1860. Image courtesy of Wilson's Creek National Battlefield, with special thanks to Alan Chilton.

Library of Congress Cataloging-in-Publication Data
Names: Garrison, Zachary Stuart, 1985– author.
Title: German Americans on the middle border : from antislavery to reconciliation, 1830–1877 / Zachary Stuart Garrison.
Description: Carbondale, IL : Southern Illinois University Press, [2019] | Includes bibliographical references and index.
Identifiers: LCCN 2019013292 | ISBN 9780809337552 (pbk.) | ISBN 9780809337569 (e-book)
Subjects: LCSH: United States—History—Civil War, 1861–1865—Participation, German American. | German Americans—Missouri—History—19th century. | German Americans—Politics and government—19th century. | Antislavery movements—Missouri—History—19th century. | Middle West—Race relations—History—19th century. | United States—History—Civil War, 1861–1865—Middle West. | United States—History—Civil War, 1861–1865—Missouri. | United States—Politics and government—1857–1861. | United States—Politics and government—1861–1865. | United States—Politics and government—1865–1877.
Classification: LCC E540.G3 G37 2019 | DDC 973/.0431—dc23
LC record available at https://lccn.loc.gov/2019013292

Printed on recycled paper ♻

To my papa, Joe Gohn

And for Liz and Graham, who reminded me that the sun also rises

CONTENTS

ILLUSTRATIONS

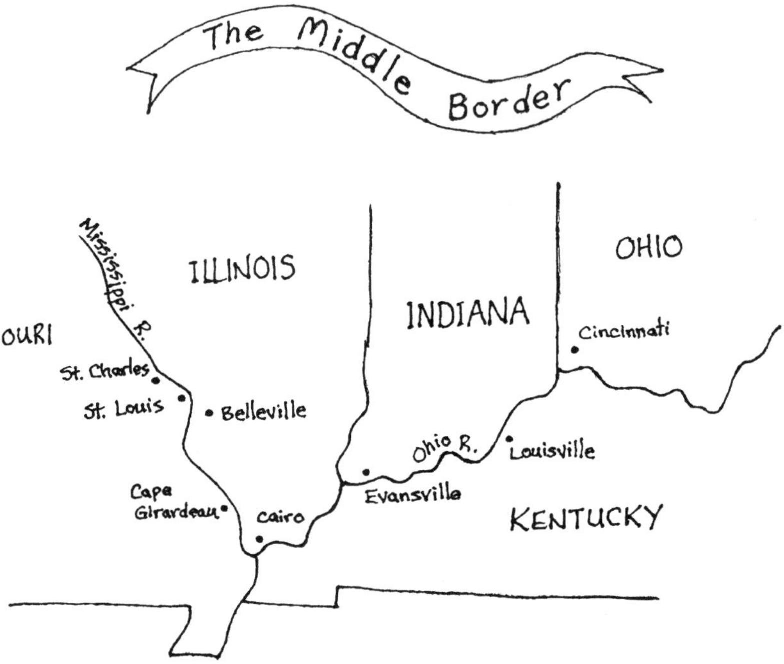
The Middle Border
MISSOURI
ILLINOIS
INDIANA
OHIO
KENTUCKY
Mississippi R.
Ohio R.
St. Charles
St. Louis
Belleville
Cape Girardeau
Cairo
Evansville
Louisville
Cincinnati

ACKNOWLEDGMENTS

I once wrote that writing history “means a sort of self-imposed isolation, and so it is often described as a particularly lonely endeavor.” That changed, however, with this book. Instead of spending my days in libraries and coffee shops, I found myself in classrooms and faculty meetings. Rather than taking sequestered research trips and transcribing sessions, I monitored chess club and went for walks with my wife, our newborn son, and Walt, the dog. All this is to say that this book was an entirely different, and far more enjoyable, experience. The writing came during the quiet hours before school, downtime on vacations, and holiday breaks; in moments between big, life-changing events. In the end, I think the work improved because of this and because of the people surrounding me along the way.

From this project’s beginning, Chris Phillips provided opportunity and guidance, and he was always there with a gentle nudge that would lead me back to the path. On many occasions, Chris went above and beyond, and then went a little farther, all to help me stay the course. Without his encouragement, I never would have attempted this book, let alone completed it. My gratitude extends far beyond the limits of an acknowledgments page, and I hope one day I’ll find a way to repay him for all the kindness he has shown me.

Regarding the oh-so-needed financial support, during the dissertation stage the Taft Dissertation Fellowship provided a year of research and writing that proved tremendously valuable. Several research and travel grants from the History Department at the University of Cincinnati also afforded key opportunities to track down distant collections. Beyond monetary backing, the department’s faculty treated me with kindheartedness. David Stradling in particular set an example that I’ve tried to emulate. While sitting in on his lectures as a graduate teaching assistant, I witnessed some of the best storytelling I’ve ever seen, and I did my best to steal what I could. Maura O’Connor, Willard Sunderland, and Kate Sorrels also stepped in to accommodate an at-times-unconventional graduate career. Without these institutions and these individuals, I would have found myself in serious trouble.

It’s important to also note the many libraries and coffee shops where I sat quietly for hours sipping lukewarm coffee while reading old newspapers, staring at illegible nineteenth-century handwriting, and using their Wi-Fi. Red Tree Café in Cincinnati was a home away from home. I probably played too much chess while there with Tom, but the work was a close second. The Cincinnati History Library and Archives, the Western Historical Manuscript Collection at the University of Missouri, the Abraham Lincoln Presidential Library and Museum, the Filson Historical Society, and the St. Louis County Library, along with several others, provided resources, copies, and solitude. I am especially indebted to the archivists and researchers who transcribed and translated many collections, which allowed this book to reach publication before the year 2030. Finally, I wrote large chunks of the last few chapters at Heavy Riff Brewery in Dogtown.

In many ways, I need to also recognize the contributions of a place. I grew up in an interesting and, as it turns out, inspiring cultural confluence in southeast Missouri. To the north, up the Mississippi River, I found towns scattered among the hills with names like Altenberg, Frohna, Wittenberg, and even Dutchtown. Heading south, I'd soon hit the beginnings of the Mississippi Delta, better known as the Bootheel, marked by long flat stretches of cotton fields and towns called Sikeston, Malden, and Charleston. Not long ago, old men would sit in the small taverns to the north, drinking lager beer and using bits and pieces of a near-forgotten German dialect. Thirty miles in the other direction, barbecue pits and drawling accents redolent of the Deep South were commonplace. Stuck somewhere in the middle, with familial ties to both sides, I found it curious until I was encouraged to try researching a bit deeper—maybe even write a paper on what I found. That was roughly eleven years ago.

When I walked into LeeAnn Whites's office at the University of Missouri to ask if she would direct my undergraduate honors thesis, it must have been painfully clear that I had no idea what I was doing. Professor Whites took pity and suggested a topic, saying something like "What about those Germans?" And off I went. Professor Whites's guidance and encouragement meant the world to me and provided the confidence I needed to apply to graduate school—even though I had no clue what that really meant or would involve. Luckily, one of Professor Whites's graduate students at the time took me under his wing. Sitting at the Heidelberg in Columbia, Missouri, Joe Beilein gave me a glimpse of the graduate student's life and convinced me it was worth pursuing. I haven't entirely trusted Joe ever since.

On arrival in Cincinnati, I made friends with fellow graduate student Matt Stanley. Our shared passion for the St. Louis Cardinals and the Civil War meant that at the very least we always had someone to talk to. Matt's guidance, in both navigating conferences and approaching historiography, was something like an apprenticeship, and it made me a much better historian. Other comrades at UC, including Charlie Lester and Nate McGee, made trudging through grad school far more enjoyable.

I also want to credit Chaminade College Prep for giving me a place to teach history. Having excellent students and colleagues makes a world of difference. I don't think most of my students believe me when I say I wrote a book, so now I'll have evidence. Hopefully, Mr. Z will put up a display in the library.

Whenever my own academic interests threatened to consume my daily existence, my friends—for going on two decades and longer—were there, and have always been there, to point out the absurdities. I could attempt to dramatically encapsulate what their friendship has meant to me, but they would laugh at me for even trying.

My immediate family provides yet another endless source of support and happiness. I've been incredibly lucky to have such a supportive group cheering me on, in particular Nanny and Papa, who together have done so much for me, and Grandma, who possesses perhaps the world's kindest heart. I wish Gramps were around to see this thing get published, but I know he'd be pretty dang proud. My grandparents are joined by a host of aunts, uncles, cousins, and in-laws who all mean a great deal to me. My younger brother, Hunter, has given me so many reasons to be a proud big brother. Topping it all off are my parents: Simply put, there are none better, of that I am convinced. Together, they all add up to one lucky guy. And as Dad would say, "Wherever you go, there you are."

Finally, there is Liz. All the pieces fit together. And now there is Graham. More pieces, better fit.

GERMAN AMERICANS ON THE MIDDLE BORDER

INTRODUCTION

IM ABENDLANDE

In April 1861, amid the chaos and confusion following the attack on Fort Sumter and the commencement of the American Civil War, the *Mississippi Blätter* could see a clear line drawn in the sand. The St. Louis German-language newspaper explained that two sides, freedom and slavery, undeniably rushed toward each other "with unswerving harshness of logic." This logical dialectic, the paper reasoned, was the result of historical forces finally meeting: liberalism's rising tide confronting an aristocracy's coerced labor system, an Old World struggle playing out on the New World's frontier. The two foes could no longer coexist, and consequently, "the very existence of a system of popular government has been placed in question." At all costs, the historically minded editorial insisted, the nation should avoid ancient Rome's failures. Indeed, the "free-soil party of Gracchi's" defeat at the hands of a "corrupt aristocracy" led to the former republic's ultimate doom. Facing its own crisis, the *Blätter* believed that the nation was engaged in a "world-historical mission" and that only with the "party of freedom of this land stands or falls the holiest hopes." Now, confronting the American republic's moment of reckoning, along the Middle Border, the very fault line separating free and slave societies, German American liberalism made clear its ideological position.[1]

Unlike the Northeast's established industrial cities or the South's plantation economy, the trans-Appalachian West in the early nineteenth century, following federally enforced Indian removal, remained wide open in both available land and identity—still malleable enough to fit the many competing visions for its grand future. Beginning in the 1830s, following a series of failed nationalist revolutions in central Europe, German-speaking immigrants arrived in the Ohio and Mississippi River Valleys, then the locus of western settlement. Trying to explain the attraction, one immigrant wrote that he had "no other view than to enjoy liberty—liberty of conscience, of opinion and expression, of religious worship, in a word, liberty in that broad and rational sense in which it is enjoyed *im Abendlande* [in the West]."[2]

The next two decades brought economic strife and more political turmoil in the German states. The combination quickly led to another, more radical-minded wave of immigration to America that followed the same settlement paths along the West's watery highways. Along the Ohio River, which flowed from Cincinnati and continued down with the rushing currents through the falls at Louisville and past the many towns and villages scattered throughout the Ohio Valley before spilling out into the Mississippi, German-speaking immigrants clustered together in tight-knit communities. Though they remained an ethnic minority in the flourishing West, with a wide array of religious and economic constellations, their concentrated numbers proved politically effective and at times transformative, giving some native-born Americans the impression that a German bloc was taking over.

The outsized importance attached to Germans was based on their strength in select locations where they established prominent newspapers, started businesses, and voted in large numbers. By 1860, St. Louis, Missouri, was the epicenter of German American liberalism, home to a number of political refugees still simmering with an unrealized revolutionary agenda. They wasted no time, gathering in the city's many beer gardens, where they formed political and social associations, as well as militias. Arriving in force, they attended rallies and mass meetings and quickly inserted themselves into the American political drama, intent on bringing their *Landsmänner* with them. In short order, their presence was highly visible. In fact, in several major cities and towns along the Middle Border, Germans were found in such concentrated numbers that they stormed their way into the major debates of the day. After three decades of immigration, 31 percent of the population in St. Louis was German-born, as was 27 percent in Cincinnati and nearly 20 percent in Louisville. Over 45 percent of individuals in Evansville, Indiana, who listed an occupation in the census were German-born. In smaller cities such as Cape Girardeau, Missouri, and Belleville, Illinois, over half of heads of households were German-born or second generation. Whether in city neighborhoods or seemingly transplanted villages, Germans used their concerted numerical advantage to alter local and regional culture and politics.[3]

This study situates these immigrants on the Middle Border, the western boundary between slavery and freedom in the era of the American Civil War. It builds on the argument of what historian Stephen Aron has aptly described as the "American Confluence." In this borderland where the Ohio, Mississippi, and Missouri River Valleys meet, the confluence was more than geographic. In this important space and time, the distinct Northern, Southern, and western political cultures collided. And in this place where freedom and slavery had long coexisted, the smoldering debates over the nation's western expansion finally detonated in the 1850s.[4]

The coexistence of freedom and slavery defined the American republic's principal contradiction in the first half of the nineteenth century, and nowhere did this paradox manifest more than on the Middle Border. Though only in its infancy when German immigrants first arrived, the deeply divisive "slave question" became more and more problematic as the nation moved westward.[5] Carrying the Old World strife with them, Germans entered the fray by questioning slave labor's presence in a free society, as well as condemning the inequitable power slavery afforded a small but powerful elite—troublingly similar to the political situation in the world they had left behind. Crucially, these immigrants did not blindly stumble into American politics; rather, they saw themselves as an extension of European liberalism, bringing the ideological struggle to a new battlefield. In their view, it was the Americans, in fact, who naively and unwittingly entered into this contest, and the new nation would benefit from German philosophy and experience. By merging their sharpened beliefs in European liberal nationalism, which emphasized individual freedoms and opposed aristocratic rule, with the burgeoning free labor ideology and the free soil movement in America, German Americans offered their unique voices to the growing antislavery chorus.[6]

On the Middle Border, along both sides of the Ohio and Mississippi Rivers, however, a white consensus firmly opposed any federally enforced emancipation of slaves and denied African American rights of citizenship. From the 1790s until the 1820s, migrants to the Middle Border came primarily from Kentucky, Tennessee, and Virginia. Families moved to and lived on either side of the rivers, perceiving little difference between southern Indiana and northern Kentucky. While the federal government prevented slaveholding across the river, poor white people often owned no slaves, so this proved no major obstacle. Culture, family, and history unified the Middle Border as a region, producing a tightly knit worldview that included white supremacy and support for slavery, which kept black people permanently positioned on the lowest rung of the ladder.[7]

It was only in the 1820s and 1830s, when Northern and European migrants began to arrive, that the Middle Border's uniformity started to crack, which required a circling of the wagons. In line with most white westerners, who portrayed antislavery rhetoric as Northern fanaticism, the *St. Louis Commercial Bulletin* refused to discuss the issue, insisting in 1833, "We contend that no man has the right to discuss the abstract question of slavery." What made slavery an abstract question was unclear, but the newspaper's outright refusal to engage in such dialogue is unmistakable.[8] Highlighting the regional unity, Kenneth Stampp explains, "The inhabitants of [southern Indiana's] river counties often felt a warmer friendship toward their neighbors in Kentucky than toward their fellow citizens in Indiana who dwelt north of the National Road." Until the 1830s, in southern Illinois's "Little Egypt," slave auctions were not uncommon, and salt mines contracted slave labor from across the Ohio River in Kentucky. Across the Mississippi in southeast Missouri, the *Charleston Courier* spoke in no uncertain terms, proclaiming, "Our interests all bind us to the South. With the North we have nothing in common but the English language."[9]

Given that many along the Middle Border held derisive attitudes toward those who even mentioned emancipation in casual conversation, Germans constituted a prominent strain of antislavery thought. Yet historians have more recently contended that characterizations of Germans as unbridled abolitionists rely to some degree on myth, one that Germans themselves had a hand in creating.[10] The historiography has long moved beyond filiopietistic histories and largely deconstructed the mythology, making way for a new debate over the degree to which Germans committed themselves to abolition and racial equality, or whether they ever did at all. To enter into this terrain can be perilous, often requiring qualifications and careful terminology, because the German migrations transported a complex and highly diverse group, ranging from elite intellectuals to illiterate peasants. To attempt broad brushstrokes leaves one wide open to criticism and the quick production of contradictory evidence.

In general, though, a historiographic picture has emerged. Much depends on which Germans are under the microscope. Charlotte Brancaforte's *The German Forty-Eighters in the United States* focuses on the radical immigrants who started newspapers and political organizations with the intention of directly and loudly influencing the political discourse of the 1850s. Mischa Honeck's *We Are the Revolutionists* makes strong connections between radical revolutionary thought in Germany and its transference to the United States, ultimately buttressing the abolitionist crusade. Together, these and other works capture the Forty-Eighters' mentality and impact, and help explain why their exploits are so well known and documented, but also leave a somewhat skewed perspective of German immigrants as overwhelmingly in support of abolition and racial equality.[11]

Additionally, an emphasis on Forty-Eighters alone misses an earlier wave of immigration that arrived a decade before and also tends to ignore the majority of German immigrants, who were not political leaders or simply never embraced full-blown abolition or racial equality. Offering a corrective, Kristen Anderson makes the case that in the 1850s, "St. Louis Germans demonstrated very little opposition to slavery," arguing that Germans in St. Louis only "shifted their position on slavery and the place of African Americans in American society when it benefitted their own community to do so." Anderson offers a detailed case study that emphasizes the conservative forces within St. Louis's German community and takes the absence of radical support for abolition in the 1850s to indicate a "general acceptance of slavery" rather than a general acceptance of abolition or even antislavery. She concludes that most Germans opposed slavery only when events conspired to push them to do so to protect their own interests, leaving radical Forty-Eighters on the periphery.[12]

But if Germans rarely expressed a selfless devotion to African American liberation and equality of the kind espoused by abolitionists, it does not directly follow that they didn't broadly oppose slavery as an institution. This study contends that Germans who arrived along the Middle Border between 1830 and 1860 believed that destroying slavery would remove a labor system and aristocratic class wholly antithetical to the expansion of civil liberty. Yet rather than reinforce the "myth of the freedom loving German,"[13] I argue that when faced with a crisis echoing their European past and therefore capable of destroying the nation, a dominant liberal discourse emerged within the German community that brought cohesion, despite its disparate members and ideologies. This discourse produced unique critiques of slavery and stood in marked contrast to the region's dominant mentalities, pointing the way toward a viable antislavery position on the Middle Border. Understanding these critiques is critical to understanding what underlay the sectional crisis, the rise of the Republican Party, and the war and its aftermath.

A product of European experience, German immigrants grounded their opposition to slavery in the struggle for liberal nationalism. In early nineteenth-century Germany, still a fragmented collection of states, a unified nation capable of protecting individual freedom and political rights stood as the ultimate goal among liberals. Inherent in liberal nationalism was *Bildung*, a philosophical, educational, and political concept that combined the meaning carried by the English word *education* with character formation and moral cultivation into a general spirit of self-improvement and self-consciousness.[14] Among these nationalistic Germans, *Bildung* transcended its educational foundation to encompass an idealistic mission to construct a culture wherein rights and freedoms were guaranteed by the state, thus allowing for individuals to flourish.[15] Brian Vick explains that liberal nationalism "sprouted from the common soil of the late eighteenth- and early nineteenth-century culture of *Bildung*" and "required liberty, rights, broad participation, a common mind" to succeed.[16] In America, the "slavocracy," or the slave-owning elite, starkly undermined liberal nationalism and *Bildung*. As the *Hermanner Wochenblatt* proclaimed in 1848 from the shores of the Missouri River, "Slavery is a stain on our Republic, yes, a contradiction of the very principles of liberty and equal rights of man."[17] In 1833, Gustav Körner, a revolutionary university student turned political refugee in southern Illinois, recognized that slavery was "the rope by which the devil holds the American people."[18]

Within this liberal nationalist framework, German immigrants on the Middle Border understood American slavery and Southern slaveholders as an aristocratic specter of European feudalism.[19] In Europe and then later in America, Germans portrayed the conflict between liberal and conservative forces as an epic historical confrontation whose actors differed only slightly. Although Germans did not come to America specifically to end slavery, they did fully believe that immigration would allow them to cast off authoritative forces.[20] Their challenge to slavery then was broadly conceived as progressive—a dialectical step toward what they believed to be society's betterment. Ultimately, it was a self-interested desire to foster a liberal nation rather than any commitment to racial egalitarianism that guided their efforts to combat slavery. Nevertheless, a self-interested political philosophy that merely questioned slavery's existence was a revolutionary position astride the antebellum Middle Border. Once proslavery forces rose up to threaten the nation, German opposition became more pronounced and radical, but the roots of this opposition ran deep.[21]

In the 1850s, debates over slave owners' constitutional right to transport their human chattel into western territories gave rise to sectional politics and also provided the platform for German liberalism to question slavery's place in a free nation's future. Proslavery Democrats' unwavering commitment to western expansion opened the door to ascending free soil and free labor ideology capable of forging a broad antislavery coalition by advocating for free western lands.[22] Already in 1850, *Deutsche Tribüne* editor J. Gabriel Woerner campaigned in St. Louis for free white workers to flood into the West, which would "exclude slavery from all of the new states being established forevermore." Blocking slave owners would open western lands and "emancipate the white slaves; free them from the yoke of their unsatisfied needs, and on that day . . . begins the emancipation of the unjustly besieged black men in the land of the free."[23]

The real turning point came in 1854 following the passage of the Kansas-Nebraska Act. The federal government had seemingly unlocked land once designated as free territory to slaveholders. Widespread outrage among Germans quickly followed, especially within both the land-hungry working class and idealistic intelligentsia who heard echoes of 1848 and felt the closing fist of aristocracy.[24] In response to Kansas-Nebraska, St. Louis's *Anzeiger des Westens* trumpeted, "The tremendous majority of the citizens . . . are tired of the improper influence of the slavocratic interest."[25] In Evansville, Indiana, Theodore Dietsch asked, "In these days, where slavery shall lie planted into all zones, as a republican law—who in such days can wonder that only a few observe the memory of the fathers of our Republic, and the great principle proclaimed by them: 'that all men are created equal.'"[26] Such stirrings invigorated Germans and gave them a call to action.

Long mainstays of the Democratic Party, Germans on the Middle Border began to question their allegiance following Kansas-Nebraska. Though Democrats had welcomed them into the fold since their arrival, many Germans responded to the polarizing debates over slavery and the West by joining the fledgling Republican Party to support its advocacy of free soil and free labor principles. Recognizing transnational ties, Thomas Bender points out that for Germans, "It was easy enough to identify the parallels between the liberal side of the binary and the North American free labor ideology."[27] And for those Germans who found the stain of nativism and anti-immigrant sentiment within the Republican Party to be an impenetrable wall, they nonetheless severed ties with the Democrats' proslavery wing.

Following Southern secession, many Germans on the Middle Border became convinced that liberal nationalism depended on slavery's destruction, and they were willing to adopt radical measures to ensure the Union's survival. Writing to his wife from the battlefield in September 1864, Indianan Magnus Brucker, a Union soldier, expressed dismay for a war being waged because of "a few ambitious slaveholders," though the "mass of the population does not have any negroes, and slavery is the doom of a free white worker." He noted that in his hometown of Troy, some called him a "black abolitionist," even though he was initially reluctant to back emancipation and what he saw as Northern fanaticism. But he quickly explained that his earlier hesitation was "not because I abhorred slavery as [I] do now and consider it incompatible with a free Republic, but because I feared a civil war and because I thought, that with time and the progress of culture and civilization, the damnable institution would have to pass." When the "damnable institution" was not swept away, Brucker joined the radical wartime campaign to bring about its demise and secure the progress he and other Germans had chased across an ocean.[28] By advancing a radical war for emancipation to preserve the nation, Germans on the Middle Border were portrayed as the "Black Dutch," revolutionary socialists, red abolitionists, outsiders, and representatives of the dictatorial power in faraway Washington. Albert Otis Allen, an ordnance sergeant in the First Missouri Infantry, CSA, expressed concern that Germans would appropriate his property. "I am the lucky owner of a bald-hill in Missouri and if a Dutchman locates on it, if I live, he will wish himself at home on the Rhine. . . . Imagine a raw Dutchman who can't speak our language teaching me principles of Republican government!"[29]

Native-born white people like Allen feared that Germans were shock troops for a radical political and social revolution that would upend the cultural status quo, with emancipation their chief weapon and freedmen their chief allies. That many Germans did eventually embrace radical war aims confirmed those fears and cemented their role as outsiders, aligned with a tyrannical federal government. This was especially true following slavery's demise and Union victory, as racially conservative white people on the Middle Border quickly and overwhelmingly rejected the war's emancipationist legacy. Thus, when the revolution went backward following the war, Germans ironically found themselves, despite having fought on the winning side, on the outside

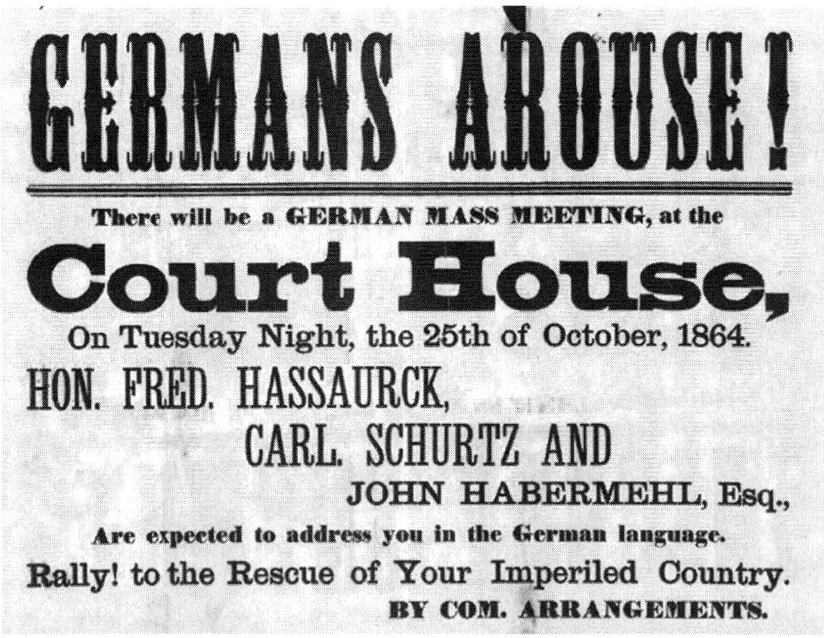

Advertisement for an October 25, 1864, mass meeting in St. Louis, where Germans represented one of the loudest rallying cries in support of emancipation and the radical war effort. German Americans held rallies and meetings in cities across the Middle Border. Courtesy of the Missouri Historical Society, St. Louis; http://collections.mohistory.org/resource/170771.

looking in. Having adopted radical war measures, they now were viewed as representing a foreign power enforcing its will on conservative white people.

During Reconstruction, Radical Republican rule, black civil rights, and federal occupation in the South were widely and often violently renounced on the Middle Border, whether in former free or slave states. Without the overarching cause of freedom and the Union, Germans in the region faced a difficult choice: continue down the radical path or accept a revolution only half complete. The fractures once hidden by a nobler cause became more visible as German socialist voices called for racial unity in preparation for the next struggle against a rising industrial elite, while simultaneously German conservatives grew bold and rejected radical politics designed, they argued, to elevate black over white. Facing this new postwar reality, German liberals began to reconstruct their own position. They argued that their opposition to slavery was pragmatic, an act to save the nation; now, that same pragmatism recognized that to move the nation forward, Radical Reconstruction's severity and divisiveness should be defeated. Arguing that liberalism and *Bildung* did not and never had equated to racial equality or federally enforced integration, they maintained that black men and former Confederates should both be given the right to vote and that freedpeople no longer needed the federal government's protection, thus ending Reconstruction.

When the once moribund Democratic Party reawakened to lead a political counterrevolution, these Germans responded by trying to reclaim the pragmatic middle ground. But they did so in a region lacking any desire to accept compromise along a hard border that as a result of the war had tilted from east-west to north-south. This new border saw Southern, or former slave, states desiring to go backward and return their society to as close an approximation of their slave past as possible; meanwhile, Northern, or free, states claimed their role in saving the Union but rejected black migrants and racial equality. Still, German leadership stood undeterred, and rather than focus on the wounds of the past, they opposed extremism on both sides, whether Northern or Southern style, in favor of national reunion and forward progress. But by 1871, having led the formation of the ill-fated Liberal Republican Party, for these Germans of the former Middle Border, no middle ground remained.

CHAPTER 1

BUILDING A *NEUEN DEUTSCHLAND*

THE DREISSIGER IMMIGRATION AND THE ORIGINS OF GERMAN LIBERALISM ON THE MIDDLE BORDER

In February 1829, Theodor Engelmann, thoroughly enjoying his college experience in Heidelberg, wrote home to relay the news that he had joined a *Burschenschaft*, or fraternity. "We are all strangers, all of us," Engelmann said, "brought together here by similar interests and wants." Providing more than camaraderie and an excuse to gather in local taverns, *Burschenschaften* initially arose in the early nineteenth century across the many German universities in response to French occupation. Later, the groups persisted as a youthful, and at times rowdy, nationalist movement bent on pursuing liberal reform, upending stifling autocratic regimes, and unifying the disjointed German landscape. While largely subdued by reactionary government censors, *Burschenschaften* nonetheless sought subtle forms of resistance as their members schemed in the backrooms of bars and coffee houses. Though unforeseeable to Engelmann and his many coconspirators, their demands for a liberal state and national unity served merely as a rehearsal for the roles they would later play an ocean away in the American West. There, in a most unlikely setting, their deeply held commitment to self-cultivation and individual freedom became embedded. Though idealistic and often naive, these immigrants nonetheless shaped early American discourse on western expansion with their thoughts on land, labor, and definitions of freedom.[1]

After arriving at the university, Engelmann was soon swept up by it all. Idealistically, he boasted to his sister, "The King would do better to concern himself with poetry rather than legislation. The latter should be in the hands of the people who know something about it—like me for instance!" By January 1832, Engelmann had been radicalized. "This may surprise you, but I am now a revolutionary through and through," he wrote to his parents, "for I am convinced that we cannot expect welfare and bliss, or quiet and peace until we, by violence have destroyed all of the old useless and incapable regime." Alarmed though supportive, Engelmann's father suggested emigration to America, hoping his son would seek out "the rich blessings that the banks of the Missouri, the Ohio, the Mississippi offer." His son flatly rejected the idea. "How is it possible that there are people in our time, fainthearted and egotistical enough to want to run away to dig for gold in America?" he asked.[2]

On April 3, 1833, Engelmann, along with his friend, Gustav Körner, led an armed revolt at Frankfort am Main. After being a dealt a disastrous defeat and facing imprisonment, the two young students joined Engelmann's entire family in their journey to the American West. Before boarding his ship, he wrote a farewell letter from Saint Avole, France, saying, "I can no longer wait in idleness—man was created for activity, and if he cannot be busy on a vast scale he must be satisfied with a small field." After traveling down the Ohio River, Engelmann soon found his new home in southern Illinois, and even the nearby bustling city of St. Louis, to be intellectually stultifying and frustrating, like many of his fellow Dreissigers (the label attached to Germans who immigrated to the United States during the 1830s) who made similarly hopeful journeys. Yet it was in Belleville, Illinois, that he would realize his youthful ambitions. As he later wrote to his fiancée in April 1845, by then as the chief clerk of the Belleville Court, it seemed incredible that "twelve years ago today I, and a group of young men who had more enthusiasm for, than experience in, the sacred cause of liberty . . . start[ed] a revolution." Now, transplanted an ocean away, he was an elected official affiliated with the appropriately labeled Democratic Party. Meanwhile, Engelmann's former college roommate and fellow radical, Gustav Körner, sat on the Illinois Supreme Court en route to his position as lieutenant governor. Both traveled a great distance from the taverns of Heidelberg, but in many ways, their vision remained intact. Their revolution, it seemed, had found a second life in the American West, along the banks of the Mississippi River.[3]

Though the idealistic emigration stories of young revolutionaries like Engelmann receive greater attention from historians, the wave of German immigration between 1830 and 1848 was a product of more than political upheaval. Displaced workers coping with protoindustrialization, a growing number of landless peasants, crippling economic downturns, and evasion of forced military service also played important roles in the rush to America.[4] Most immigrants were neither ardent revolutionaries nor middle-class intelligentsia. Still, both radical liberals and those simply pursuing a higher standard of living drew on a shared European past to construct their vision of the future. Optimistically, Engelmann believed that "the people, awakened to self-determination, can no longer remain the means for their princes' selfish purposes." Politically active Dreissigers like Engelmann and Gustav Körner articulated German liberalism's ideals, marked by belief not only in basic rights and privileges but also in democracy and universal freedom. They attached such ideas to the concept of liberal nationhood, which would simultaneously unify German-speaking peoples and protect their rights as citizens. The many German princes to whom Engelmann referred represented an entrenched landed class wholly skeptical of the citizenry. Their intransigence thwarted would-be revolutionaries, and a stagnant economy created a starving working class, sending both groups across the Atlantic. There, progress merged with belief in a national mission, a unified state free from aristocratic control. Such expectations ultimately contributed to emerging notions of American Manifest Destiny while complicating and even challenging prevailing visions of the West.[5]

Arriving at the Middle Border along the boundary between freedom and chattel slavery, German liberalism introduced a new strain of thought not entirely welcomed by a society accustomed to racial hierarchy. Espousing the benefits of a free society and free labor, Germans often explicitly critiqued the degrading effects of human bondage. Though these critiques rarely attacked slavery head-on or called for direct action against its continued existence, nevertheless Germans did not hide their general contempt and disapproval. At times, even this could prove problematic given the fact that, as historian Christopher Phillips contends, many westerners "decidedly did not reject slavery as incongruent with democratic ascendance. . . . For them, slavery was a perfectly democratic institution, consistent with the promise of western expansion." Yet whether in Missouri, southern Illinois's "Little Egypt," or Cincinnati—considered by some the northernmost city in the South—Germans recognized and embraced free labor principles along slavery's border. Though they led no marches and gave no fiery speeches, by simply articulating these attitudes on the Middle Border, the 1830s Dreissigers positioned themselves as a liberal vanguard in America's westward march.[6]

The nineteenth-century liberalism that Germans brought to the Middle Border preceded the political upheaval of the 1850s and therefore was not simply a reaction to an American crisis, but instead was a product of European Enlightenment. Rooted in an idealistic mission, German liberals sought to build a culture dedicated to self-consciousness and self-development, or *Bildung*, wherein the rights of every individual, regardless of class or background, were guaranteed and protected.[7] To ensure a free society, reformers realized the necessity of upending monarchical power and replacing it with a national political body. Uniting Germany's "patchwork of small worlds" meant challenging the chaotic array of local sovereignties that existed under the aegis of the Holy Roman Empire. Before 1806, this proved a difficult task.[8]

Conditions quickly changed after Napoleon's conquering armies marched into the Rhineland and set about dismantling the entire structure by consolidating the incoherent German territories into larger, more manageable states. The French soldiers' constant presence ignited a patriotic and nationalist fervor among German-speaking peoples, resulting in a war of liberation as well as a new sense of national pride.[9] Young university students, caught up in the enthralling rhetoric, wore red, black, and gold as a symbol of unity and heartily volunteered to fight for "*Ehre, Freiheit, Vaterland*" ("honor, freedom, fatherland"). Victoriously casting off Napoleon's domineering presence in 1815 created a shared experience and common cause. Nationalism united people and culture, becoming the framework on which a free society could securely rest, for "being a nation meant being free." Liberals saw clearly that, as David Blackbourn explains, "the nationalist cause and the liberal cause, unity and liberty, went together."[10]

In response to calls for a liberal German nation, conservative forces instead constructed largely independent, modernized states led by a hostile aristocracy intent on maintaining power and privilege within the new top-down bureaucracies. To shut out the *Burschenschaften* and other liberal nationalist groups, the Austrian minister of the state, Klemens von Metternich, oversaw the assembling of the Carlsbad Decrees. Soon unruly professors were fired, radical presses and academic lectures were censored, and a slew of political arrests flooded state prisons.[11]

In the years that followed, acts of defiance were not well received. In 1821, Albert Lange, a law student at the University of Halle, joined "a club, in which the subject of government, political economy, public education, and kindred subjects were treated in lectures prepared by one or the other of the members, and debated with great freedom." Despite the crackdown, Lange and his fellow students "resolved to do all in [their] power to put an end to that despotism, and for that purpose entered into a conspiracy to overthrow the thirty-two big and little tyrants of Germany, and establish one free constitutional government." Lange's efforts landed him in prison. On his release, Lange "repaired to the United States," which he described as "the land of my affection and sympathy, in which the true and enlightened principles of freedom were embodied in those most incomparable instruments, the declaration of independence and constitution of the U.S." Eventually, Lange made his way to Terre Haute, Indiana, where he became involved in local politics and in 1860 was elected state auditor on the Republican ticket, cutting a path other Dreissigers would follow. The key to Lange's story of disenchantment and resurgence was the setting —the American West, a stage on which his grand designs could play out.[12]

Indeed, the New World's myth and mystery acted as a powerful magnet. Nineteenth-century Germany's romantic aesthetic positioned America as the perfect foil, depicting an unadulterated alternative to the repressive, suffocating regimes of central Europe. Growing up with tales of noble Indians and adventurous frontiersmen in America left a young George Husmann longing for "this distant country, [which] had charmed and inflamed our youthful imaginations." When the Husmann family fled Germany, it was no coincidence that their destination was the West, the "promised land."[13] The language and imagery found in the reports, travel accounts, diaries, and letters written by immigrants gave the country an aura of exoticism and fed the fascination, forging powerful links in a chain of migration that stretched across the Atlantic. As information and images poured into Germany, the flow of emigration was often directed down the Ohio River, the great western highway, or up the Mississippi from New Orleans to the great western confluence.[14]

One of the earliest German accounts of the western frontier came from the pen of Gottfried Duden, a lawyer, intellectual, and travel writer. First published in the 1820s, Duden's "Report on a Journey to the Western States of North America" found a wide audience, offering readers a highly stylized and entertaining story. After spending several months in rural Warren County, Missouri, along the Missouri River west of St. Louis, Duden wrote, "I do not conceal the fact from you that the entire life of the inhabitants of this region seemed like a dream to me."[15] This rendering assuredly spoke to those who sought to leave behind Germany's ostensible inertia. Duden's primary audience, however, was not necessarily peasants and laborers. Well educated, Duden instead spoke to those similarly discouraged by Germany's frustrating and stagnant political evolution, juxtaposing that stasis with a natural landscape waiting to be cultivated by German culture and ideals.[16]

The University of Giessen in particular acted as an intellectual training ground for *Burschenschaften* liberals intent on emigrating across the ocean, which made them eager readers of Duden. Following the failed revolution in 1833, the founding of the Giessener Auswanderungs Gesellschaft (Giessen Emigration Society) epitomized the hopes of those willing to start anew. Friedrich Münch, an original member who would later take up the pen name "Far West," anticipated, "The foundation of a new and free Germany in the great North American Republic shall be laid by us."[17] In the same vein, the Giessen Society published and circulated a pamphlet titled "Invitation and Explanation regarding Emigration on a Large Scale from Germany to the North America," which described ambitions including the "founding of a German State, which naturally must become a member of the United States . . . which will assure the continuance of German customs and the use of the German language, and which creates a genuine free life, based on German ideals." Nothing if not audacious, the pamphlet's language expressed familiar sentiments, drawing on the revolutionary goals of a German nationhood.[18]

Though buttressed by sincere optimism, most of the roughly five hundred members who joined the Giessen Society left behind relatively comfortable middle-class lives and were therefore often devastatingly underprepared. A mixture of poor timing, disease, and misinformation resulted in near catastrophe. Those who struggled through took shelter in and around St. Louis's small German community and across the Mississippi River in Belleville, while the more adventurous continued on to rural Warren County, Missouri, to follow in Duden's footsteps. Here, they were somewhat derisively referred to as "Latin farmers" (suggesting that they knew more of Latin than farming; this nickname made clear that the German intellectuals who spearheaded the Dreissiger immigration were not well suited for the endeavor). Their original mission proved naive and ultimately impossible. In fact, after confronting Missouri's harsh conditions, Gustav Körner fell into retreat, settling in Belleville, an area Charles Dickens once described as "oppressive in its barren monotony."[19] Once established, Körner began preparing a correction to Duden and, more specifically, the grandiose depiction of the West. Still a proponent of immigration, a sobered Körner now understood Duden's report to be "excessively bright and much too highly colored."[20] Despite their disappointment, Körner and a sizable number of other Dreissigers continued on to form the German community's political backbone in Missouri, southern Illinois, and Cincinnati.[21]

Notwithstanding the Dreissigers' cultural impress, Belleville, which included an extensive German library, still proved too provincial for Theodor Engelmann. In 1836, he left for the humming city of St. Louis. Writing to his sister, Engelmann praised his new home: "Here in the West, St. Louis must be considered the gathering place of the Germans. . . . There is no lack of German shops, of inns, and beer houses, and new ones arise daily." Like Körner, he encouraged continued immigration, though only after careful planning and establishing more realistic prospects. Seizing on the times, he opened an information agency for German immigrants and, in a stroke of entrepreneurialism, began locating farmland for prospective German buyers, attaching a 4 percent fee. As part of his real estate business, Engelmann also began publishing *Das Westland*, a "North America journal for Germany." It was printed and sold in Germany, where "its usefulness," as outlined in its inaugural issue, could be found "in destroying wrong concepts and exaggerated views of America, and in furthering a correct and clear conception of the country." The truth, though, was that little could be done to temper the grand expectations that easily muffled voices of caution.[22]

Despite the proliferation of rags-to-riches tales, journeys across the Atlantic often ended with a jarring reality that left immigrants scrambling. Many Dreissigers simply lacked the resources to purchase land immediately or make the connections needed to find skilled, high-paying employment. They were forced instead to work menial, labor-intensive jobs for low wages. Left exposed, German immigrants were apt initially to jump at whatever offer was presented. American businessmen hoping to commercialize the West recognized an opportunity in the wave of immigrants pouring down the Ohio River. In November 1838, J. B. McCall wrote to a business partner about his concerns over finding cheap laborers to work on the Wabash and Erie Canal. Fearing that a current contract wouldn't be agreed on, McCall proposed using a new labor source: "If the former and latter [laborers] decline entering into contract . . . I will put on to it a number of Germans and push the competition." The immigrant workers, McCall believed, could undercut negotiations with Americans already on the job. "If the reports are true we shall be overrun with immigrants," he predicted, and if so, they would soon "eat Sourcrout with the Dutch." The forecast proved prescient. As Germans flooded down the river valley, they concentrated around likely job opportunities, forming small German communities in the process.[23]

Dreissigers also fled central Europe to avoid forced military service, furtively avoiding local authorities by boarding a ship bound for America. In Hanover, much to his chagrin, Bennet Baumer Jr. found himself conscripted for a five-year service period. Soon after, in 1833, he and his parents, along with an aunt and uncle, fled and ultimately settled in Richmond, Indiana. Within six months, five more young men also arrived in Richmond after escaping the army, encouraged by those who had already successfully absconded.[24] Carl (Charles) Mayer left Darmstadt in 1839, dodging the draft and leaving behind the authoritarian society he loathed. Writing from his new home in Cincinnati to his half-brother, Gustav, he asked, "Are your prospects better than they were when I left? If not," he suggested, "come to America, if the parents have no objection. I'll be willing to share with you. . . . A young man without money has a better chance here than in Germany." What he particularly enjoyed was the relaxed social decorum, which hinted at an underlying egalitarianism. "If a Lady or the Governor or a Negro comes in the store, you keep your hat on the head and do not make compliments," he boasted. In 1840, he received a letter from Gustav, who remained enamored with the idea of emigration but had not yet decided to leave his home. "You can imagine the joy [your letters] gave us to hear of your continued welfare, and they also furnished me with another reason in my determination to follow you to America."[25]

The great pull of immigration evoked powerful narratives disseminated in many forms, whether through a relative's epistle, an engrossing work of fiction, or simply word of mouth. Among an audience craving the knowledge that a better world existed, success stories found the greatest reception. According to these stories, work was plentiful, the pay was higher, and land could be purchased in dazzling quantities. Such stories were not necessarily false or aggrandized; they just ignored or understated the possibility of dissatisfaction. But wealth and property were quantifiable measures of success, whereas the promise of democracy and freedom proved more abstract and undefined, though no less tantalizing.

Writing home from Missouri in 1838, August Blümmer distilled the Dreissiger wish list: "I invite you to come over here, should you want to obtain a clear notion of genuine public life, freedom of the people and sense of being a nation."[26] Lottchen Engelmann, living outside of Belleville, referenced the cultural and nationalist mission in a letter to her oldest sister, still in Germany: "As to the latter three [culture, art, and science], I hope we bring them along with us to our new country and our new Germany, as we call the region we inhabit now." The outcome, she anticipated, would be wholly successful, and the German community would "grow in time as it takes in all those who sacrificed their security for the liberty of the land across the seas." But she then confessed, "The laments that touch our ears here concern the household, the empty pantry, the boredom, the load of work, the poor quarters."[27] Pursuing an ideal was often undermined by tedious daily chores and western living's requirements; nevertheless, the promise of realizing the Dreissiger ideal continued to attract and inspire.

Hoping to deter emigration, government officials in Saaz, Bohemia, in the Austrian Empire, attempted to change the narrative by writing a tragedy. They published a series of letters written by Jacob Schramm to his family after his immigration to Hancock County, Indiana, in 1835. The government-written preface warned those considering exodus, "It is not uncommon for men, like children, to throw aside what they hold, and grasp at a remote uncertainty."

Schramm's letters, the preface argued, attested to the crude conditions on the American frontier and the grim disappointments that would surely be found by any foolish enough to follow. Those who sought a quick fortune, the preface continued, "have thought to find mountains of gold, and have actually found what they shunned here—work and hardship."[28]

Schramm's experience started with a horrible sea voyage replete with seasickness, vomiting, thievery, and mistreatment from the ship's crew, and his disillusionment only grew after settling in southern Indiana. "In everything written about North America which I have read so far, I have found mistakes, and matters of importance unmentioned," including greedy land speculators, nativism, and an undeniable lack of highbrow culture. "I and my family will be with you again in 7 or 8 years, God willing. I am not disposed to spend my life here in the wilderness." Tellingly, while noting the incongruities between America's promise and its bitter reality, Schramm intentionally avoided slavery's troubling presence. "One could settle in a slave state," he wrote, but advised, "I would never do this. I have no desire to be a taskmaster, and the blacks do little without whipping." No abolitionist, and only vaguely sympathetic to the plight of slaves working on plantations south of the river in Kentucky, Schramm nevertheless articulated the Dreissigers' liberalism. Slavery corrupted both the laborer and those who wielded the whip. Most important, enslaving human beings undermined both the cultural and national missions. One could not claim to live in a free country while simultaneously owning slaves. Schramm would not soon escape this paradox. Rather than retreat to Germany, he remained in southern Indiana and eventually made a small fortune on land investments. Two decades later, Schramm's two sons fought for the Union Army in the Civil War.[29]

For German Dreissigers on the Middle Border, addressing slavery as an idea proved problematic—its mere existence challenged basic expectations of American liberty and life in a democratic society. Yet in the West, whether in southern Illinois or northern Kentucky, the institution was widely accepted. On a basic level, this contradicted the Dreissigers' belief that to progress, all members of a free nation would pursue self-improvement, or *Bildung*; if an entire class were permanently held in bondage, the whole nation would crumble. In 1830s Germany, Johann Jacoby outlined "two opposing parties confronting one another: . . . the rulers and the aristocracy with their inclinations toward caprice and their commitment to old, irrational institutions" and "the people with their newly awakened feeling of power and their vital striving toward free development."[30] Having failed in Europe, the Dreissigers touted German liberalism's potential to realize this free development in the American West.

The Giessen Society's immigration pamphlet anticipated finding "the spirit of freedom," officially prohibited "the legal existence of any kind of aristocracy," and "renounc[ed] the introduction of slavery." Outlawing aristocracy and slavery was a given. Cornelius Schubert, a member of the Giessen Society, described the ship taking him to America as a "stately Medora, which was to take us to the land of freedom and equality, our new Fatherland."[31]

Freedom and equality, however, were incomplete thoughts when set next to chattel slavery and thus proved elusive, as Eduard Zimmermann discovered while traveling down the Ohio River. In a diary meant for future publication in Europe, Zimmerman announced his intention "to spend a few weeks wandering through at least a part of the new *promised land* of the state of Missouri" and discover for himself whether the state, indeed the West as a whole, were truly the place for Germans to settle. Yet Zimmermann's effusive praise for the many natural advantages turned to scorn when he confronted "the shameful practice of slavery." "Against this sin committed against humanity," he exclaimed, "one must strive with all energy." Although later in his diary Zimmermann again referred to Missouri as his "promised land," only a few pages afterward he admitted, "No German ought to live in a slave state."[32] Zimmermann's account suggested the problem of expectation versus reality and the disillusionment felt on discovering slavery deeply entrenched in a land of supposed liberty.

German literature focused squarely on this American contradiction, filling pages with descriptions of bucolic landscapes marred by enslaved Africans. In Heinrich Zschokke's 1832 novel *Der Pflanzer in Cuba*, the protagonist, after immigrating across the Atlantic, decides to continue on to the American frontier. "It will surely become a true Promised Land," he pontificated, "the only country in the world, so far as we know, where men (to be sure, only white men, so far) can breathe freely and enjoy without fear the privileges bestowed upon them." Yet a few years later, in Zschokke's *Ein Buckliger*, a German immigrant in the American West found the "promised land" wanting. While America claimed to be a free country, he instead saw a "land where a colored man is repulsed, despised, excluded from the society of white people, and public republican opinion finds this quite sensible." In J. C. Biernatzki's 1839 novel, *Der braune Knabe, oder die Gemeinden in der Zerstreuung*, a German traveler is shocked to discover that "in the southern provinces the lynch-law, applied to the slaves, is so cruel that every interest shown on behalf of the negroes is severely punished." After traveling through several plantations, he concludes, "Slavery is a poison which, with its blight, dries up every pure, warm, and true sympathy."[33]

But slavery's degradations were not confined to the slave South; the border that separated slave and free was far from impenetrable. Along the Ohio and Mississippi Valleys, where German immigrants settled in concentrated numbers, slavery's presence could be felt on both sides of the rivers' banks. As Stephen Rockenbach explains, "The farmland and communities flanking the river formed an area where the lines between slavery and freedom blurred."[34] Given this proximity to and tenuous separation from slavery, the true danger was slavery's potentially uninhibited expansion and the danger such a scenario posed to a free nation of free workers, the type of nation German liberals expected to discover.

After first arriving in Cincinnati in the late 1830s, Edward Mühl stumbled across the city's canal into the German neighborhood known as Over-the-Rhine. Astonished, he wrote, "It is like a second Cincinnati, or a new German city." Likewise, arriving in the city a few years later, travel writer Friedrich Gerstäcker called Cincinnati "the Eldorado of the German immigrants." Yet Gerstäcker was shocked to see plantations right across the river, plainly visible on the opposite bank. "Slavery, the stain upon the free states of North America," he predicted, "will sometime be the cause of their dissolution, at least of the separation of the Northern and Southern states."[35]After working for five years as a farmhand in Paducah, Kentucky, in 1834 fellow Dreissiger Emil Klauprecht made his way to Cincinnati, where he helped form the German Society. There he also became increasingly aware of the city's precarious position on the border as the debates over slavery began to simmer in the late 1830s and 1840s. "Cincinnati was the main battlefield between freedom and slavery," he later wrote. "Not a month passed when some occurrence refocused attention of this great conflict; often there was the destruction of an abolitionist press, then the mob would demolish the house of a free black man."[36]

In 1840, nearly 20 percent of Cincinnatians were German, and over the next decade, more than 40 percent were either German-born or of German parentage. Drawn to the cultural flowering and financial opportunity associated with the "Queen City of the West," the Dreissiger immigrants quickly established strong roots. These early arrivals, in the words of Bruce Levine, "left a deep impression on the politics of German Cincinnati, providing the city with an able, sophisticated, and energetic group of liberal intelligentsia."[37] Hailing from Württemberg and educated in Heilbronn, Karl Reemelin devoured Gottfried Duden's account along with the letters of a friend who had already immigrated and subsequently became convinced that his future resided in the American West. He spent a year in Philadelphia before setting out for Cincinnati in 1833. Initially, his travel plans included a stop in Wheeling, Virginia, but outside of

Baltimore, he witnessed "the whipping of a female slave." "I regarded this as barbarous," Reemelin wrote, and he changed course to travel strictly north of the Ohio. "I was outside of slave, and inside of free territory," a distinction that meant a great deal. "I came to America with the idea, that here liberty had its last refuge, and that, if it were lost here, it would never be recovered. I believed therefore, that its defense was the first and highest duty of immigrants, that had come here from countries, whose liberty had been destroyed." Within a year of his arrival, Reemelin and Heinrich Rödter, a fellow liberal, founded the German Society, meant to ensure German immigrants could immediately "take part in the people's government." Though far from abolitionists, they worked to enflame democratic institutions, which meant shunning the decidedly unfree institution as much as possible.[38]

For German Cincinnatians, the Ohio River, at least in their minds, provided a physical separation from slavery, but in Missouri, Dreissigers directly confronted the paradox of western progress and democracy existing ostensibly in harmony with chattel slavery. But recognizing the problem did not necessarily create an immediate impetus to correct it, especially for an ethnic minority unfamiliar with the institution's deep roots on the Middle Border.

After moving across the river from Belleville to St. Louis, the young radical refugee Theodor Engelmann had his first experience with enslaved human beings in 1837. "You can discuss this subject [slavery] among acquaintances freely and without restraint," but not in public, he informed his sister. "The main excitement is against people who either try to stir up the colored people directly and incite them to violent uprising against their masters, or those who make it a business to preach liberation of the slaves." Though very much a newcomer and unacquainted with the culture surrounding slavery, Engelmann at the very least understood the inherent dangers of mounting a public critique. Thus he expressed restraint and pragmatism, noting, "The evil cannot be eradicated all of a sudden, but only with the greatest caution." Abolitionists, as he saw it, "are religious fanatics, whose humane thinking I respect, but whose ways and means cannot of course appeal to the Germans." Abolitionists' disapproval of slavery originated from a deeply religious feeling that did not appeal to German rationalism, according to Engelmann, though he still believed that "somebody who is up to the task could, with due caution, set forth these reasons without making the people furious against him," though it remained a risky mission. Still, as offensive as slavery appeared, he admitted, "Since I came to St. Louis I have had very little cause to complain about brutal or harsh treatment of the slaves." But two conditions remained disturbing and stayed with him for years to come: "The worst to my mind is that nothing is done to raise them from the low level of education where they stand (and must stay) and that slaves are very frequently the children of their masters!" Slaves who were offspring of white masters nevertheless could not achieve independence or pursue *Bildung* and would therefore perpetually reside on the lowest rung of the ladder. The system was much like European feudalism with its rigid class hierarchies—only more permanent and lasting. The moral question of masters fathering slave children only added to Engelmann's general abhorrence of slavery.[39]

For immigrants desperately attempting to acclimate to their new home, slavery's incongruities with liberalism could initially be overshadowed by the West's opportunities and even led to benign characterizations and tacit acceptance of slavery as a social and labor institution. The Bruns family came to Missouri as part of the group of Catholic settlers who founded Westphalia in Osage County. They eventually purchased a slave couple along with their child, making them one of the only German families in the county to own slaves. But the Bruns were careful to differentiate their ownership of another's labor from owning another's freedom. Henrietta, or Jetta, the matriarch of the family, wrote to her brother in Germany, "I'm sorry if . . . you were offended that we had some blacks. Indeed, I do not feel very good about it either." But, she continued, "white girls are very pretentious and rarely stay very long." Several years later, however, Jetta reported that their slaves had *elected*, of their own free will, to move on to a new owner. Undaunted, the Bruns simply sought new workers, equating their slaves to the European notion of domestic servants. More telling, after becoming better acquainted with the institution's true nature, Jetta and her husband went on to serve as major advocates of antislavery legislation in Missouri.[40]

Gradually, as Dreissigers gained a clearer picture of slavery, actually becoming a slave master seemed reprehensible. Living in Belleville, Gustav Körner had his own brief contact with slavery in Missouri, which led him to conclude, "No German will find it easy to be comfortable south of the Ohio River in the alien region of the plantations." If a German did buy a slave, the immigrant "must be reviled, twice and thrice over." Körner was most likely referring to Ludwig Eversmann, an original companion of Gottfried Duden and one of the very few Dreissigers to own a slave.[41] In his memoirs, Gert Göbel revealed that Eversmann "became rapidly Americanized. He married an American girl of a very good family and very soon became one of the first German slaveholders." By owning slaves, Eversmann, in the eyes of his fellow countrymen, forfeited part of his identity, for a German and a slaveholder were mutually exclusive. For Göbel, Eversmann was an aberration: "To the credit of the Germans it must be said that there were few imitators in this respect among them."[42]

Such categorical statements suggest the contradictory nature of Germans choosing to settle in a slave state. Friedrich Münch saw the irony and acknowledged, "Most of our countrymen seem to think: 'If I can have the same advantages that a slave state offers, in a free state, I prefer the latter.'" Yet Missouri, Münch argued, was the frontier, a western state where, compared with free states farther east, there was "still the possibility of purchasing land without having to pay the staggering prices."[43] An immigrant living in St. Charles County informed a visiting German pastor, "You see, Herr Pastor, America is indeed a splendid land. Here a person can still acquire something. In Germany, I didn't have as much property as I could hold in my hand."[44] Such possibility seemed to hinge on the belief that the West remained malleable, still open and undetermined, where slavery was perhaps only a temporary condition. At the very least, the cheap and abundant land helped Germans convince themselves that slavery would eventually be crushed by progressive western settlement. Potential rewards, then, outshone distant dangers.

The experiences of two immigrant families support the contention. The Schlebbe family left Lower Saxony specifically for the opportunity to purchase land in Stallostown, Ohio. The family learned of the small colony from neighbors who had immigrated years earlier. Though the colony had initially been successful, by the time the Schlebbes arrived, conditions had changed, leaving the family gravely disappointed. Land speculators purchased the most desirable tracts, and within two years both the mother and father died during an outbreak of typhoid. The family splintered and several continued westward, seeking the land and opportunity that appeared out of reach in Ohio.[45] Conversely, in 1837, Friedrich Freking, a soldier in the army of the Kingdom of Hanover, deserted and immediately made plans for emigration. He managed to persuade his uncle Friedrich Dierking to sell the family farm, gather up a collection of family members and neighbors, and set out for the American frontier. In all, fifteen individuals put their faith in the stories they heard of promising virgin land that sat there waiting. After arriving in Lafayette County in central Missouri, Dierking pooled all his profits from the sale of 50 acres in Esperke and quickly purchased 880 acres of government land in Freedom Township, a savvy move that increased his property holdings by 1,300 percent.[46]

Still, however alluring the draw of available and cheap land, slavery's presence could not be ignored forever. Further exposure to fields filled with black laborers and a growing awareness that the state's political machine was driven by slaveholding families challenged the liberal Dreissigers' idealization of Missouri and the West in general. While contemplating moving his family to Missouri, Frederick Steines succinctly summarized the dilemma: "I cannot see how a freedom-loving German can subscribe to the principles of slavery, and it certainly must require a great deal of Americanization in order to start a negro factory."[47] Despite this, German immigrants did settle in Missouri in large numbers, themselves producing a paradoxical arrangement bound to create tension. And in fact, rather than subscribe to slavery, many subtly undermined it. As historian Alison Clark Efford outlines, over the next three decades, antislavery in Missouri became "more closely identified with German ethnicity than in any other state." Just as upland Southern slaveholders and ambitious northeastern merchants understood the state's significance to western expansion, German liberals believed that free land and free labor's western progression were the crucial elements to securing a free nation.[48]

After his initial journey to the frontier, Eduard Mühl depicted Missouri as "unspoiled," the perfect place to transplant his young family. But after arriving in 1843, he was deeply disturbed by the sight of enslaved men and women. In the 1820s in Germany, Mühl had attended the University of Leipzig, an epicenter of rationalist thought, and promptly announced his new status as a "free-thinker." When it just as promptly resulted in his censure, Mühl set out for America and the freedom to say and preach whatever he so chose. In Cincinnati, he established the *LichtFreund* (Friend of Light), a rationalist newspaper that he continued to publish in Hermann, Missouri. In the new iteration, though, he added antislavery editorials, making the *LichtFreund* one of the earliest antislavery papers in the West. In one of the first editions, Mühl announced, "People and animals are here not for the purpose of slavery." Shortly thereafter, along with surviving members of the Giessen Society, then living in nearby St. Charles and Warren Counties as well as St. Louis, Mühl formed the Freie Männer Verein (Free Men's Society), which discussed as one of its topics the corrupting influence of slavery.[49]

Though the Dreissigers' clear disapproval of slavery rarely took the form of public rebuke or political protest, their position was more than just a harmless curiosity to many American-born settlers, slave owners or not. Already in the 1830s, slavery was highly politicized in the West. Slavery's presence by means of the Missouri Compromise was in reality a fragile balancing act, achieved only through the machinations of national proslavery politicians and careful placation of Northern dissenters. Dreissiger Gert Göbel noted that even the subtlest critique of slave labor could ignite a firestorm. "As friendly and hospitable as these people [American or native-born] were with strangers," he explained, "this friendship soon ceased as soon as they suspected [Germans] of being abolitionists . . . they regarded with distrust every stranger who came from a country where slavery was not permitted."[50]

Confirming Göbel's assertion, Gustav Körner recounted the infamous 1836 McIntosh incident, in which a free black man in St. Louis was arrested after allegedly stabbing and killing a police officer. Despite conflicting reports, a mob kidnapped the man, chained him to a tree, and burned him alive. William Weber, the editor of the *Anzeiger des Westens*, one of the largest Germans newspapers in the country, published an editorial that condemned the mob. "Last night we were eye witnesses of the most gruesome thing," he wrote. "Citizens of St. Louis! The blot with which your city was sullied last night, you will not be able to wash away." In response, another St. Louis paper, the *Commercial Bulletin*, expressed outrage at the *Anzeiger*, warning that Weber ought not "insult the community, in which he himself is a stranger," and suggested the paper's offices be stoned.[51]

Rather than back down, Weber rejected the suggestion that as a foreigner he had little right to criticize his American neighbors or their institutions. "Though we know how to treasure the kindness and magnanimity of the American People, nevertheless we are by no means dependent upon them," he wrote. Though Germans "came to these hospitable shores as fugitives," they fled "for the sake of freedom" and therefore could not be silenced. Months later, the *Anzeiger* came out emphatically against the nomination of yet another Democratic presidential candidate, Martin van Buren, who opposed any limits placed on slavery and insisted on its protection under the Constitution. As far as the *Anzeiger* was concerned, here was a candidate "whose interests favor the principle of slavery." As Weber made clear, Germans sought freedom in America, while Van Buren and slavery labor's proponents seemed to be offering the opposite.[52]

Well before the 1850s sectional crisis, the Dreissigers made their aversion to slavery well known along the Middle Border as their own interests and expectations increasingly intersected with national confrontations over western expansion. To be sure, local concerns surrounding issues like temperance or German-language instruction in schools garnered much attention, but burgeoning debates over slavery, territorial expansion, and the right of foreign citizens to decide such national issues held the potential to unravel *Bildung* and liberal nationalism. In 1834, it was already clear to Gustav Körner that "no parties in the United States stand so starkly against one another than those for freedom and slavery," and he predicted that "a division of the country into two or three parts could be made, which would naturally only take place as the result of a major civil war."[53] Past European experience had taught the importance of an organized, cohesive effort when facing such a dialectical confrontation. The liberal cause in Germany had splintered, leaving progress and reform to die a quick death, but the Dreissigers in America recognized that the war was not over.

The Dreissigers' liberal nationalism articulated an ideal—pursuing a free society wherein all citizens would play a role in moving the nation forward. In many ways, such efforts contributed to early expressions of Manifest Destiny, while emphasizing far more intensely the necessity of free labor and free soil, well before such phrases entered political parlance, to fulfill the national mission and a culture of *Bildung.* As western expansion forced the rest of the country to finally confront the great contradiction of liberty and slavery as it played out on the frontier, the Dreissigers found themselves in the unlikely position of shaping the discourse and perhaps even tilting the balance. Arriving at a remarkable moment and in a remarkable place, German immigrants in fact constructed an early articulation of liberal Unionism along the very lines and borders where the nation slowly began to fracture.

CHAPTER 2

THE POLITICIZATION OF GERMAN LIBERALS

THE REVOLUTION OF 1848 AND THE SECOND WAVE OF GERMAN IMMIGRATION

Founded in 1835 in St. Louis by liberal Dreissigers, the *Anzeiger des Westens* immediately courted controversy by denouncing a mob execution of a black shipyard worker accused of murder. Continuing on in this fashion, the newspaper made persistent jabs at slavery at a time when such talk often led to violent reprisals, signaling a determination to shape regional culture and politics. But by the summer of 1848, the *Anzeiger des Westens*, the largest German-language newspaper in the West, had lost some of its edge.[1]

Though the newspaper served as German liberalism's outspoken voice in the West, the *Anzeiger* slowly became mired in the demands of America's Second Party System. During the 1840s, Germans on the Middle Border were drawn to the Jacksonian Era's egalitarian themes and overwhelmingly threw their support to the Democrats. Through this affiliation, they successfully entered the political fold. But their ascendance came with a price: an expectation to maintain a general silence on the divisive issue of slavery. Territorial expansion and growing sectional tensions in the West during the late 1840s, however, posed a challenge to German party loyalty, a dilemma the *Anzeiger* would not easily escape. It was at this moment of heightened sectional anxiety that the failed German Revolutions of 1848–49 initiated a second wave of immigration to the United States. A new generation of radical thinkers and a host of disgruntled, politically conscious laborers, together known as Achtundvierzigers, or Forty-Eighters, arrived at a time when German American liberalism was at a crossroads. Though far from harmonious, the combined efforts of Dreissigers and Forty-Eighters pushed forward a broadly conceived version of liberal nationalism that wove together individual freedom and self-improvement with emerging calls for free land and labor in the West.[2]

By the mid-1840s, national party politics was entirely dependent on sectional compromise. But this fragile equilibrium began to crumble when the Mexican-American War broke out in 1846, and as a consequence, slavery was at the forefront of every partisan discussion. With the expectation of future territorial acquisitions extending to the Pacific Ocean, slavery's expansion to the West gained new traction. David Wilmot, a Democratic congressman from Pennsylvania, hoped to stymie such a scenario by proposing a bill prohibiting slavery from any new western lands. After passing the House, Wilmot's proviso died in the Senate, but the furor that erupted suggested a growing sectional rift.[3]

Two years later, with the war concluded, the *Anzeiger* reasoned that there was no need for the federal government to legislate against slavery in the former Mexican territories. The institution was already outlawed there, especially in California, where "no one, despite every form of permission, would carry slaves." Conceding to Wilmot's concerns, the *Anzeiger* was thoroughly "averse to the principle of slavery," but its editor, demonstrating a keen faith in nationalism, insisted, "Above all else we wish to keep our Union, unbroken and undivided, and in its continuance alone can we perceive security and freedom and for the gradual development of freedom throughout the whole world." But just a few months later, the *Anzeiger* eagerly dismissed the slaveholder and Whig presidential candidate Zachary Taylor, lamenting that "a man who is running for President of a free country makes money by selling human beings." In desperation, the liberal mouthpiece of German Americans in the West sought to somehow reconcile antislavery feeling with party fealty, a denunciation of slavery with national union. But such neutral ground was quickly disappearing.[4]

Two developments in 1848 altered German American liberalism's course on the Middle Border: the free soil movement, which emerged to defy slave labor in the new territories, and the uprising in Germany. The unrest consisted of students and intellectuals renewing the call to expand individual freedoms and middle-class liberals seeking broader political representation with constitutional reform. But workers and laborers, displaced by Germany's painful industrial transition, along with socialist activists who welcomed the class conflict as necessary and inevitable, insisted on profound socioeconomic change. The demand for broader, more inclusive representation briefly brought together these varied strands of political consciousness, but the revolution's inchoate makeup led to internal strife and ultimate collapse.[5]

Like the Dreissigers before them, the Forty-Eighters ultimately set their sights on America, the grand republic across the sea. They brought with them a magnetic intensity and zeal for reform, the rights of free citizens, and equitable opportunities to pursue self-improvement, which they quickly, and often bombastically, reconfigured in the context of their new homeland. For the *Anzeiger*, free soil ideology offered the first glimpse of an alternative to western proslavery expansion, but it took the arrival of a Forty-Eighter journalist and erstwhile playwright to steer the most-read German newspaper in the West directly into the eye of the storm.[6]

In July 1850, months after assuming the editor's duties at the *Anzeiger*, radical journalist Heinrich Börnstein published his thoughts on an upcoming election in a city where he had only recently arrived. In his "Address to the German Citizens in the Counties of Missouri," Börnstein argued that beyond nativists, or anti-immigrant, Whigs, Germans ought to consider a new threat, "those seceders from the great Democratic party." For Börnstein, "seceders" threatening to dissolve the nation trumped all other concerns. For a Democratic paper to instruct its reader to turn against Democratic candidates identified as potential "seceders" and yet remain loyal to the Democratic Party seems antithetical. But as Börnstein later explained, "I was bound by the fact that my paper was a Democratic mouthpiece. My readers and subscribers all belonged to the Democratic Party, and the Democratic Party was none other than the slaveholders' party." The solution, Börnstein believed, lay with Northern antislavery Democrats like Missouri's Thomas Hart Benton, who had broken away from proslavery colleagues and opposed slavery's unrestrained spread by subtly embracing free soil ideology.[7]

Northern antislavery Democrats strictly adhered to Jacksonian political thought but emphasized an egalitarian democracy incompatible with slavery. As a result, they broke away from their Southern colleagues, at least in principle, well before the cataclysms of the 1850s, by "linking their antislavery opposition to a land reform agenda that pressed for free land for poor settlers, in addition to land free of slavery."[8] Overlooked by historians is the impact made by German Democrats on the Middle Border, often the strongest supporters for free soil within the Democratic Party. When Börnstein implored his German audience to seek out these progressive Democratic candidates lest they "be governed from above, as you were in Germany," he drew on the collective experience of two generations of liberals who had fought this fight once before. Forty-Eighters' zeal combined with the reach of an established Dreissiger newspaper pushed

Germans to embrace free soil, opening the door to a new and more acceptable critique of American slavery, one that combined Jacksonian democracy with the universal pragmatism of *Bildung* and liberal nationalism.[9]

In many ways, the Forty-Eighters' agenda in America developed its rationale in a European context. The revolutionary outbursts in 1848 and 1849, which nearly brought down German monarchies, worked as a continuation of the liberal nationalism expressed in the 1830s. Inspired by the abdication of France's king Louis Philippe and the resignation of Austria's widely disdained prince Klemens von Metternich, the movement had an intensity and breadth that indicated heightened participation. To press back against emerging ills of industrial capitalism, which empowered the aristocratic class and created fundamental economic dislocations across Europe, "the nation emerged as the principal nexus with the ability to bind together an imagined people across a given distance." The liberal nation could guarantee political and natural rights for all. What exactly this meant, or what that nation might look like, was up for interpretation.[10]

The mounting pressure for such a framework culminated in the Frankfurt Parliament of 1848, bringing together delegates charged with replacing the outmoded German Confederation with a liberal nation-state. For the majority of representatives, "nationhood required liberty, rights, broad participation, a common mind and will, if it was to have any real meaning, any real existence, at all."[11] The challenge would be defining the proposed nation's boundaries and, just as important, who qualified as a German citizen. Tracing the evolution of citizenship and national identity in Germany through the first half of the nineteenth century, Brian Vick argues that generally, across the spectrum of liberal representatives, biological or racial qualities as a basis of national belonging appeared far too immutable and counterproductive. Instead, most representatives "preferred to emphasize the role of human freedom over natural necessity." As a result, Vick maintains, free will rather than biological determinism influenced thoughts on race. "No one denied inequality—they were not that relativist—but neither did they feel they had to accept the situation as permanent or rooted in the blood." Through *Bildung*, through self-improvement, any man (those calling for gender equality were very much in the minority) could belong to the nation-state. To think otherwise would suggest the legitimacy of a hierarchical society and lend credence to the notion that some were meant to rule while others were only to serve. Many of these same representatives would confront similar questions of belonging in America, but in the immediate moment, they faced the task of hammering out a clearly demarcated German nation and people.[12]

Initial uprisings and protests proved successful, even forcing Prussia's king Friedrich Wilhelm IV to support unification, but there remained a great divergence of expectations. The movement's fundamental weakness was the separation between moderates who cautiously believed in the idea of a constitutional monarchy and radical democrats who sought nothing less than a true republic.[13] But the revolution broke down further, relying on a coalition of peasants, artisans, and laborers hoping to dismantle the great estates and reduce taxes and debts—essentially, break the grip of the landed aristocracy—alongside the budding bourgeoisie (*Burgertum*) consisting of liberal intelligentsia, activist students, and professionals who desired, largely for themselves, a broadening of civil rights and general political representation. The clash between modest liberal aims and more ambitious democratic demands stalled debates at Frankfurt. Radical displays seeking full male enfranchisement and complete popular sovereignty only increased general fears that the whole endeavor might go too far. Fissures widened and moderates retreated behind traditional powers. The Frankfurt delegates broke into squabbling factions, losing the strength of a united front. With blood in the water, conservative forces swooped in for the final victory.[14]

In the aftermath, many of the most radical and voluble Forty-Eighters dramatically began the exodus to America. But despite all the passionate ideological rhetoric and political theorizing, the bulk who left Germany after 1848 did so in reaction to a combination of a depressed economy and a complacent elite who made no attempt to ameliorate the financial hardship. To make matters worse, the uneven and rapid industrialization that eroded traditional trades only worsened after the revolution's collapse. Historian Bruce Levine's careful analysis of Germany's economic landscape demonstrates the direness of the situation on the eve of the revolution. For one example, by 1848 in the Kingdom of Saxony, 70 percent of families owned no land, and nearly a third lived in cities where they found employment only in low-paying wage work in small-scale manufacturing. For many, this dramatic transition from an agrarian workforce to a new urban industrial reality proved debilitating. The customary guild system's undermining by wage labor and piecework was the grand symbol of disruption. Conversely, those who did not leave for cities and towns often remained mired in feudal-like conditions governed by landed aristocrats, relying on cottage industries to survive. One German contemplating immigration to America offered the full range of motivating factors: "the ease with which land can be earned there, the absence of restrictions on commerce, trade, and traffic; low cost of living, political and religious freedom, absence of a standing army, and, at the same time, the undisputed internal as well as external peace."[15]

Because so many immigrants located their motivation to emigrate within the maelstrom of Germany's punishing economy, many historians assert a lack of ideological or political engagement. Marcus Lee Hansen's influential article "The Revolutions of 1848 and the German Emigration" completely dismisses a direct connection between the social revolution and the economic emigration that followed.[16] Historian Theodore S. Hamerow argues that most Forty-Eighters were not radical democrats motivated by ideology, but were instead "interested in economic rather than political improvement." He acknowledges intellectuals' and radical orators' presence but insists that they constituted a minor element. Hamerow suggests that radical Forty-Eighters were simply far more verbose and visible than the mass of German immigrants after 1848, who focused first and foremost on securing a wage.[17] As a result, these and other historians have concluded, radical Forty-Eighters garnered more attention and came to inaccurately represent immigration writ large. The problem with this characterization is not demographics or the emphasis on economic push factors, but the narrow definition of political activism.

While more celebrated German revolutionaries pursued political upheaval, vast numbers of shopkeepers, workers, and peasants protested economic oppression. Their end game was not so different. Such a claim does not mean all who left the German states in 1848–49 were driven purely by ideological reasons, but rather widens the definition of protest. Historian David Blackbourn finds numerous examples of mass popular participation, as "peasants, rural laborers, journeymen and industrial workers demanded redress of their grievances and engaged in direct action." Though historians might dismiss such popular action as the result of empty stomachs and empty pockets, Blackbourn insists, "We should not overlook the powerful moral categories that underlay popular anger: the right to the fruits of one's labor and a fair wage."[18] Indeed, class antagonism, anger directed toward political nobility, and demands for new forms of political representation were broadly expressed—if many rural peasants were not outright radicals, they nevertheless reacted and participated in a less obvious capacity. Levine describes the local workingman associations (*vereine*), singing societies, and other social organizations as the "shock troops" of the revolution. Carl Wittke, a leading scholar on the Forty-Eighters, contends that "more of the revolutionary forces were drawn from the rank and file than from the intellectual or upper classes."[19]

While serving a brief imprisonment following his participation in the storming of the Dresden arsenal in May 1849, University of Leipzig student Frederick Behlendorff studied American history, later claiming the experience "opened new visions to me and directed my attention more and more to that land of supposed liberty." After his release, Behlendorff immigrated to southwestern Illinois and later enlisted in the Thirteenth Illinois Cavalry. But his memories of the revolution and his fellow dissenters remained inspiring. "This revolution was headed by substantial citizens and supported by armed men from all ranks of life. But principally," he insisted, "the young men from the agricultural districts, mechanics, and some students." He also remembered peasant women who "poured boiling water and pitch on the heads of the advancing Royal troops," and one young woman, Pauline Wunderlich, "divested the corpse of her betrothed of his uniform which she donned herself. She took up his rifle and ammunition and followed us behind the barricade."[20]

By merging political and socioeconomic conflict in Germany, historians can likewise expand the definition of the politically conscious Forty-Eighter immigrant beyond the gallant radical exile. James F. Harris insists, "Political motivation must be seen as including those who took issue with restrictions and controls in nonpolitical areas like religion, as well as those irritated with the economic policies of the German trades . . . [and] those frustrated by the class structure of the political world."[21] And when protest failed, emigration itself was in fact a political act.[22] Thus, when many ultimately settled in the American West, both the German artisan and radical newspaper editor could blend social and economic concerns with ascending free soil and free labor ideologies: a landed aristocracy that used slave labor could not be allowed to dominate free western lands meant for free workers. To be sure, racial egalitarianism was not the driving force; abolition was almost entirely absent. Instead, by destroying slavery, German liberals believed the doors would be thrown open for free white workers, laborers, and farmers. This was a political and economic position that nearly all Forty-Eighters, regardless of class, supported.[23]

Germans who arrived in America from the 1848–49 emigration cannot be sharply divided into the intellectuals, fleeing from failed revolutionary efforts and seeking to pursue their political ideals as refugees in a democratic nation, and the struggling masses, completely lacking political consciousness. Such an approach is far too limiting.[24] Forty-Eighters established newspapers, formed political associations, and demanded a reinvigorated liberalism from the German community—often to the annoyance of their countrymen. But it is impossible to see the number of newspapers sold, memberships added, or elections won and conclude that the German immigrant community remained entirely segregated from or apathetic about political causes.

Importantly, as the seasoned Dreissiger generation was quick to remind, Forty-Eighters did not enter into an enervated German American community lacking political will. Gustavus Wolfing left Germany along with his two brothers in the late 1830s, originally settling in Indiana before heading successively to Cincinnati, Louisville, and St. Louis in 1842. He followed the news of unrest in Europe closely, advising family in Germany, "As long as there are emperors and kings there can be no freedom. I am sure that you would share my point of view, if you had been a citizen of our fortunate free America for thirteen years, as I now I have been." The American experience transformed Wolfing into a free citizen, a status the Forty-Eighters couldn't yet entirely comprehend. In fact, the Dreissigers maintained that it was only because of their previous activity and engagement with American politics that the Forty-Eighters could find a solid entry point.[25]

The chronological gap between the early 1830s and 1848, then, is crucial to understanding the environment the Forty-Eighters so confidently inhabited. As sectional debate ignited in the mid-1840s in the Ohio and Mississippi River Valleys, the Dreissigers began to find space to maneuver. With western territories cut up and reorganized, old questions concerning slave labor reemerged with a vengeance. In search of answers, new fringe political platforms began to form solely around the issue of slavery, sending the two traditional political parties, Democrats and Whigs, furiously counting votes. Suddenly, thanks to the almighty power of the ballot, German Americans could leverage their small but growing numbers. This was true for the liberal Dreissigers on the Middle Border, who found western Democrats especially welcoming. In addition to the loyalty of St. Louis's *Anzeiger des Westens*, in 1843 Cincinnati's *Deutsche demokratische Verein* announced its unqualified support for the Democrats and the belief in "equal rights and complete justice for all men, irrespective of religious or political beliefs."[26] The Dreissiger Friedrich Münch based his political ideas on a combination of Jefferson's faith in the independent farmer and Jackson's support for the common man. "Withdraw from man the right of property," averred Münch, "and you snatch away from him the strongest lever upon profitable activity and purest source of happiness." Extending his argument, and essentially outlining an early form of free soil in the West, he reasoned that democracy could continue its destined course "as long as public lands set aside for settlement are available."[27]

For Germans, the Democratic Party's western branch during the 1840s did not yet represent slavery's protector, but rather the common man's benefactor. Conversely, the Whigs far too closely resembled the Fatherland's erudite nobility. And as the Democrats enlarged the electorate by expanding male suffrage, they fashioned a political rhetoric meant to attract workers and small farmers, as well as immigrant voters. In 1839, Bazil Edmonston, a staunch Jacksonian Democratic politician in southern Indiana, cheered German immigrants' arrival because he believed they would tip the balance in his party's favor. "We have hundreds of Germans pouring into our country," he reported. "In a coming day they will be the strongest party, all Democrats." With the immigrants' help, Edmonston felt confident, asserting, "The Germans will soon outnumber the Americans and they nearly to a man are Democrats."[28]

An entirely new and foreign population along the Ohio and Mississippi Valley was not a welcome sight for all, especially as political affiliations and cultural preferences became more evident. Characterizations of Germans as Europe's financially destitute, drawn from the lowest classes, proved an effective tool for those who perceived a political and even cultural threat. Chronicling his travels down the Missouri River, Solomon Eby expressed disgust with his fellow passengers. "The boat was crowded with German immigrants on deck who were filthy in the extreme, shamelessly picking lice from their bodies and heads."[29] By the mid-1840s, nativism, an anti-immigrant ethos, began to employ such representations to actively work against German political involvement, all while enjoying the Whig Party's tacit support. The *St. Louis American* grumbled over steamboats carrying German immigrants who seemed incapable of ever truly becoming Americans. "This Bremen hive seems in no danger of being emptied of its serf and pauper hordes. They come in swarms, like Egypt's locust—but the locusts change their character—annually; the Germans never. Once a Dutchman, always a Dutchman."[30] The following years brought even larger numbers of Germans to cities such as St. Louis, Louisville, and Cincinnati, leading nativists to amplify claims that immigrants stole job opportunities, drank copiously—even on the Sabbath—and, most regrettably, threw their votes away to the Democrats.[31]

Yet if Germans found animosity on one side of the widening two-party aisle, they could by no means ignore complications on the other. Cincinnati Dreissiger Karl Reemelin enjoyed great success with Democrats, including his election to the Ohio State Legislature, where he saw to it that all public documents were also printed in German. But with continued genuflections to the southern wing of the Democratic Party, such affiliations proved a millstone for Reemelin and other idealistic Dreissigers who, after all, had fled Germany as "refugees for the sake of freedom." During the debates over Texas's annexation as a slave state, Reemelin, who felt no sympathy for abolitionists, prepared a report announcing that he "was not in accord with any of the movements, that would convert the United States into an agency for furnishing lands to slave-holders, and for colonizing them with negro slaves." Constitutionally, Reemelin would never suggest the federal government possessed the right to abolish slavery in the South, but as the nation moved west, he could not support the institution's perpetuation and thus undermine progress by propping up an elite class that threatened the Union's destiny. Such a predicament continued to haunt Dreissiger Democrats as they navigated the increasingly muddy waters of sectional politics on the eve of the March Revolution.[32]

Since March 1848, when news of an uprising first crossed the Atlantic, finally reaching Gustav Körner's home in Belleville, Illinois, excitement spread among the city's predominantly German population. On learning of five hundred liberals and democrats in Frankfurt who gathered with the intention of forming a national parliament, Körner wrote, "I must say, my heart swelled with joy at the intelligence. The ideal of my youth for which I had sacrificed all, seemed in process of realization." After his own revolutionary attempt fifteen years earlier ended ignobly, Körner narrowly escaped and joined Theodor Engelmann, a close friend and fellow subversive, in search of asylum in the American West. There, aspirations of living in a free republic soon materialized, though very quickly, Körner saw his expectations subverted while traveling down the Ohio River. In Louisville, he recounted, "we put our feet for the first time on slave soil. What we heard here and what we saw, (for instance, negroes chained together hauling water from the river) contributed to our detestation of the institution of slavery" and ultimately led to his settlement in the free state of Illinois. After leaving Kentucky soil, he wrote in his daybook, "As long as the Southern States uphold the institution of slavery, so long shall I believe that this beautiful structure of the United States will break down, and so long will the liberty of the whites, in which they now rejoice, be only a half-deserved boon." But in his immediate environment, such thoughts found no audience, and after settling in a free state unencumbered by slave labor, Körner joined the Democratic Party. The ability to collect German votes resulted in his election to the Illinois House of Representatives in 1843 and the state supreme court two years later, his star quickly rising.[33]

But the distant rumblings in Europe reminded Körner and other Dreissigers of their own youthful causes and sacred vows. Matching efforts in St. Louis and Cincinnati, Belleville Germans offered financial support to the revolution and also attached an encouraging message, drafted by Körner. The address acknowledged—drawing on firsthand experience—that joining the cause would be difficult while many still "hesitated to take the decisive leap from the darkness of slavery into the clear light of liberty, [yet] we feel prompted to urge this upon you." So stirred by early victories, Körner even contemplated returning to join the fight. But before serious preparations could be made, a letter from his brother Charles, still in Germany, warned, "Don't leave your free sphere. . . . The revolution has halted half way." Regardless, the revolutionary spirit made its way to Körner and southwestern Illinois, and if it could not reach fulfillment in Europe, America would have to do.[34]

Back in his university days, Gustav Körner had once experienced an unpleasant run-in with a younger student during which insults were traded and honor was besmirched to the point that a duel was required to settle the dispute. In a swirl of veteran swordplay, Körner cut his upstart opponent badly enough to end the contest. Over fifteen years later, after Körner returned home one evening, his wife announced that he had a visitor. Waiting inside was Friedrich Hecker, still bearing the scar inflicted by Körner's dueling sword. Since their last meeting, Hecker had gained fame and hero status after leading an armed peasant uprising in southwestern Germany. Charged with treason, he fled Europe and made his way to, of all places, Belleville, where he believed like-minded friends could be found.

While he toured across the country en route to Belleville, adoring crowds met Hecker at every major city. The *Cincinnati Freie Presse* recorded, "Festival welcomes were staged for him, with parades, flags and music. The most prominent men addressed him with flattering speeches, thousands and tens of thousands gathered in his honor." After delivering a celebrated address in St. Louis, Hecker crossed back over the river into St. Clair County, his journey complete. The *Belleville Advocate* approved, assuring that "on no spot in the wide world could he have chosen an asylum where a warmer grasp of the Republican hand is ever ready for freedom's devoted friend." Körner could not help but admire Hecker's blend of charisma and audacity, and he agreed to help the refugee select adequate farmland for permanent settlement. Yet almost immediately, on learning of a renewed uprising in Baden, Hecker attempted to return to the fight, only to discover the rebellion died out before he could hope to arrive. Devastated, Hecker finally abandoned Europe completely, explaining in a letter, "I look across to the far West and my woodland solitude with true longing. . . . With bitter feeling I take the end of the pencil and erase twelve years of valiant, restless action from my life, starting over at 38, working and creating in the small world of a Western farmer." Retired to relative isolation by 1849, he determined to rarely make public appearances, content, or so he claimed, to sit on the sidelines of history.[35]

In a comprehensive biography, Sabine Freitag outlines Hecker's belief that American republicanism presented the best chance for "a prosperous, independent, stabilizing middle class . . . a society whose core as ever would be farmers as small, independent entrepreneurs and into which the workers in urban centers would somehow find their way by means of the American slogan 'help yourself.'" Such a viewpoint and confidence in upward mobility would sound familiar to free labor's adherents.[36] In fact, Hecker drew from years of university training that fostered a high regard for the American constitution and Jeffersonian republicanism. His close relationship with the historian Carl von Rotteck would bear heavily on Hecker's idealization of America. In *General History of the World: From the Earliest Times until the Year 1831*, Rotteck supported immigration to America, reasoning, "For the resident of the Old World there lay in the unmeasured regions of the New . . . [a] secure place of refuge for oppressed right and for the outlawed love of liberty." Taking Rotteck's advice, Hecker found such a refuge and intended to live out the republican ideal on a small farm, far removed from political duels and hopeless uprisings.[37]

But like the majority of Forty-Eighters, Hecker was soon drawn into America's great struggle to define its western boundaries and the rights of workers, both free and enslaved—how could he not be? Such a contest was easily recast as the natural protraction of European liberalism, an elusive second chance suddenly within grasp. It came as no surprise then that just a few short years after his self-imposed sequestration, Hecker sharpened his rhetorical sword, comparing "the Bourbons and Hapsburgs," the European aristocracy he loathed, "with the plantation-masters of the South." Later he warned, "The victory of the proslavery party, indeed, would make European oppression seem benign by comparison."[38]

From the onset, the brashness of Hecker and many other leading Forty-Eighters came as somewhat of a shock to the Dreissigers, now characterized by the newcomers as out of touch and even dangerously Americanized. Editor Heinrich Börnstein bragged of the Forty-Eighters' ability to "furnish the kindling ideas that set the masses into action," implying that the current German leadership lacked spirit. After his arrival in St. Louis, Börnstein calculated a new path, intending "to organize the Germans in the west into a great strong unit, in order that they might gain power and influence in the internal affairs of their new homeland," ostensibly dismissing similar efforts of those who came before.[39] Though several years older, Börnstein went so far as to label Gustav Körner "Der Graue Gustave" (the Gray Gustav), indicating that the older Dreissiger generation had lost its enthusiasm. Körner struck back, referring to Börnstein as "Green" and totally unfamiliar with American institutions or politics. In his memoirs, Körner wrote of Forty-Eighters that while "there were many amongst them who were worthy of all esteem," many others were "full of the most fantastic and Utopian ideas," including "not only to revolutionize Europe but also this country." Fellow Bellevillean Dreissiger Theodor Hilgard similarly believed that the Forty-Eighters would soon "learn what our German heroes of liberty in general do not know . . . that a true republican must, before all else, submit to the majority, even when it appears to him that it is a hundred times wrong." And in Cincinnati, Emil Klauprecht reminded that Forty-Eighters had arrived in a city where already "the German heart greeted the essence of the Fatherland in a thousand forms, and where the German ethic was presented with an opportunity for rapid advancement."[40]

The wedge between "Greens" and "Grays" was largely a product of individual rivalries and an experiential divide across two revolutionary generations that would gradually dissipate as national debates over immigration reform and temperance rose to prominence. Far more important was the synthesis of the Dreissigers' acquired wisdom and hard-won political power within the Democratic Party, with a renewed sense of purpose and destiny that Forty-Eighters undoubtedly brought to the table. Following the Forty-Eighters' arrival, Friedrich Münch recognized an enlivened spirit, "which suddenly asserted itself," pointing to the "aspirations of the Germans in recent times to form a political power."[41] Despite their irreverence, Münch admitted that Forty-Eighters "tried above all to reawaken in us a more ardent German national feeling."[42] Encouraged by the new, more incendiary atmosphere, the Dreissiger rationalist Eduard Mühl cranked up his own critique of slave society in 1850, announcing, "We hold ourselves as free men, who did not escape slavery in our old home lands to support it here in America."[43]

While their opinions were diverse and ran the full gamut of European liberal ideology, in America the Forty-Eighters constructed a broad, encompassing culture of liberal nationalism, blending *Bildung* and conscious citizenship with republican self-improvement and independence. The perfect embodiment of this cultural mission was the Turnvereine, or Turner Societies. The Turners' roots stretched back to the Napoleonic Wars and Friedrich Jahn's decision to resist the occupying forces through athletic display and achievement as a form of national pride. Jahn in his *Deutsches Volkstum* argued for a German national consciousness and unity that included bringing an end to involuntary servitude (*Knechtschaft*)—essentially authoring the foundation of Forty-Eighter *Weltanschauung* (ideology) in America.[44]

When revolutionary hero Friedrich Hecker made his tour through America in 1848, his stop in Cincinnati inspired a group of young immigrants to form an American version of the Turner movement. The day after giving a rousing speech, Hecker agreed to meet with the youthful Forty-Eighters, including the Tafel brothers, Rudolf, Gustav, and Albert. The brother's father, Leonhard, as a radical student and Turner in the 1820s, was taken prisoner for two years, during which he translated James Fenimore Cooper's *Leatherstocking Tales*. Regarding his imprisonment, Leonhard Tafel pointed to his "participation in a student club, whose object was to bring about the unity of Germany and freer institutions," saying, "I dreamed, at the time, as so many others did, of the unity of Germany and of Liberal institutions and would have made every sacrifice for their realization."[45] Continuing their father's mission, and with Hecker's encouragement, the Tafel brothers agreed to establish the first Turnverein in America. Gustav Tafel's membership card depicted the German tricolor and the American flag alongside weightlifting and vaulting gymnasts. Cincinnatian Heinrich Rattermann later outlined the association's envisioned function as aiming at the "cultivation of rational training, both intellectual and physical, in order that the members may become energetic, patriotic, citizens of the Republic who could and would represent and protect common human liberty by word and deed."[46]

Cincinnati's Turner Society signaled the association's America renaissance. Nearly every major city in the North and West soon established its own Turnverein, creating an impressive organizational network whose impact over the next decade would be incalculable. At a combined meeting with the German Free Men's Society (Freie Männer Verein) in Cincinnati in 1853, the Turners endorsed a political platform that opposed slavery in the Western Territories, while promoting a liberal homestead bill and public schools—articulating free soil and free labor with a German accent. As the "Song of the Turner" promised, "Man's Eden will return, Slavery's yoke will break." And when civil war threatened to divide the nation, Turners on the Middle Border's major cities formed the first Union regiments.[47] But the organization's membership was not composed entirely of those who once manned the barricades. Membership rolls included those from all walks of life, from craftworkers to middling business owners to celebrated intellectuals. Though their emphasis on rationalism often put them in conflict with conservative German Catholics and Lutherans, Turners delivered a clear and inclusive outline of what German liberalism hoped to accomplish in American political culture.[48]

In cities and towns throughout the Middle Border, Forty-Eighters expanded German involvement in the sectional discourse of the early 1850s, hoping to make the New World match their ideal. For Ludwig Stierlin, a Prussian radical who narrowly eluded a prison sentence, Louisville, Kentucky, was the place to start anew. In 1851, Stierlin accepted a position as editor of Louisville's *Anzeiger*, the city's leading German-language newspaper founded by Dreissigers. The paper remained staunchly Democratic throughout the 1850s, yet Stierlin supported moderate antislavery efforts while strongly opposing nativist activities threatening to engulf the city—a delicate balancing act for a Democratic paper in a slave state.[49]

Walking the fine party line would only become more difficult when, in 1852, Karl Heinzen, a far-left participant in the 1848 revolutions, joined Stierlin in the burgeoning city. Heinzen's arrival came after he found little success in New York, which led him to look west and accept the editor's desk at the *Herold des Westens*. Displaying the idealism mixed with pompous ignorance that typified many Forty-Eighters, Heinzen landed in Louisville and promptly announced his antislavery views. In 1852, speaking at an Ohio state convention of African Americans in Cincinnati, Heinzen declared, "Tyranny in Russia, Austria, and America is the same . . . and therefore the Russian serf, the Hungarian Peasant, and the American slave and all other oppressed people, should unite against tyrants and despotism."[50] Soon after, the *Herold des Westens*' offices mysteriously burned down. Undeterred, Heinzen began issuing *Der Pionier* in late 1853. It quickly claimed the mantle of the most radical newspaper in the West and gained a far-flung readership. Building momentum, Heinzen, Stierlin, and a core group of supporters soon began work on a German-American reform movement in Louisville destined to send shockwaves.[51]

Loud and outlandish, Forty-Eighters like Heinzen and Heinrich Börnstein presented a sensationalized rendering of German-American liberalism pitted against an oppressive foe—David and Goliath, republican and aristocrat, slave and master. This hero's narrative resonated with the majority of immigrants who did not regularly correspond with Karl Marx or theorize on republicanism. In Louisville, Ludwig Stierlin wrote for craftworkers and small business owners, well aware of his readership's socioeconomic makeup. When first traveling to Louisville on the *Midas*, he was surrounded by fellow Germans of whom few shared his education or partisan past. "The steamer had packed the poor immigrants like fish in a barrel," he later wrote. "Forty had died on the way." By 1852, one local historian estimated that eighteen thousand Germans resided in Louisville and the surrounding area, and they turned to Stierlin's *Anzeiger* for the region's only stable, continuous source of the German-American perspective.[52]

While nearly all of Stierlin's readers lacked a university education, they well understood the connection between Germany's failed economy and the desperate condition of its working people, with the intransigence of princes and landed aristocracy. These tens of thousands of immigrant workers on the Middle Border recognized the dangers slave masters posed, and as their political consciousness grew, so too did their impact on local politics. Across the river from Louisville, in New Albany, Indiana, Germans made up 52 percent of shoemakers and 61 percent of tailors. Downriver, the rapidly industrializing city of Evansville, Indiana, perhaps benefited most from the 1848 immigration.

Over the next decade, the city's population ballooned to twelve thousand, with 45 percent of the workforce born in Germany. The inundation shifted the city's politics, leaving candidates reliant on the German vote and therefore empowering the German perspective.[53]

In the early 1850s, as sectional interests threatened to subsume traditional party loyalties, the flood of German immigrants held the potential to reconstitute politics in key cities and towns throughout the Middle Border. During the 1852 election in St. Louis, Germans marched to the polls to cast their votes for Thomas Hart Benton, the veteran Democrat advocating for limiting slavery. Expecting the Germans to arrive in full force, a crowd of native-born rowdies gathered in German city wards to prevent the ballots from ever reaching the box. A destructive riot soon broke out, ravaging German neighborhoods and businesses. The next day, a pamphlet circulated the city, forcefully crying out, "Americans! The events of yesterday must teach you that the institutions of our republic cannot be preserved unless you do your duty. Yesterday the slogan was: 'Germans and other foreigners versus native-born Americans.' What happened yesterday was only the beginning."[54] The combination of nativism and proslavery sentiments suggested the dangerous waters the German immigrants had waded into and also signaled a growing perception that the Germans possessed the ability to alter local politics should they go unchecked.

The question was how far German-American liberalism was prepared to go for the cause of free soil and free labor. Democrats on the Middle Border, meanwhile, anxiously wondered to what degree antislavery would factor into the German position within their party. In 1850, the editor of the Democratic *Missouri Courier* in Hannibal, Missouri, took notice of German political activities in St. Louis, condemning "[an] association formed by some of the German population," which the editor accused of being "exclusively political." The paper denounced the "impolicy of [Germans] separating themselves from the native-born brethren and forming separate and independent political cabals" and predicted "that so soon as the tens of thousands of foreigners who were crowding every ship thought themselves strong enough, they would band together and make an effort to control our elections so as to alter and change our institutions." The context of the *Courier*'s warning is significant: 1850 marked the Forty-Eighters' appeal to Germans to reconsider their alliance with proslavery elements. The clarion call accompanied the Compromise of 1850 and the growing sectional schism within the Democratic Party, which only added fuel to the fire.[55]

Despite Forty-Eighter leadership's antislavery insinuations, it would be inaccurate to place German Americans on the Middle Border in the same camp as northeastern abolitionists or identify them as enthusiastic allies of Southern slaves. Kristen Anderson makes the case that as late as 1850, "St. Louis Germans demonstrated very little opposition to slavery," arguing that Germans in St. Louis "shifted their position on slavery and the place of African Americans in American society when it benefitted their own community to do so." This initially meant a "general acceptance of slavery," but only until the peculiar institution "began to seem like a threat to the German population"—specifically, to Germans as white citizens interested in preserving the West from slave labor.[56]

Yet German immigrants, both Dreissigers and Forty-Eighters, did not suddenly adopt free soil ideology in America; they brought it with them. Well before their arrival in America, German liberals, whether college students or day laborers, embraced ideas antithetical to slavery and slave masters. Relative to the conservative forces in the region, German liberalism did in fact constitute one of the strongest drivers of antislavery. To say Germans were not radical abolitionists or in full support of emancipation until late in the game is correct, but abolition was entirely untenable in the West, especially for an ethnic minority. Movements to improve the condition of slaves or free black people on the Middle Border were essentially nonexistent. No major party platform even considered an antislavery plank until the mid-1850s. Yet from an ideological position, Germans in both free and slave states denounced slavery and the "slavocracy" as antithetical to a free republic. They therefore did not embrace free soil ideology explicitly for political expediency or white racial privilege; rather, they did so to shape the discourse to meet the deeply ingrained vision they carried with them. Rather than a moral or abolitionist critique of slavery, Germans constructed a rationale for opposing slavery that relied on *Bildung* and liberal nationalism combined with free land and labor policies in the West. The goal was racial equality not to benefit Southern slaves, but to create a free nation unencumbered by slave barons.

In 1850, the *Wochenblatt*, a central Missouri paper edited by the rationalist Dreissiger Eduard Mühl, presented the contest in stark terms. Outright abolition certainly presented a difficult set of problems—namely, that "black men were systematically bred as cattle and consequently were incapable of estimating their duties and rights as free citizens." Yet for Mühl, there was no denying that ultimately, "the slavery of the blacks will destroy the Union."[57] Whether from the perspective of a rationalist journalist, a shoemaker in Evansville, or a former revolutionary hero seeking the Jeffersonian ideal in Belleville, individuals could become citizens and improve their condition, and the nation that protected such possibilities must remain intact or all would be lost.

CHAPTER 3

"I WAS AN ENTHUSIASTIC DEMOCRAT IN THOSE DAYS"

FREE SOIL, FREE LABOR, AND THE REALIGNMENT OF GERMAN LIBERALS, 1852–1856

The 1850s ushered in lean times for the *Evansville Daily Journal*, a Whig newspaper surrounded by Democratic readers, many of whom were German immigrants who arrived en masse in Vanderburgh County, Indiana, throughout the 1830s and 1840s. But the tumult of the times potentially offered hope—divisive, unresolved disputes capable of upsetting the political status quo in southern Indiana presented an opportunity to improve the *Journal*'s prospects. As the national Whig Party fractured along sectional lines, it became clear that if the *Journal* wanted to survive, it would have to reinvent itself. One key ingredient, the editors knew, involved persuading local antislavery Germans to reconsider their political affiliation with proslavery Democrats. To that end, the *Journal* presented Germans with an alternative, a new political organization advocating free soil, free labor, and on some level, free men. Within the coalition that became the Republican Party in the West, many believed, as the *Journal* did, that winning over German voters was crucial. To do so, Republicans would have to convince Germans that the new party had erased the stain of nativism and was sincere in its advocacy for a free West.[1]

How exactly Republicans mounted a challenge to the slave South constitutes the Northern prelude to Civil War, yet the party's antecedents remain undefined, especially on the nation's periphery.[2] On the Middle Border, Germans harbored vague, often grandiose notions of progress and destiny that meshed with free soil and free labor, but by the early 1850s, no national party offered a legitimate platform. As the national Democratic Party succumbed to sectional infighting, breaking apart along a hardening north-south border, Germans found an opportunity to shape the new political reality by demanding a complete separation from proslavery elements. Their growing aversion to the old Democratic Party amplified as proslavery leaders seemed to seize the reins of power. When slave masters threw open the door to western territories, Germans along the Middle Border pressured local Democrats to denounce their party's Southern wing or face a difficult reelection. As a result, several key Jacksonian Democrats in the West, buttressed by German voters, abandoned their political ties and jumped to the rising Republican Party. This development did not mean that all or even a majority of Germans suddenly forsook the Democrats, but it did begin to significantly alter the political dynamic.[3]

When sectional politics arose in 1850, a compromise materialized that pleased neither side but seemed to lean decidedly to the advantage of Southern Democrats. That slavery might spread unencumbered following the Mexican-American War reignited debates over the nation's westward advance. The likelihood of slave labor invading territorial lands proved troubling to Germans in the West who saw the machinations of an aristocratic class at work. Hoping to drive a wedge between local Democrats and the Germans, who represented a formidable voting bloc in Evansville, Indiana, the *Evansville Daily Journal* wrote, "[We] are not surprised that the Germans should rebel against this spirit of dictatorship." The Germans "know they have the power and seem determined to act independently." Moving swiftly, the newspaper suggested Democrats might be wolves in sheep's clothing. "The readers, and especially the German readers of the [Evansville] *Democrat*, will recollect the gross epithets applied to them by it, simply because they were foreigners. They will recollect being termed a 'horde of savages.'" Here on display was local politics at its best. The *Daily Journal*, itself once loosely connected with nativism, hoped to turn the tables, recasting local Democrats not only as the party of slavery but also as reactionaries who shouted down German dissenters.[4]

The *Journal* initially fought an uphill battle. In preceding decades in Dubois and Vanderburgh Counties, the Whig majority had completely lost its footing, overwhelmed in part by German voters won over by local Democrats. It all began when a German Catholic priest arrived in southern Indiana. A nationalist poet during the German uprisings of the 1830s, Joseph Kundek embarked on a new mission to form a Catholic colony along the banks of the Ohio River. In 1840, Kundek advertised in Cincinnati's *Der Wahrheitsfreund*, promising, "The region is healthful, the soil fertile." Two years later, Matthew Hassfurther, a German Methodist, wrote to his son-in-law relaying the priest's success. "In general, the Germans came flying like snowflakes and buy up the land."[5] Though he believed the colony was divinely inspired, Kundek also found nonsectarian motivations for encouraging immigration. A devout Democrat, Kundek worked behind the scenes to unify the German Catholic vote. In 1848, he advised, "Catholics never do well at an election unless they hold together."[6]

In addition to political organization, Kundek also oversaw many local land sales. Hassfurther reported of one town in southern Indiana, "Jasper will probably be cleaned of Americans," saying that "those with property the priest buys out and resells it again to Catholics."[7] In 1850, when equipment arrived for a cotton mill in Cannelton, the owners immediately advertised for German workers.[8] Assisting in the search was Father Kundek, who devised a plan to attract immigrant laborers. "I wrote a letter to his excellency the Governor of Indiana offering him my services as a state agent to induce the Germans to emigrate to our state," Kundek informed. "I will have to disseminate the pamphlets in order to let the seeds take root."[9]

Following suit, Germans continued to flock to southern Indiana into the 1850s, drawn to the sparsely settled land along the lower river valley suddenly booming with trade and agriculture. One description, published in Westphalia, Germany, emphasized that the region had "not yet increased as is already the case in Ohio, so this state is even more suited for the German settler," and advertised that "Congressional land can still be had in quantity in this state for 1.25 dollars per."[10] Hermann Bullermann and six companions traveled to Evansville in late 1848, all wearing red military jackets. Bullermann wrote home to describe the German community outside of Evansville, amazed that "almost all of them arrived here without property and by now they have acquired enough so that they can have a comfortable existence." Adding further enticement, he continued, "By the way, there are many farms for sale because all the Americans want to sell."[11] By 1860, in Dubois County Germans constituted 25 percent of the population while claiming 53 percent of the total property valuation. As Adolf Brandeis wrote, "I am in a part of the country inhabited, for a distance of about 60 to 80 miles, exclusively by Germans and since I left the steamboat I have not heard a single word of English."[12]

Heavily concentrated German settlements in southern Indiana, much like southwestern Illinois, could transform and then dictate local politics.[13] As the 1852 election cycle approached, the *Evansville Daily Journal* struggled to win German support for Whig candidate Winfield Scott. "No intelligent man we say," the paper asserted, "can or should believe that Gen. Scott . . . ever entertained nativist feelings toward foreigners." The paper cited Charles (Karl)

Heinzen, a Forty-Eighter and "radical Democrat" who nevertheless "*tells the truth*." In Cincinnati, Heinzen declared, "Most Germans tend to the Democratic Party. But they allow themselves to be deceived through the great names of the past . . . now the Democratic Party is entirely rotten, and has completely gone over to slaveholding hunkerdom." Heinzen represented the first sign that Germans would disassociate themselves from a party run by a slave-owning aristocracy, and the *Daily Journal* was ready to offer an alternative.[14]

Evansville's Democrats, however, did not sit idly by, as the *Journal* noted with frustration. "Perhaps there never was a time in the history of this city when the foreign vote was so much courted by the Democratic party." It was plain that their opponents were "trying to deceive Germans and other foreigners into believing that the Whig party from Gen. Scott down is opposed to foreigners." When election returns revealed a trouncing at the state and local levels, the *Journal* knew where to locate its defeat. "In this county, about six hundred foreigners, Germans principally, have declared their intention of becoming citizens within the last two months." German immigrants' last-minute naturalization in Vanderburgh County and across southern Indiana brought the Democrats victory, or so the *Journal* had it.[15]

Similarly, the German enclaves in southwestern Illinois provided a strong Democratic base stretching back to the 1830s, with Germans arriving in dizzying numbers that overwhelmed the original settlers. In Macoupin, an American-born minister commented in 1850, "Each new [German] family in turn brings a circle of relatives and friends who settle around them. . . . Americans do not like them for neighbors and some sell out and leave the place on that account. Thus the effect of this immigration to diminish our neighbors will soon be quite apparent." In St. Clair County, where Germans constituted 55 percent of the adult white male population (not counting second generation) by 1850, the Democratic Party thrived, particularly in the city of Belleville.[16] Located in the fertile American Bottom, Belleville was described by the *Belleviller Zeitung* as "essentially a German city, and for that very reason it exerts a definite power of attraction upon the German immigrant . . . for we all know quite well that we and almost all Germans prefer to live among countrymen."[17]

So concerted and reliable was the German Democratic presence that in 1852, respected Dreissiger Gustav Körner received the nomination for lieutenant governor. Körner cemented his long relationship with state Democrats and Stephen Douglas after using the *Belleviller Zeitung* to garner support for the 1850 Compromise among Germans in southern Illinois, while denouncing Forty-Eighters who assailed the act as submission to Southern slave owners. Though Körner had long criticized slavery, he was not yet willing risk his political prospects by opposing his own party leadership. Körner instructed the *Zeitung* to take the position that because of the climate, slavery was essentially useless in the new southwestern territories, and thus compromise to preserve the Union was entirely acceptable. Therefore, the *Zeitung* wrote, "We hope that the German element especially will rise up strongly in support of the Union." Hence in 1852, despite undermining efforts by Whigs on the local level, in southern Indiana and southern Illinois Germans offered a solid bloc of support to western Democrats.[18]

After thirty consecutive years of serving as a U.S. senator, Thomas Hart Benton, once the unchallenged leader of Missouri's Democratic Party, was shocked to find himself defeated in the 1850 election. Benton's unseating was the product of one massive political miscalculation: he simply underestimated Missouri's devotion to the institution of slavery and the lengths to which his fellow Democrats would go to protect it. A Southerner by birth, Benton was never antagonistic toward slavery in the early stages of his political career and fought tooth and nail to defend the slaveholders' rights during Missouri's march to statehood in 1820.[19] At the time, Benton argued, "It might be that the people of Missouri would go *voluntarily* as far . . . as any other portion of the union [in abolishing slavery]; but until that time arrives, no process of reasoning can make it right that they should be *forced* to the surrender of their slaves."[20]

As the years passed, Benton came to believe that Missouri belonged fully to the West rather than the South. In line with his Jacksonian roots, he saw Missouri as the crucial piece to a grand vision of western progress: a land destined for free white men, furthering the republican mission.[21] As he continued to develop his arguments, Benton understood slavery to be an impediment to that vision. Consequently, in the early 1840s he subtly turned a deaf ear to the proslavery chorus by advocating against slavery's westward movement. This situated Benton among the Jacksonians whose emerging free soil arguments expressed a desire to prevent slave labor from invading newly acquired territories. But in a state dominated by a proslavery elite, as historian Benjamin Merkel succinctly concludes, "Out of this issue was to arise serious trouble for Benton."[22]

On the national stage, in January 1849, a collection of Southern congressmen met to discuss the threat to slavery. In a dramatic gesture, they resolved in what would later be known as the Southern Address that the federal government possessed "no right to extend or restrict slavery, no more than to establish or abolish it." Though Benton represented slaveholding Missouri, he refused to attend or lend his support. Instead, he stood firmly in the path of Southern Democrats. Soon enough, Benton came under attack from fellow party members in his home state. In March 1849, the Missouri State Assembly adopted the Jackson Resolutions, named in honor of proslavery stalwart Claiborne Fox Jackson. Unabashedly promoting slavery's expansion, the document promised that Missouri would be in "hearty cooperation with the slave-holding states" should there be "encroachments" by the North. In essence, the Jackson Resolutions served as a formal declaration of war against Thomas Hart Benton.[23]

With the middle ground quickly receding, Benton continued to hold firm, boldly proclaiming, "If there was no slavery in Missouri today, I should oppose its coming in; if there was none in the United States, I should oppose its coming into the United States; as there is none in New Mexico or California, I am against sending it to those territories."[24] With the 1850 Compromise, Benton further separated himself from his base when he declared the act "a capitulation to those [Southerners] who threatened secession."[25] The result was his defeat at the hands of an alliance between Southern Whigs and anti-Benton Democrats. As the Washington, D.C., paper the *Union* eulogized, "He had made an issue with the Democratic party" and "with the people of his own State."[26]

In defeat, Benton discovered his most ardent supporters: German Democrats who shared his discomfort with their party's increasingly Southern character. Heinrich Börnstein, the *Anzeiger des Westens'* controversial editor, led the way, seeking to escape a hierarchy dominated by slaveholders. Börnstein made it clear that Germans must vote for Benton because his enemies aspired to turn Germans into "laboring slaves without political rights." In 1850, after the German Social Reform Club and the German Shoe-workers' Association formed the German Free Land Association, with the motto "free land, cultural progress, and betterment of the workers," Benton lent his approval, gaining admiration from German workers.[27] As Benton began to campaign as a free soil Democrat in preparation for the 1852 congressional election, his efforts at wooing Germans were out in the open. The *St. Louis Republican*, then the city's leading Whig voice, accused the veteran of pursuing "Socialism, Red Republicanism, Infidelity, Communism, [and] Free Soilism," and of "trying to Germanize St. Louis," insisting, "The American people will not stand innovations upon their rights, their principals, their institutions."[28] One anti-Bentonite openly denounced the attempt at "pandering to the foreign prejudice against slavery." Indeed, with the *Anzeiger*'s support, the German vote swung nearly unequivocally in favor of Benton and his protégés, Frank Blair and his cousin B. Gratz Brown, who founded the *Missouri Democrat* to support Benton's new party and successful election to Congress.[29]

By 1852, German Democrats on the Middle Border recalibrated but ultimately maintained their alliance with western Democrats, supporting those candidates who upheld Jacksonian principles and advanced free soil policies. Arnold Krekel, lawyer and editor of the newly established *St. Charles Demokrat*, assured readers in the paper's first edition on January 1, 1852, "In politics . . . the 'Democrat' will side with the party known by its name. I will advocate all measures and support men to carry them out, that are truly Democratic." But with continued genuflections to the interests of the slave South, the *Demokrat* would begin to question its party's commitment to free soil and free labor and start to consider alternatives.[30]

The catalyst for German Democrats arrived in 1854 after Stephen Douglas, the powerful western Democratic senator from Illinois, authored a piece of legislation meant to end sectional tension. The Kansas and Nebraska Territories, Douglas proposed, would individually decide whether to allow slavery based on popular sovereignty, theoretically allowing the people to decide. Although some western Democrats praised the compromise, others, particularly Germans, saw it as yet another submission to the Southern slave power and a threat to free soil and free labor in the West.[31] Seizing the opportunity, the *Evansville Journal* denounced Douglas's efforts, decrying the bill as "nothing more nor less than a truckling to the unjust demands of the South." Significantly, the *Journal* noted it was not alone in its disapproval. "We are glad to see the Germans speaking on this subject. We learn that a great many German Democratic papers are opposing the Nebraska Bill. In our city they are speaking out." Seeking a new partnership, the former Whig organ reached out to the Democratic Germans of Evansville and southern Indiana, paving a path to a new political ideology.[32]

Though still in its infancy in 1854, the Republican Party attracted voters because of its ability to pull together the broken pieces of the Second Party System. Republicans offered opposition to slavery's expansion based on the simple premise that free white labor trumped coerced slave labor. Disparate parties could perceive the idea of free labor whichever way they chose—as an antislavery measure, purely a protection of white working men, or some combination of the two. Either way, under the Republican Party's big tent, all understood "that free labor was degraded by slavery, and the corollary that if slavery were allowed to expand into the territories, Northern laborers would be effectively barred from settling there."[33] To Northerners, western expansion represented a panacea, possessing almost mythic qualities. Their cities were teeming with wage workers and immigrant families, and homesteads, property, and resources waited in the vast expanse of western lands. Set against these prospects, the threat of slavery became all too real after the passage of the Kansas-Nebraska Act. Suddenly, slave masters could flood into land destined for free white workers. Thus the singular cause of free labor echoed throughout the North and Northwest, where the first Republican organizations slowly built a new party platform.[34]

The threat posed to free labor by the Kansas-Nebraska Act ultimately led a significant number of German Democrats to demand a new direction. In St. Clair County, Illinois, Lyman Trumbull, a longtime Democrat reliant on the German vote, firmly opposed Stephen A. Douglas and based his campaign for Congress strictly on his anti-Nebraska position in hopes of solidifying German support. Such maneuvering stole German Democrats away from Douglas and proved German fealty was not unconditional. Similarly, Thomas Hart Benton harangued the act as a violation of Western interests, eliciting praise from the *Anzeiger des Westens*, which called Benton "the people's candidate of the progressive Democracy," while declaring that "it is as if the few thousand slaveholders in Missouri had totally forgotten that they constitute a tiny minority in the state, or as if they considered it a trifle to rule the vast majority of the people of Missouri like white niggers."[35]

Crucially, the Kansas-Nebraska Act awakened German Americans, particularly those along the border, to the immediate dangers slavery posed. This realization instigated a definite shift toward more direct opposition by "fusing the issues of free soil and antislavery with those of land reform and free labor in the West." At a German protest in Evansville, one resolution read, "To open the door to slavery in the territories . . . is to close it upon the free labor and free laborers of the Northern States and of the old world."[36]

The resulting political upheaval invigorated German opposition but also created uncertainty and dislocation. Dreissigers on the Middle Border, who held the strongest ties to Democrats, especially in Cincinnati and southern Illinois, saw a threat to party unity as well as national stability. Karl Reemelin, a staunch Democrat, could no longer support "any compact made with slavery," declaring Germans had for too long "been deluded with the idea that slavery was temporary." No friend of abolition, Reemelin nevertheless warned, "The South thinks they are secure, but let them pass this bill, and the whole slavery question will again be open."[37] In Belleville, Illinois, Gustav Körner, once a major ally of Stephen Douglas, was placed in an uncomfortable position. The *Belleviller Zeitung* tried to maintain neutrality, but anti-Nebraska fervor led the paper to conclude, "We believe very firmly, that a vast majority of the people of the United States not only does not want, but also hates and detests this law, in so far as it annuls the Missouri Compromise and at least makes possible the introduction of the curse of slavery upon free soil." Fearing a backlash in his home state, Douglas positioned himself as an opponent of proslavery forces in Kansas, even printing his speech against their Lecompton Constitution, a document intended to open the state to slavery, in German. But the damage was done; here was a candidate few Germans could comfortably support.[38]

Even among Germans who rarely engaged directly in sectional politics, the prospect of slavery extending its reach provoked concern. Though many rural German Catholics remained mostly agnostic in regard to slavery, and with large segments of the more conventional German Lutheran community criticizing their radical countrymen, a general antagonism toward slave ownership still existed. *Der Lutheraner*, a newspaper published by the church, advised that while little could be done to counteract slavery, as it was "a visitation of God upon sinful men," readers still should "do all they could to mitigate its abuses." In *Die Abendschule* (*The Evening School*), a Lutheran family journal in Missouri founded in 1854, the response to Kansas-Nebraska was clear. "It is almost incomprehensible how, in a country based on free principles, the most enormous servitude, slavery, not only exists but even finds defenders!" A few issues later, the journal printed an image titled *Branding of Black Slaves*, writing, "Imagine, dear reader, you have black skin rather than white, and your homeland is not Europe or America but Africa—you would still be a human being like any other, a living soul . . . only your dark skin and your curly, wooly hair would differentiate you from other human beings." Refraining from politics, *Die Abendschule* instead crafted a moral critique in the aftermath of Kansas-Nebraska. Suddenly, it appeared as if slavery loomed within striking distance, invading the lives of German immigrants who had heretofore done their best to ignore it.[39]

While some Germans approached their opposition to Kansas-Nebraska cautiously, those Forty-Eighters intent on kicking the hornet's nest mounted a full frontal assault. At an anti-Nebraska meeting in Cincinnati's Turnhalle, Douglas's bill was labeled a "disgrace to America" and met with a "call on the friends of liberty, without distinction of party or country, to unite with us in putting down the aggressions of slavery." After leaving New York to man the helm of the liberal *Pioneer* in Louisville in 1853, Karl Heinzen immediately courted controversy as a radical. One of his first editorials took on slavery, arguing that in America, it represented a shocking contradiction to freedom. "They call slavery a blessing and declare it a necessity for the Republic," he wrote, "making it a national institution by fire and sword, carrying shiploads of unfortunates here from Africa, whom they educate with the whip and torture into working, like cattle." But it was Kansas-Nebraska that propelled

Heinzen to more direct action. With the support of a small but vocal coterie of Forty-Eighters in Louisville, Heinzen called for a mass meeting to organize the Louisville Platform. The measures adopted argued that true freedom in America had yet to be realized, citing slavery as well as class division, and the meeting officially opposed the Fugitive Slave Law and slavery's western expansion, all while calling for some form of gradual abolition. Most controversially, the platform demanded equality for women and free black people. Such an ambitious pledge found patchy support—many agreed with portions, but few approved all measures.[40]

The Louisville Platform did, however, have far-reaching impact, with meetings in Indiana, Illinois, and Ohio employing similar language. Consensus most often revolved around western land policy. The platform's demand for "free cession of public lands to all settlers" received broad support—land reform shone brightly for those seeking a new life and opportunity. That the burgeoning Republican Party was founded on the principle of free western lands combined with a call for free soil, or territory unpolluted by enslaved labor, was enough to persuade many Germans to contemplate a new political alliance.[41]

After condemning Kansas-Nebraska, the *Evansville Daily Journal* enjoyed a growing German readership following years of having rather unsuccessfully vied for their attention. Embracing a free West, the *Journal* strongly denounced Stephen Douglas and popular sovereignty, despite the large number of Democrats in the region and the paper's proximity to a slave state. "We don't care a fig whether those Kentuckians in Evansville like our position or not," the *Journal* declared. "If the interests of the North are not paramount with them to the interests of the South, it is time *they* were changing." The *Journal* then lauded local German Turners, who "turned out in large numbers in an imposing torch-light procession," protesting Kansas-Nebraska. Still, clarifying its free soil position, the *Journal* avowed it was not interested in radical antislavery measures. As one editorial reassured, "We again say, as we have said before, there is no spot in the whole North freer from the taint of abolitionism than Evansville—even *slaves* know this." This flourish went to great pains to demonstrate a strictly free soil position, or land preserved for free white labor, which appealed to Germans hoping to constrain slavery in some capacity.[42]

Though they favored antislavery policies, many Germans negatively associated abolition with New England evangelicalism, a dangerous sect with little to offer. As the *Belleviller Zeitung* made clear, "We are not abolitionists, we have nothing in common with those crazy, Bible-quoting fanatics." Still, this did not erase the need for proactive antislavery programs. The *Zeitung* made its case, explaining, "We perceive the dangers which are presented by the extension of slavery too precisely for us not to expose the pressures of the South." The *Zeitung* insisted that the real danger could be found in "the concentration of the property in the hands of a few, the ever increasing number of 'King Beasts,' [which] must in the short or long run produce in the South an aristocracy, compared to which all the types of our European aristocracy are to be preferred." The goal then was to limit slave owners and prevent their western movement, focusing not directly on emancipating black slaves but on preventing an aristocracy, which fell within the purview of free soil and free labor. This allowed Germans to develop antislavery arguments with antecedents in liberal nationalism while denouncing abolition, crafting a far more acceptable message wrapped within free soil and free labor ideology.[43]

Though Forty-Eighters' critique of Kansas-Nebraska resonated with German and Anglo free soil advocates throughout the Middle Border in 1854, the movement remained disorganized, lacking cohesion across the disparate groups attracted to the free soil and free labor message. The challenge was to fuse free soil and free labor's moderate aims with the more radical antislavery vision. Individually, and with only limited support, Forty-Eighter leadership began to lay the groundwork for a new political strategy. In a speech to the Evansville Turners following their march in celebration of George Washington's birthday, Theodore Dietsch harked back to Jeffersonian democracy: "In these days, where slavery shall lie planted into all zones, as a republican law—who in such days can wonder that only a few observe the memory of the fathers of our Republic, and the great principle proclaimed by them: 'that all men are created equal.'" Dietsch tucked his antislavery position into the more traditional and revered folds of the Founders' republicanism, making his conclusions appear natural despite the potential radical underpinnings.[44]

By framing the free soil and free labor argument as a logical and necessary counter to a landed, antirepublican oligarchy, Germans on the Middle Border began to cut a path to the Republican Party. In St. Louis, *Anzeiger des Westens* editor Börnstein expressed that he was "tired of the improper influence of the slavocratic interest." Yet he carefully assured readers, "We are for the abolition of slavery in Missouri, but only constitutionally and in a manner to pay due respect to the just claims of the citizens of this state." Such language served to separate the leading German newspaper in the West from northeastern abolition, while still maintaining the necessity of limiting slavery's expansion to secure the institution's eventual demise. "The establishment of slave states on our western border will make the abolition of slavery in our own state still more difficult, if not entirely impossible," he reasoned, subtly suggesting that slavery's days in Missouri were numbered. But given the lack of unity among western free soil and free labor Democrats in support of such measures, Germans who either opposed the growing national power of Southern slave owners or abhorred the idea of slavery's extension into the western territories seemed politically adrift. "The fact is: There is no party at all present with which one can go," lamented the *Anzeiger des Westens*. "Therefore, break party ties altogether and give preference to those candidates whose political creed corresponds to our own." Increasingly, such candidates joined the Republican ranks.[45]

After 1854, the Republican Party offered itself as a viable home for free soil and free labor. The audacity of a third party presenting a singular, unifying program aimed specifically at limiting slavery even gained the attention of Friedrich Hecker, the people's hero of 1848 who had resigned himself to isolation in southwestern Illinois. Hecker was especially intrigued by a meeting of German Republicans in Chicago, where attendees professed that as "Pioneers of the West as we [Germans] are, we have lost our confidence in, and must look with distrust upon, the leaders of the Democratic Party, in whom we hitherto had confidence enough to think that they paid some regard to our interests." Inspired, Hecker increased his public appearances and regularly expressed his belief that within the Republican Party, Germans could become "united for liberty against the aristocratic power of the slaveholders and their characterless Northern satellites." Through this new alliance, he saw great opportunity, believing American politicians would "seek the German vote more militantly."[46]

Looming in the background, threatening to undercut the blossoming relationship between western Germans and Republicans, was a virulent groundswell of nativism. The antiforeigner ethos predated the Republican Party, sweeping across the country in the early 1850s, targeting recent European immigrants, especially Catholics, and culminating in the secretive American, or Know-Nothing, Party in 1854. Emerging from the chasm left by the Second Party System's collapse, Know-Nothings captured the antislavery and free labor momentum among Northerners and, to some degree, native-born laborers on the Middle Border. Nativists despised foreign workers, who not only competed for jobs but also overwhelmingly supported the Democratic Party. For a short period, the Know-Nothing Party found incredible success, winning major elections by positioning itself as a new party willing to shift the focus to issues of immigration, temperance, and the plight of white workers in industrializing cities. Nativism in fact proved most successful in the Northeast, where workforces in major urban centers vied against immigrant throngs for well-paying jobs.[47]

In the West, where growing cities and towns offered less economic competition and, more important, were home to established concentrated immigrant populations, nativism took on a different form and function.[48] From cities such as Cincinnati, St. Louis, and Evansville to more rural St. Clair County in southwestern Illinois and Cape Girardeau in southeastern Missouri, Germans made up one-third or more of the total population and were therefore better able to assert their own interests. Indeed, nativism owed its rapid decline in these western states to German voters. If the nascent Republican Party were to succeed in specific areas where Germans constituted significant portions of the population, it would have distance itself from explicit nativism.[49]

Often appearing as propaganda and a tool for political manipulation, the specter of nativism in the West was often used to win over Germans by either accusing or repudiating the Know-Nothing label. Following Kansas-Nebraska, the contest in southern Indiana pivoted once again when local Democrats scrambled to recapture German support by portraying the Republican Party as Whig nativism in disguise. The Democratic *Evansville Enquirer* warned, "We have heard a good deal of speculation in reference to the probable organization of a lodge of 'Know Nothings' in our city. . . . This is a new and mysterious organization for the resuscitation of the Whig and Native American parties." Hoping to quickly dissociate itself from Know-Nothings, the *Journal* fired back, insisting, "We recognize all foreigners as AMERICAN CITIZENS," but after years of professing Whig and nativist proclivities, shedding the past would not be easy.[50] In Alton, Illinois, Henry Weigler hoped to start an anti-Nebraska newspaper but feared that while local Germans opposed slavery in the West, they were "very liable to be led away by the cry of Know Nothings."[51] Dreissiger Friedrich Münch expressed his growing concern: "Next to slavery as the most damnable abuse of social life stands nativism." At the moment when Germans on the Middle Border began shifting their allegiance in response to slavery's amplified presence, nativism endangered the entire realignment.[52]

Unlike their northeastern counterparts, one nativist branch along the border also embraced the movement as a viable defense of slavery. Know-Nothings in the North claimed a firm antislavery stance in hopes of elevating the free white worker. Therefore, they often cast German and Irish immigrants as ignorant supporters of proslavery Democrats. But in the West, following the Kansas-Nebraska Act and the outbreak of violence in Kansas, antislavery Germans—aligned with anti-Nebraska Democrats—began to work with free soil Whigs to combat proslavery forces, which included many Upper South Know-Nothings. Nativists in Louisville and St. Louis rarely supported antislavery and in fact were far more likely to condemn Germans as the greatest threat to slavery. Thus western nativists who opposed slavery found it increasingly difficult to stay united with their Upper South proslavery allies—an indication that sectional borders were hardening.[53]

For free soil Whigs in southern Indiana, the Ohio River increasingly represented a wall of separation from Kentucky. The *Evansville Daily Courier*'s overtures to local Germans signaled a shift away not only from nativism but also from their proslavery brethren across the river. The Democratic *Evansville Enquirer* reported with glee after northeastern Know-Nothing leadership had forbade "the admission of any slaveholder to membership," concluding, "Such resolutions do not go down quite as well in Evansville and other cities bordering on slave states. . . . Our Kentucky neighbors who have been mixing with the Order on this side of the river can't come any more." The American Party's success relied on the plasticity of nativist Know-Nothing ideology. But nativists could not stand on both sides of the slavery question, forcing proslavery nativists in Kentucky to part ways with fellow Know-Nothings in Indiana. This left free soil Whigs in Evansville to appeal to their German neighbors in hopes of a new alliance.[54]

For proslavery Whigs in Louisville, however, Germans went from a mere nuisance to a very real threat. After years of Whig Party prominence in the city, Germans' sudden political participation in the 1840s and early 1850s threatened to tilt the balance to local Democrats. Whigs drove Germans from the polls as early as 1844 in an effort to stave off such incursions and continued to intimidate foreign voters in the years to come. Germans responded by forming the National Guarde militia two years later, and newly ensconced Forty-Eighters only boosted German activity. Gustav Körner wrote that with the advent of the energetic Forty-Eighters, "Louisville became for a time, one can say coincidentally, a gathering place for some of the most intelligent, indeed one could even say, most fantastic elements, which the waves of reaction in Europe had thrown upon the American shores." Attracted to the party of Jackson's democratic principles, the new arrivals immediately began to combat the nativist and Whig elements in the city. As was often the case, however, slavery made the situation far more complicated.[55]

Emblematic of national fragmentation, sectional disputes soon problematized the German-Democratic partnership in Louisville. After initially focusing their attention on countering early Whig and nativist assaults, Forty-Eighters became entangled in territorial debates and slavery's future. Karl Heinzen's radical antislavery Louisville Platform combined with the fallout of Kansas-Nebraska rocked the German element in the city. Though only a short-lived publication, the *Freie Zeitung* led the way with the motto "free soil, free labor, free education, free men," voicing a strong antislavery philosophy. Simultaneously, and not coincidentally, nativism soon swept through Louisville as proslavery Whigs adopted nativism as a way to combat any sign of antislavery expressed by Germans.[56]

In Louisville and throughout Kentucky, Southern Whigs voiced anxiety over foreign influence and often perceived German and antislavery to be synonymous. A pamphlet addressed to "Native Americans" in Fayette in 1848 warned, "All the states of Europe are emptying upon our shores the contents of their poor houses and jails," and predicted that "no less than five hundred thousand, the refuse population of the world, will be landed upon our soil."[57] W. Darrell Overdyke contends that Know-Nothings in the Upper South "received Americanism with a growing consciousness of their outlying position adjacent to free states rapidly filling with antislavery immigrants." In 1849, Whig congressman Garret Davis called for stricter immigration laws in Kentucky, pointing across the river to an example of the potential danger: "Look at the myriads who are perpetually pouring into the North-western states from the German hives—making large exclusive settlements for themselves. . . . Living in isolation, speaking a strange language, having alien manners, habits, opinions and religious faiths, and a total ignorance of our political institutions." "In less than fifty years," Davis predicted, "they will number millions and millions, and they will be essentially a distinct people, a nation within a nation, a new Germany."[58]

One year later, the census revealed that the German-born population in Louisville had reached eleven thousand, or nearing 30 percent.[59] As German households and businesses flourished, so too did Southern nativist apprehension. In 1853, the *Louisville Daily Courier* lambasted the city's Turner association as European rabble-rousers. The entire city administration, all with ties to the American Party, likely agreed. The tipping point, though, came with the 1854 Louisville Platform and its radical antislavery stance, which, as Forty-Eighter and platform supporter Ludwig Stierlin explained, "brought forth unintended consequences . . . [and] only helped to accelerate eruptions of Know-Nothingism."[60]

On Election Day, August 6, 1855, German voters in Louisville went to the polls determined to influence the heated congressional race but found a body of armed men equally determined to stop them. Joshua F. Speed, close friend to Abraham Lincoln and brother of recently ousted mayor James Speed, watched in disgust as the democratic process degenerated into a violent, chaotic riot. "Irish and German voters were chased from the courthouse yard," he later wrote, "while a crowd of armed Americans stood inside the Court House."

Later in the afternoon, one man justified the violence, telling Speed that "the Germans 200 strong, singing and armed with double barrel shotguns had taken possession of the polls in the first ward." Speed doubted his informer but then saw the crowd pursue "a little German who was going up Jefferson Street—they rained the shout 'move him.' He was pursued by the crowd—he was stricken many times." Mob activity exploded in the German Uptown neighborhood as Know-Nothing bands tore through German businesses and homes. By the riot's end, twenty-two had been killed and scores more injured. Shortly after the Bloody Monday rioting, Louisville's German-language *Anzeiger* proclaimed, "The whole population is to decide whether Louisville still should rank among the civilized and civilized cities in the world. Anyone considering this question, if we have a majority against us, then we waive all claims to be citizens of this town." In fact, some Germans did decide to abandon Louisville in the riot's aftermath, though most resolved to stay and rebuild. Those who remained, however, would continue on under proslavery nativism's enduring shadow.[61]

Following the riots, Know-Nothings in Louisville continued to openly support the institution of slavery. The animus directed at German immigrants, then, originated in their loyalty to Democrats and was augmented by their lack of enthusiasm for slavery. Louisville's nativist congressman Humphrey Marshall gave a speech that listed "Reasons for the formation of a Native American Party," including "The ignorance exhibited in the proposal of political privilege illustrated by atheism of the free German [Louisville] Platform." In an exchange of letters between Marshall and fellow nativist Henry Middleton, Middleton condemned the "anti-Americans" who would be given "no quarter—whether they sail under the Abolition, free soil, Democratic, or any other flag."[62] The *Louisville Daily Journal*'s editor, George Prentice, denounced any ties between Know-Nothings and abolition. In July 1855, a month before Bloody Monday, he had made the case that since "the most ominous and momentous question now agitating is that of slavery," the "American Party is the only one that can be relied upon to save the country." Prentice argued, "Nothing is to be hoped by the South from any party in the North except the American Party. If that party cannot save the Union, the Union is doomed." The thinking behind such a statement came from the realization by Southern Whigs turned Know-Nothings that nativism could unite the national party by emphasizing the dangers of foreign influence over the discord inherent in slavery.[63]

In the end, the Know-Nothings could not escape the sectional divide they sought to ignore. At the 1855 American Party convention in Philadelphia,

Northern delegates walked out in protest of perceived proslavery conciliations. W. Darrell Overdyke explains the intractable stance taken by Southern delegates by saying, "There was little doubt in the minds of Southern Know-nothings that three and a half million Europeans . . . meant ill to the South." The root cause of Southern nativism, then, was not simply immigrants, but the threat they posed to slavery's survival. A leading Know-Nothing advocate, the *Louisville Journal*, sounded the alarm after Illinois free soiler John Wentworth advocated, "If people wish to drive slave labor from free territory they must look to foreign labor as the best means of doing it."[64] It wasn't long before the *Louisville Daily Courier*'s Walter Haldeman severed ties with the American Party's Northern branch because it did not come out strongly in support of slavery.[65] Crucially, for the remainder of the 1850s, proslavery Know-Nothings in Louisville held the reins of power, leaving Germans without a Free Soil Party or the possibility of a Republican alliance.[66]

For Whigs and nativists in St. Louis and across Missouri, the Know-Nothings' ascendance also signaled an opportunity to concentrate efforts against antislavery Germans. At an American Party meeting in central Missouri, members condemned government interference with slavery in the territories and supported the fugitive slave law. As historian Michael Fellman explains, "Most southern-born Missourians coupled nativism to politics, targeting Germans, the largest immigrant group, as the greatest foe." Reminding its readers of the dangers posed by the combination of proslavery and nativist Whigs, the *Anzeiger des Westens* warned, "There is a Whig ticket for the city of St. Louis upon which appear the proud names of slave-raising millionaires."[67] Desperately, Germans in St. Louis and other enclaves throughout Missouri sought a political platform that promoted their free soil and free labor, opposed the slavocracy, but also denounced nativist policies.

The unique formation of the Republican Party in St. Louis, with its roots in Thomas Hart Benton's free soil branch of the Democratic Party, offered antislavery Germans a platform largely free of nativism. German Republicans then originated from Benton's free soil movement as early as 1852 and began to abandon the Democratic Party following Kansas-Nebraska.[68] Surveying the profoundly altered landscape in 1854, Frank Blair, prominent Democrat and Benton's loyal adherent, saw the potential in Missouri for the free soil cause unencumbered by nativism.[69] While his proslavery Democratic foes focused all their energies on defeating Benton Democrats, and with the Whig-nativist coalition in tatters over slavery, Blair envisioned a new alliance. The key was persuading German free soil Democrats to support *local* Republicans, many of whom, including Blair, were rooted in the Jacksonian Democratic tradition, had no ties to nativism, and sought to limit slavery. In 1856, Blair won election to Congress, becoming the only Republican from a slave state to do so before the Civil War. By combining Benton's Democratic Germans with emerging free soil advocates under the aegis of the Republican Party, along with an intentionally vague program of gradual abolition, Blair secured the greater St. Louis region. By 1858, Benton lost his battle with intestinal cancer, but Blair's tactics would prove successful, ushering Benton's many supporters, especially Germans, into the folds of the Republican Party. This strategy served as a blueprint throughout the Middle Border.[70]

Across the river in southwest Illinois, Republicans also concluded that to embrace nativism within their ranks was to kill any chance of gaining German free soil Democrats. Former Illinois Whig Abraham Lincoln, in one of many examples of his advocacy against nativism to win the German vote, wrote to Joshua Speed, "I am not a Know Nothing. That is certain. How could I be? How can anyone who abhors the oppression of negroes, be in favor of degrading classes of white people?"[71] As one Republican politician argued at an early party convention in Bloomington, Illinois, in 1856, "There should be some distinct ground assumed on which the 20,000 antislavery German voters of this state can stand, or we will lose them in a body." The convention was not well represented by southern Illinois counties, with the exception of heavily German St. Clair County, with Gustav Körner and Friedrich Hecker in attendance. Hoping to entice Hecker to return to a more public and visible life and therefore gain German approval, the convention chose him as an independent presidential elector. One approving German commentator optimistically suggested, "If [Hecker] enters the field for the Republican cause, for freedom of speech, individual liberty, freedom in the territories, free Kansas and opposition to the slaveholder oligarchy, what German will go against him?"[72]

After officially joining the Republican ranks in 1856, the *Evansville Daily Journal* once again made its case to Germans in southern Indiana by warning that because they did not support slavery in the western territories, Democrats would inevitably turn on them. Finally, a substantial number of Germans seemed ready to listen. The paper reprinted an editorial from the *Indianapolis Freie Presse* that strongly advised, "Germans! Will you continue to give your vote to a party that makes an alliance with the Know-Nothings? Think about this before it is too late. Think about which party is better for you: The Republicans, who are authentic, or the Democrats who stand in union with the Know-Nothings."[73] In this leading German Republican newspaper distributed throughout southern Indiana, Democrats were suddenly cast as nativists who hoped to silence any and all opposition.

A lifelong Democratic lawyer, Oliver P. Morton, rode the momentum and joined Indiana's Republican Party. Aware of the considerable German presence in central and southern Indiana, Morton astutely noted, "Free labor will not go to any considerable extent where slave labor exists, because it is degraded and dishonored by the association." Those who sought to prevent free labor in the West, he insisted, would not stop short of disunion. And if South Carolina moved to secede, the West would be doomed to resemble "the principalities of Germany." Such a calculated reference was meant to remind Germans of *Kleinstaaterei*, or small-statism, which left Germany a fragmented collection of states and kingdoms ruled by aristocrats and nobility. Republicans, as Morton and other western leaders conscious of the German vote put forth, offered the best defense of a free republic, occupying ideological ground previously the domain of Jacksonian Democrats. After a total rearrangement of political life on the Middle Border, it was the Republicans who afforded the best chance for securing a free West and the liberal nation.[74]

As western Republicans absolved their party of Know-Nothingism and aggressively pursued German voters, pockets of support began to appear in a region where little progress had been made. In the major cities along the Middle Border, including Cincinnati and St. Louis, and in smaller cities such as Cape Girardeau, Evansville, St. Charles, and Belleville, German Republicans began to organize. In a letter to his brother Hugo, Gustav Tafel, a founding member of the first Turner organization in America, recounted with glee Germans' shifting alliances in Cincinnati's 1856 municipal elections after the Tenth, Eleventh, and Seventh Wards all went Republican. "The greatest jubilation in Over the Rhine was due to the abolishment of the Democratic police," Tafel wrote. "Now we have one that is totally Republican."[75]

Many Germans remained skeptical, suspecting nativism in disguise, or they feared Republican ties to radical abolitionists in the Northeast who risked disunion in pursuit of religious zealotry. In southern Indiana, William (Wilhelm) Hofmann attempted to disentangle American politics' messiness in Posey County for his brother in Germany. He listed the three major candidates, happily noting that even before the election, it was clear the "Know-nothings are defeated," before moving on to present the German perspective: "The Germans, who earlier were usually on the Democratic side, have split this year, and many of them have joined the Republicans." Writing again after the election, Hofmann clarified that while Republican candidate John C. Fremont was popular in Europe, in America "it is not the case, since the Democrats are for slavery and the Republicans are for freeing them." As if imagining his brother's shock that he had not joined the antislavery movement, Hofmann quickly asserted, "But there is more to it." The complications arose from the fact that "the Republicans want us immigrants to be in the country 21 years before we have the right to vote, while the Democrats place the time at five years. For that reason down with the principle and let us be concerned for our own freedom before we make the Negro free, since this can only happen by and by and not all at once if we want to avoid an out and out war in the Union." Though he seemed to agree with the principle of emancipation and certainly supported free soil, Hofmann pragmatically continued to attach himself to the Democrats, hoping to further his own interests.[76] If nativism had not reared its head at the moment when the Second Party System began to crumble, then it was likely many free soil and free labor Germans would have abandoned Democrats in greater numbers in 1856. Instead, many Germans continued to believe the Democrats best represented their and the nation's interests. But as proslavery Democrats revved up their fiery secessionist rhetoric, this confidence would rapidly fade.

Recalling his experience as an editorial assistant in central Missouri leading up to 1856 election, William Schrader remembered how he and his German friends "were invariably referred to as the 'Damn Dutch,' and although many [of us] voted the Democratic ticket, [we] were suspected of being 'Black Republicans,' at heart." Such accusations stemmed from Schrader's support for free soil and Thomas Hart Benton; that he did not support attempts to expand slavery made him a Black Republican. Four years later, during Missouri's secession crisis, this suspicion, Schrader proclaimed, "was gloriously verified in the almost unanimous rally of the Germans in defense of the Union." Still, in 1856, Schrader remained in the Democratic Party, which had best supported his interests as an immigrant in the years and decades prior. But as central Missouri's Democrats began to threaten secession, all in slavery's name, Schrader changed course. Charting the rapid evolution of the late 1850s, Schrader recounted, "I was an enthusiastic Democrat in those days and it seems queer to me now that before [Democratic president] Buchanan's term expired I could have seen him hanged with great pleasure and that within a year after he went out of office I was shooting at some of the companions with whom I celebrated his election."[77]

By 1856, whether Democrat or Republican, Germans overwhelmingly pursued free labor and free soil and opposed the Kansas-Nebraska Act. As Bruce Levine reminds, by pursuing German voters, "Northern Democrats did not, to be sure, depict themselves as enthusiastic champions of slavery's expansion. They took their stand, rather, as dauntless guardians of national unity, popular rights, and regional diversity," all of which appealed to free labor Germans wary of Republican nativism.[78] But the opposite proved just as likely, with German Democrats abandoning their party and its attachment to the slave South in favor of free soil Republicans whom they had once voted for under the Democratic banner. Either way, Germans on the Middle Border searched for the best strategy to secure liberal nationalism through free soil and free labor leaders and legislation. Increasingly, slavery appeared to be the largest impediment, the most glaring contradiction, and the gravest threat.

In southern Indiana, the *Evansville Daily Journal* reported that during a German Republican meeting in 1856, the audience resolved, "We regard slavery as a moral evil, and a political curse in any country and especially in a Republic; we therefore solemnly protest against any further extension of slavery in the territories." The meeting concluded only after inviting "all Germans who are of our mind to unite with us and deem it the special duty of every adopted citizen to work against the extension of slavery, and at the same time for the perpetuation of the Union."[79]

CHAPTER 4

"CONTINUOUS VIGILANCE IS THE PRICE OF FREEDOM"

ANTISLAVERY GERMANS AND THE ELECTION OF 1860

With the 1860 presidential election approaching, a disruptive decade had left Germans on the Middle Border without political cohesion or consensus. For over two decades, beginning in the 1830s, their allegiance had remained firmly with the Democratic Party. But entwined antislavery causes in the western territories—free soil and free labor—and the rise of the Republican Party presented a framework to challenge the contradiction of coerced labor in a free society, the liberal nation a fait accompli. Still, while discomfited by the principle and proximity of slave labor, many Germans did not see the situation in such stark terms. Rather, they remained far more concerned with the strands of temperance, nativism, and abolitionist zealotry found within the larger Republican coalition. To overcome these reservations, antislavery Germans emphasized the pressing danger slavery represented and, with growing urgency, insisted that the best means for preserving the Union required a clear road to emancipation.[1]

Few understood the precarious path to the Republican Party on the Middle Border better than Illinois's Gustav Körner. Once a likely candidate for the Democratic nomination for U.S. senator or even governor, he cut ties with the Democratic Party following the passage of Stephen A. Douglas's Kansas-Nebraska Act. "On all other questions which had divided the two great parties, I was as sincere a Democrat as ever," he avowed. Yet the nagging incongruity remained between his beliefs on individual freedom, cultivated during his tenure as a student radical in 1830s Germany, and his party's ties to slavery. "I always hated slavery," he said, "and while constitutionally I saw no way of abolishing it, I could not prevail myself to favor it in any way whatever, or to extend it into any Territory heretofore declared to be free." The cause of antislavery taken up by Körner and other leading Germans emphasized the necessity of containing slavery until its eventual and expected demise. Though in pursuit of a pragmatic path to emancipation, they nonetheless represented radical change in a region rapidly succumbing to sectional division.[2]

Consistently, Civil War studies not directly focused on the involvement of Germans often categorize them primarily as antislavery radicals and abolitionists. But in reality, on the Middle Border, their political position most often favored free soil, free labor, and the end of slavery by some type of gradual emancipation. The *Anzeiger des Westens* made clear that "the German is no border raider and no thief of Negroes . . . nor has he ever disturbed the borders of a slave state in the guise of an abolitionist leader."[3] Still, when slave labor threatened free labor, the *Anzeiger* maintained, "the German is an opponent of slavery" and would be "unfailingly there when free labor is being defended through law and Constitution against the pressure and dominance of slavery and the despotic principles of government it brings with it."[4] The *Anzeiger*'s critique was couched in terms of free soil and free labor, but by articulating its clear antislavery stance on the Middle Border, the popular German newspaper walked a fine line between moderation and radicalism. To those in the region vehemently opposed to emancipation in any form, the *Anzeiger* appeared to be dangerously swerving toward the latter.

As antislavery Germans well understood, the Middle Border's pervasive racial hierarchy was rooted in a shared sense of western identity based on white supremacy. On both sides of the lower Ohio and Mississippi Rivers, in the upper South and the lower North, white residents viewed slavery mostly in the abstract. Many on the northern side of the rivers abhorred African Americans, insisting that black people and slavery as an institution remain outside of their own white communities, while those to the south believed that their own elevated place in society was predicated on the permanent enslavement of black people. As long as slavery remained a nonissue, compartmentalized, white people on each side of the border could stand united. To insist on a final referendum on slavery was to breathe fire into sectional divisions and disrupt the delicate balance.

As a result, while antislavery received only limited acceptance in the North after 1830, it was virtually outlawed on the Middle Border, whether in free states or slave. Antislavery politician George W. Julian considered southern

Indiana "an outlying province of the empire of slavery," and in Illinois, where the institution came remarkably close to legalization in 1818 and 1824, a form of de facto slavery called "contract apprenticeship" remained legal until the late 1840s, especially in southern Illinois's cotton-producing counties of "Little Egypt" and the American Bottom.[5] In 1820, the Missouri Compromise had seemingly decided the state's slave future. Opposition was quickly shouted down. As the *St. Louis Commercial Bulletin* announced in 1833, "We contend that no man has the right to discuss the abstract question of slavery." Abolitionist editor Elijah P. Lovejoy's press was destroyed multiple times by mobs in St. Louis throughout the 1830s, forcing him to relocate across the river in Alton, Illinois. There, a proslavery mob once again attacked, this time murdering Lovejoy, martyring him for the antislavery cause in the West and elsewhere.[6]

In such an inhospitable climate, self-preservation alone indicated the logic in avoiding public expressions supporting emancipation. Germans' moderation was then in part an acclimation and deference to the engrained racial hierarchy, but this is not to say it was acceptance. Beginning with the Dreissigers of the 1830s, Germans constructed an ideological opposition to slave ownership rooted in European liberalism, which found full expression with the arrival of Forty-Eighters in the sectional debates surrounding free soil and free labor in West during the 1850s. Thus as antislavery Germans, bolstered by the Republican Party's ascendance, amplified their attacks, they nevertheless remained mindful of the racial politics that still dominated the region.

Conscious of the resistance to antislavery policies, German Republicans on the Middle Border sought to maintain equanimity as the 1860 presidential election approached. After listening to one visiting speaker condemn local Black Republicans as abolitionists, pro-temperance, and Know-Nothings, Gustav Körner incredulously asked the largely German Catholic audience, "Don't they kiss their wives every day, and don't they like lager beer or good whiskey as well as you do—and yet they are all Black Republicans?" Sensitive to the abolitionist stigma, Körner encouraged the *Belleviller Zeitung* to sustain a moderate tone when dealing with slavery. Though the paper was thoroughly Republican and was operated by outspoken antislavery Forty-Eighters, its editorials attacked Southern aristocrats and their reliance on coerced labor but refrained from calling for immediate abolition. Körner explained that the new editor, Franz Grimm, "had practical sense enough to know that as a journalist, particularly in Southern Illinois, he should not go too far and make the paper a rank abolition-organ."[7]

Whether a result of political expediency or disregard for abolitionist religious zealotry and claims of racial equality, avoiding a radical position did not undermine or derail Germans' attack on the plantation system. From the German perspective, slave owners, like their European equivalents, constituted an aristocracy that monopolized political and economic power, threatened western progress, and limited individual improvement through self-cultivation. Friedrich Hecker easily discerned such parallels. "A Southerner is like a Baron," he concluded. "He looks upon an emigrant as he would look upon a nigger."[8] St. Louis's *Anzeiger des Westens* portrayed the struggle as a familiar one, avowing "the battle of the slaveholders against free labor is the old battle of privilege against freedom in new garments." By rooting their cause in a struggle between free labor and slave labor and the preservation of free soil, Germans offered what they believed to be a rational rather than an emotional criticism of slavery. Yet by promoting a vision for slavery's decline, Germans found themselves steadily adopting a radical position within the context of sectional antagonisms.[9]

As sectional ideologues thrust slavery into the forefront of daily political life, St. Louis emerged as the epicenter of the German antislavery movement. Leading the discussion was the *Westliche Post*, a newly established Republican organ under Carl Dänzer's direction after he broke away from the *Anzeiger des Westens* in 1857. "The influence of the German element is rising, and nowhere more than in the western states," Dänzer proclaimed in the inaugural issue. "It is up to the Germans to incorporate German achievement into the American way of life."[10] A veteran of the 1848 revolution and a former member of the Frankfurt Parliament, Dänzer voiced forceful editorials, reasoning that "the slavery question is likely to provide grist for the mills of political parties for years to come. German immigration into the northern slave states, as well [as] into the newly formed territories, is one of the surest ways of establishing more free states." Outlining a strategy for limiting and eventually eliminating slavery, the *Westliche Post* believed Northerners and German migrants would overwhelm Southern planters, resulting in a free West. Appropriating an American notion of progress, the *Westliche* declared, "It is the 'manifest destiny' of slavery to be pressed southward."[11]

By the late 1850s, antislavery Germans continued to emphasize the threat slavery posed to a free society, but more immediate and personal concerns, such as nativism or Sabbatarianism, continued to lead many Germans to discount the exigencies of antislavery activity. Seeking a more palatable rationale, the *Westliche Post* reasoned that "the slavery of the black man will lead to the slavery of the white worker" and asked, "Are you willing to continue to hold the chains for the southern slave owners and thereby . . . continue to pay tribute to European despotism?" Thus antislavery did not mean a fight for slaves, but rather a struggle for free labor.[12]

By positing coerced labor as anathema to free labor principles, Germans could remain generally silent on the condition of black slaves while still working in support of antislavery. William (Wilhelm) Palm, a conservative Dreissiger, insisted he would support emancipation only "if [it] can occur without any injustices against the slave owners, and under the additional stipulation that we get rid of the Negro." For Palm, both the institution of slavery and African Americans writ large needed to be removed from the equation.[13] Promoting antislavery as a boon to the white worker, the St. Louis Arbeiterverein (workers association) prioritized its own interests by endorsing the Republicans in 1858 and offering the slogan "Missouri für freie weiße Arbeiter, und freie weiße Arbeiter für Missouri" (Missouri for free white workers, and free white workers for Missouri).[14] That same year, the *Anzeiger des Westens* stipulated that "above all it is the white laborer, the free white population of Missouri, who must be emancipated from slavery, from the slave-oligarchy of the slave aristocrats. . . . To emancipate the state from a beastly system is the priority; to emancipate the Negro slaves in the process is only one aspect of this."[15]

From antislavery Germans' perspective, that the sectional crisis continued unabated only strengthened their contention that slave owners threatened to undermine free workers' rights. In July 1858, the German-led Union Party, organized in St. Charles, Missouri, announced that "the National Democrats of Missouri had sinned against the people." The group cited the Dred Scott decision and the proslavery Lecompton Constitution in Kansas as evidence of Democratic transgressions. The party's goal was not emancipation measures; rather, it insisted that "the preservation of the Union should be the highest goal of every patriot." "While, on the one hand, we clearly damn abolitionism," the group said, "on the other hand we condemn nullification [of federal law] equally." Safeguarding the Union secured free soil policies in the West but did not lead to untethered abolition. Antislavery Germans instead made clear that slavery's unchallenged proliferation would ultimately destroy the Union. As the *Westliche Post* astutely asked, how could the peculiar institution continue exist in the "freest country in the world?"[16]

The antislavery sentiments expressed by Germans did not go unnoticed and soon came to represent a highly conspicuous and radical threat to proslavery forces. Shortly after his return to the Missouri Supreme Court in 1857, William Barclay Napton assessed emancipation's emergence within his state's rapidly evolving political landscape. Topping his list of concerns was a growing antislavery contingent "whose announced object is to convert our state into a second Illinois." Napton represented the anxieties of a small but influential segment of slaveholders and proslavery advocates who sensed their longtime power slipping away in Missouri and the West in general. "I have no fear of the fanatics," he said. "The danger lies in another direction." Napton was undoubtedly right in his appraisal of western abolitionists, who lacked both numbers and resources. Instead, he broadened his gaze. Joining "the little band of Yankee abolitionists" were "German Radicals" who had "gotten possession in St. Louis and have made that place as thoroughly hostile to slavery as Chicago."[17]

Confirming Napton's suspicions, in 1859 Friedrich Münch issued a clarion call to Missouri's German citizens. "The important thing now is that the political power in the state be taken from the hands of proslavery men," Münch announced, "and that to this purpose the freedom-loving German element must be strengthened." He contended that there existed a small number of slaveholders who "strive to maintain here a tone of aristocratic refinement, a kind of superciliousness; but they are not succeeding." Münch had spent decades deploring slavery and promised that Germans were "working toward the gradual abolition of slavery" but stopped short of advocating immediate, revolutionary measures to accomplish the feat. It would take secession and civil war for Münch to forcefully advocate for abolition, the emergency of disunion outweighing any lingering reservations.[18]

Though they resided in free states, Germans in southern Illinois and Indiana also mounted a challenge to proslavery policies, advocating for free soil and limitations on slavery's western extension. In the 1830s, Gustav Körner chose to remain on the Illinois side of the Mississippi River rather than live in close proximity to slave owners. Based on his first encounter with Missouri slaves, Körner observed that "the negroes hereabouts are generally treated very kindly," though he was immensely troubled by the fact that slaves "are looked upon as a lower race, destined by nature to serve a higher. . . . Their comparatively satisfactory status does by no means excuse the principle of slavery, and it must be combatted with all our might." Nearly thirty years later, Körner remained firm in his disdain for slavery but pursued a calculated course.[19]

Together with Lyman Trumbull, one of his closest allies, Körner assessed central and southern Illinois Republicans as largely anti-Nebraska free labor advocates and not racial egalitarians. Working to further dissociate himself from Northern abolitionists, Trumbull reassured his constituents, "When we say all men are created equal, we do not mean that every man in organized society has the same rights. We do not tolerate that in Illinois." Cementing his point, Trumbull insisted, "I know there is a distinction between the two races because the Almighty himself has marked it upon their faces; and, in my judgment, man cannot, by legislation . . . produce a perfect equality between the two races, so that they will live happily together."[20] Far from campaigning on an abolition platform, Körner and southern Illinois Republicans guided Germans to either shun Stephen Douglas's popular sovereignty or abandon Democrats altogether to ensure free labor in the West. The *Belleviller Zeitung* was quick to remind that "no Republican can forget that it was the 'reckless hand' of Mr. Douglas which overturned the hallowed Missouri Compromise, a document so salutary to the peace of the Union," implying that if war came, it would not be a product of free soil policies, but rather a result of blatantly abusing historical legislation meant to ensure harmony in the name of protecting slavery.[21]

Even more so than in Illinois, German Republicans found direct inroads difficult in southern Indiana as a result of overt racial hostility. Johann Heinrich zur Oeveste's letter to a brother in Germany explained that in Bartholomew County, "Many people now favor total abolition, but one is worried that two nations, namely blacks and whites, cannot coexist but much rather destroy each other. . . . The Negroes living in free states are no slaves. They pay their taxes and other dues, but they are not entitled to vote. And nobody wants to hire them. In short, they are Negroes." Outside of Evansville and New Albany, many Germans identified as rural Catholic Democrats who were more concerned with combating surviving elements of nativism, a prominent temperance movement in the state's Republican Party, and felt little sympathy for black slaves. An 1860 meeting in Dubois County, led by native-born locals but attended by a large number of German Catholics, concluded, "We hold no equality with the Negro, and we will have no social intercourse with them, for we look upon them as an inferior race and believe that the Almighty never intended the races to amalgamate."[22]

But even those conservative Germans who rejected free black people within their communities often detested slavery. Joseph Thies recounted his father's temporary foray away from the Democrats "on the promise that the slaves were to be set free—and settle in a state out west all by themselves." German Catholic Christina Katterhenry feared that a coming war was a manifestation of God's wrath for the "abominable traffic in human beings," saying, "The slaves have been too terribly oppressed [and] I believe nothing else than that God has heard their screams and will free them." Though they preferred separation from black people, German Catholics nevertheless harbored little love for slavery. Such sentiments were in part the product of the unique perspective Germans carried across the ocean. As Richard Nation explains, "Having left Europe with its caste system still quite intact, German Catholics had embraced the equality espoused by the Democratic Party; they did not wish to return to the kind of world which they had left behind." Though growing German Republican organizations in urban centers failed to attract a significant number of rural Catholics, whose primary interest remained focused on nativism and temperance, conservative German Democrats still opposed the idea of slavery, suggesting that locally the difference between the two parties on this issue was often only by degrees.[23]

As the undulations of the 1850s wore on, transformative events following the Kansas-Nebraska Act heightened sectional antagonism for Germans living along the Middle Border. Throughout the turbulence, political loyalty remained fluid. Though the American Party's nativism waned after 1855, remnants continued on within the Republican Party, making free soil and free labor Germans hesitant to jump aboard. In 1857, the U.S. Supreme Court's *Dred Scott v. Sandford* ruling essentially declared the Missouri Compromise unconstitutional, indicating that as property, slavery would be protected in the territories. As a result, German Democrats could no longer ignore their party's ties to proslavery.[24] A year later, Democratic president James Buchanan, buckling under the weight of the Southern wing of his party, approved a proslavery constitution in Kansas written by a proslavery minority. These episodes loosened Germans' moorings to the Democratic Party in the West but did not signal a complete break. Stephen Douglas's forceful opposition to Buchanan and the proslavery Lecompton Constitution argued the merits of uncorrupted popular sovereignty, while Douglas made a conscious effort to mollify antislavery Germans by appointing a number to small state positions in Illinois.[25] When Massachusetts nativist Republicans pushed forward the Two-Year Amendment, which would prevent naturalized citizens from voting or holding office for two years following citizenship, this led to renewed accusations of Know-Nothingism. Given these twists and turns, Germans could not easily feel at home in either party.[26]

By the end of the decade, neither the Democratic nor the Republican Party offered antislavery Germans an unblemished record or a clear choice. Thus it became a question of which path better secured the "free soil, free labor, free men" version of the Union they had long envisioned. Joining the Republican ranks represented a more aggressive position on slavery, but to remain within the free soil Democratic fold was not to enlist in its proslavery wing. Rather, German Democrats could argue that they pursued the strongest course for compromise and preservation of the Union, while at the same time believing firmly in free soil policies.

Conversely, within the German Republican ranks, western members led the way in advancing the party's 1860 platform as the most viable vehicle for a free West. They pointed to the removal of nativist policies along with strong support for a homestead bill in the territories as evidence. Held in the West's fastest-growing city, Chicago, in Lincoln's home state, the Republican Convention revealed Germans' growing influence. While their countrymen in the East—where nativism persisted—felt ignored and mistreated by the party, Germans in the West were awarded seats on Republican councils and received nominations on local and state tickets. The situation was made evident by the fact that while no German delegates hailed from New York, eight represented Missouri.[27]

Citing their highest level of participation in any national convention, and hyperbolically touting the likelihood of bringing tens of thousands of votes with them, western German representatives threw their support to the Republican cause. In the end, such claims translated into only moderate support for Republican candidates.[28] For some Germans, the Republican platform did not go far enough, evidence of the growing radicalism among Germans in the region. The *Anzeiger des Westens* expressed general ambivalence following the convention, noting that the final party platform "did not succeed in laying a foundation for universal civil rights on the basis of universal human rights. It did not succeed in obtaining any written guarantee for the abolishment of slavery." While the *Anzeiger* did not expect immediate abolition, it desired a plan of eventual, constitutionally directed emancipation. Yet the platform adopted what were known as the "Dutch planks," which condemned nativist legislation seeking to limit foreign citizens' rights and supported a western homestead bill, and thus received the paper's recommendation along with that of other prominent western German leaders.[29]

Abraham Lincoln's nomination likewise generated diverse opinions. The *Cincinnati Volksfreund*, a Democratic paper that cared little for antislavery, believed "the immigrant citizen should . . . know from experience how to protect freedom and never forget continuous vigilance is the price of freedom." But the newspaper did not necessarily equate freedom with enslaved black workers. Rather, it believed in the perpetuity of the liberal nation state as the best protection of the rights of white workers. From the *Volksfreund*'s perspective, Lincoln, whom they conflated with overzealous abolitionists, appeared likely to dismantle the nation over slavery, while Northern Democrats sought to hold it together. In September, when Stephen Douglas visited the city, the *Volksfreund* declared, "Since the days of Jackson . . . no other presidential candidate or statesmen of America has ever enjoyed such general popularity."[30]

Countering the *Volksfreund*'s efforts was August Willich. Encouraged by respected Dreissiger Joseph Stallo, the Prussian intellectual came to Cincinnati to oversee the *Cincinnati Republikaner* and write prolabor editorials. As sectional politics engulfed the border city, Willich gave his support to the Republicans. Despite hesitations over the party's Whiggish and nativist tendencies, he believed it was far better than the "Slavo-Democratic" Party.[31] In the wake of the fiery abolitionist John Brown's execution following his failed raid on the federal arsenal at Harpers Ferry in Virginia in 1859, Willich and other Germans participated in a mournful demonstration attended by a diverse crowd that included local African American leaders. Willich gave a speech in which he advised his audience "to whet their sabers and nerve their arms for the day of retribution" and afterward led a torchlight protest march through the streets of Cincinnati. The Democratic *Cincinnati Daily Enquirer* condemned the Germans who participated, incredulously declaring, "They recognize no distinction of color in their social intercourse, and, if anything, consider a negro little better than a white man." Embarrassed by their countrymen's activities, the *Volksfreund* distanced itself from such extremism. Undeterred, in the protests' aftermath, Willich continued to push the Republican cause. Given his radical stance, Willich considered Lincoln too moderate in his slavery politics, but he nevertheless encouraged Germans to "battle for Lincoln" as "soldiers of freedom."[32]

With few exceptions, German Republicans on the Middle Border considered Lincoln an adequate candidate but far from an ideal leader. With Germans increasingly calling for an assault on Southern aristocrats as a roadmap to emancipation, Lincoln seemed shrouded in ambiguity and likely too moderate to be a viable candidate. After backing John C. Frémont for the nomination, the *Anzeiger* reminded disappointed readers that Lincoln would nonetheless push through a homestead bill that would "fill the west with immigrants from the older states and from the old continent." As a consequence, "slavery will lose its offensive nature."[33] On the other hand, newly elected southern Indiana Republican congressman George Julian warned Forty-Eighter Theodore Hielscher that Lincoln might be too easily influenced by "old Whigs," who sought "to kill our party by injecting in its veins old Hunker [aristocratic] blood."[34] The *St. Charles Demokrat* decided to take Lincoln's nomination in stride, throwing its full support behind the greater cause that the paper believed his election would represent. "Yes, go into all the districts of Missouri and preach the gospel of freedom to all our citizens and baptize them in the name of Lincoln and Hamlin," the *Demokrat* declared. "German countrymen! It nears, the great battle day, on which it must be decided if freedom or slavery shall be victorious."[35]

Within his own state, Lincoln did have a strong ally in the formidable Dreissiger Gustav Körner, whose path to such a position said much about the realignment of German political identities in southern Illinois. In 1858, Körner witnessed the first Lincoln and Douglas debate in Chicago and concluded, "What made Lincoln vastly more effective in this contest was that even the most obtuse hearer could see at once that Douglas spoke for himself, and Lincoln for his cause." Körner admired Lincoln's ideological opposition to slavery, yet he also possessed a firm grasp of Illinois and western politics and the need for diplomacy.[36] Likewise, revolutionary hero Friedrich Hecker became an early supporter, though he expected Lincoln would act with purpose against Southern extremists. In 1856, after Hecker's home outside of Belleville, Illinois, was purportedly burned to the ground by individuals who disapproved of his Republican campaigning, Lincoln wrote asking for Hecker's presence at an upcoming rally and suggested the possibility of providing funds to rebuild his home. Beyond this, Hecker was impressed by Lincoln's "House Divided" speech, which he witnessed firsthand, along with the backwoods rail-splitter turned successful lawyer narrative, which reminded Hecker of his democratic hero, Andrew Jackson.[37]

Generally, outside of Illinois, German Republicans on the Middle Border were less familiar with Lincoln's political background and were motivated instead by the momentum building behind antislavery. Ideals seemed to direct Johann Bauer's interests when he cast his ballot for the first time. He ultimately voted with the Republican Party because it believed "in the idea that all men are created equal before God, with the same rights."[38] Political action spurred Gustav Tafel, who, while speaking to Turners in Cincinnati, bemoaned German Democrats' continued allegiance to a proslavery party. "Why stand by the Democrats?" he asked. "The only alternative remaining is whether to join the Republicans, or to continue in skillful idleness."[39] In the *Daily Missouri Democrat*, a Republican paper despite its name, B. Gratz Brown skillfully incorporated the *Westliche Post*'s message when suggesting slave owners sought to build their own empire much like "the reign of some Louis Napoleon." Planters, Brown contended, hoped "to be a duke or a count—to wear the insignia of an order, and strut in the court of a monarch." As the election neared, the Republican Party's broadly defined ideology was further molded to fit the concerns and interests of Germans who might have remained less impressed with Lincoln but believed in the party's ability to challenge the Democrats in the slave South.[40]

The presidential election of 1860 ultimately served as a referendum not on German attitudes toward slavery, but rather on their confidence in the Republican Party. The question was not whether to oppose slavery's western diffusion; in that regard, a near unilateral opposition prevailed in the German ranks. Up for debate was whether they should give support to an antislavery Republican coalition that ostensibly courted nativists, Sabbatarians, and New England abolitionists. Persuading Germans along the border to alter their conception of western Republicans would prove a significant task. While crisscrossing Illinois in 1858 as he sought Stephen Douglas's U.S. Senate seat, Republican Abraham Lincoln sent a letter to Gustav Körner. Aware of his vulnerability in southern Illinois, Lincoln explained, "I write this mostly because I learn we are in great danger." Lincoln asked whether Körner would "set a plan on foot that shall gain us accession from the Germans."[41]

Lincoln also reached out to Theodore Canisius, a Forty-Eighter and publisher of the Republican *Alton Freie Presse* who was battling, with great difficulty, for the allegiance of Madison County's German Democrats. Canisius wrote to Lyman Trumbull, one of Lincoln's few Republican supporters in southern Illinois, "The Democratic Party is losing ground fast here since the [Democratic president Buchanan's] Cabinet has taken the position in regard to Kansas." A year later, after he lectured German Turners on slavery's origins and history in America, Canisius relocated to Springfield, where, with Lincoln's financial backing, he renamed his paper the *Illinois Staats-Anzeiger*. Lincoln thus gained antinativist credentials from the paper's support for German-American causes. In March 1859, Lincoln declared admiration for the German "love of liberty and hatred for doctrines and acts tending to subdue and crush the spirit of universal freedom and liberty." He went on to admit that the Republicans were "not perfect," referencing the Massachusetts naturalization legislation, "but all these errors dwindle down to a shadow, compared with the monstrous atrocities of the 'Slave Democracy.'" Though Lincoln lost to Douglas in 1858, he believed future Republican ambitions required German voters' support.[42]

Historians' general acceptance that German voters in the West secured a victory for Lincoln in 1860 likely has its roots in claims made by both German Republicans and native-born Republican leadership. On the senate floor in 1862, Charles Sumner proclaimed, "Our German fellow-citizens, through the long contest with slavery, have not only been earnest and true. . . . Without them our cause would not have triumphed at the last Presidential election."[43] Contemporary and early historical accounts insist the 1860 election hinged on the German vote in the West. Kentucky Republican iconoclast Cassius Clay outlined what he believed to be one of his party's greatest unrealized strengths. Writing to a Northern colleague, Clay claimed, "The Germans about New York may partake of the prevailing spirit of Democracy there: but in Cincinnati and the Great West they are nearly all for us."[44]

While Germans' contributions in the West to Lincoln's victory were exaggerated, in some cases wildly, their impact remains profound. In the Illinois election, German voters truly did matter. In southwestern Illinois, of St. Clair County's total population of 37,694, 43 percent were German, though this does not include the region's considerably large second generation, likely pushing the number to more than 55 percent. In 1860, Lincoln received 54.8 percent of the vote in the county. The native-born population in St. Clair and neighboring counties in southern Illinois were heavily Democratic before and during the war, making it unlikely that Lincoln received many votes outside of the Germans.[45] While a highly diverse German community ultimately prevented a unified vote, key islands of German Republican voters provided a significant boon. As in St. Louis, Illinois Republicans, motivated by their belief that the German vote was essential, had largely shed any nativist or temperance labels. Based on a wide survey of precincts and townships in both Chicago and southern Illinois, James Bergquist determined that in 1860, roughly 65 percent of Germans voted Republican. Looking again at St. Clair County, he estimated that 77 percent of Germans voted Democratic in 1852 but only 38 percent did so in 1860, indicating a significant shift. Still, the final tally fell far short of any uniform German vote. Republicans struggled to win German Catholics and rural pockets throughout the state.[46]

Taken as a whole, the 1860 election results on the Middle Border indicate that where German voters felt their interests were aligned with and protected by the Republican Party, they continued to embrace free soil, free labor, and antislavery ideology. In Evansville, Indiana, Forty-Eighter Theodore Dietsch weighed nativism and temperance against antislavery and free soil before promoting the Republican ballot. Though he had once labeled the local Democratic paper "an infamous hunker sheet, a slavery and Nebraska swindle paper," in 1855 Dietsch resigned himself to work with local Democrats, as he could not abide the sudden rise of nativists who "proscribe a whole religion, a whole sect and thereby abolish the truly republican principle of religious freedom." But after a dispute over tax assessments in regard to the Straight Line Railroad left Democrats attempting to defend city leaders putatively at the expense of public schools, Germans revolted. This local measure, combined with Democratic support of slavery in the territories and the despised Lecompton Constitution, pushed Dietsch and many Germans in Evansville to the Republican Party, which ascended into power in 1858. Thus Lincoln fared well in southern Indiana in the city of Evansville and Vanderburgh, Spencer, and Perry Counties, where Republicans convinced Germans that they represented their best interests. Conversely, Republicans did less well in southern Indiana among rural German Catholics and in counties where temperance and nativism remained prevalent.[47]

Crucially, Lincoln won Ohio but likely split the German vote with Douglas. In Cincinnati, however, though Lincoln received only 46 percent of the vote, the overwhelmingly German Tenth and Eleventh Wards gave him over 60 percent of the ballots, and four out the five predominantly German wards went with Lincoln.[48] Directly across the Ohio River, Germans in northern Kentucky gave Lincoln what little support he received from the Bluegrass State. Of the roughly two thousand votes cast for Lincoln in Kentucky, the overwhelming majority came from Campbell and neighboring Kenton County, along with Louisville, the state's other major German concentration.[49]

In Missouri, Germans were Lincoln's strongest and nearly sole source of support. In St. Louis and the nearby counties to the west and south, the majority of Germans abandoned the state's proslavery Democratic Party in favor of Thomas Hart Benton's old free soil coalition, which now wore the Republican moniker. Walter Kamphoefner's detailed analysis of St. Louis Germans' voting patterns demonstrates that roughly 80 percent voted for Lincoln. Outside St. Louis, Lincoln won the heavily German Gasconade County and did well in other counties, such as St. Charles, where the German township Femme Osage and town of Augusta voted overwhelmingly Republican. Beyond the heavily German communities, Stephen Douglas received the greatest support and won the state.[50]

Often lost in studies attempting to ascertain exact voting practices is that on the Middle Border, Germans did almost uniformly cast their vote for free soil Unionism by voting for either Lincoln or Douglas. They eschewed entirely John Bell and John C. Breckinridge, who received votes nearly exclusively from non-Germans on both sides of the Ohio. Validating those free soil German Democrats who maintained their faith in Stephen Douglas, Douglas proclaimed immediately following his defeat, "We in the Mississippi Valley cannot allow this Union to be broken up. This valley must forever remain one and indivisible." Douglas went on to support Lincoln, denounced secession at every turn, and diligently traveled throughout the region to encourage his former supporters to back the new administration.[51] In agreement, Germans on the Middle Border, both Democrats and Republicans, began to organize around the principle of unconditional Unionism. At a pro-Union meeting in St. Charles County, native-born organizers, believing themselves an island in a sea of Southern sympathizers, claimed that "if the German population of this country were not so through and through for the Union, without any 'ifs' or 'buts,'" native-born Unionists' immediate future appeared grim, and "they would have stood alone." Following the Unionist meeting, the *St. Charles Demokrat* boasted that Germans "came gladly to the meeting from all parts of the county, regardless of which party they belonged to, for they have recognized the danger in which their new fatherland is suspended." Frustrated with conditional Unionists' equivocations and outright secessionists' boldness, party identities gave way as Germans overwhelmingly rallied to prevent disunion.[52]

In response to calls for secession, Germans' Unionism converged with their antislavery impulses, contrasting sharply with the rhetoric of conditional Unionists, who sought compromise and the maintenance of both the nation and slavery. The *Westliche Post* believed, "The threats of the southern aristocrats, to separate themselves from the Union . . . are as despicable as they are presumptuous."[53] Yet only months later, Missouri politician James Moss promised that his state would "stand by the gallant men of southern Illinois, who have declared that they will never suffer a Northern army to pass the southern boundary of Illinois for the purpose of invading a Southern state." With disunion stirring among neighbors to the south or surreptitiously from those within their own communities, German antislavery grew bolder and more defiant. The *Belleviller Zeitung* declared, "The antislavery principle has triumphed over the region of the slaveholders and Southern aristocracy. The principles of true democracy as understood by the founding fathers of the republic will now be reestablished."[54]

By promoting an antislavery vision, Germans were at odds with a significant number of their neighbors and consequently were cast as a dangerous radical element. At the southern tip of Illinois, the *Cairo City Gazette* announced, "Let her [South Carolina] in God's name go peacefully, the sympathies of our people are mainly with the South." The *Indianapolis Sentinel* acknowledged the regional separation within that state: "The business and social interests of the people of South-western Indiana are largely identified with the South, and as a consequence their sympathies are strongly enlisted in whatever may affect that section of the nation." In southeast Missouri, the *Charleston Courier* stated in no uncertain terms, "Our interests all bind us to the South. With the North we have nothing in common but the English language." With the Germans, they often lacked even that. Indeed, from the Southern perspective, Germans were most to blame for western radicalism. *Debow's Review* tied Germans to the antislavery movement in St. Louis, while the *Southern Literary Magazine* argued that part of the Confederate mission was to fight against the influence of the "reddest of all German red republicans" in the West.[55]

With the nation teetering, lines were drawn in the sand, eliciting increasingly radical responses from Germans. Meyer Friede, a Jewish German immigrant representing St. Louis as a Republican in the state legislature, explained German liberalism's position: "I wish to say a word about my own countrymen, who are so often referred to here as 'Black Republican Dutch.' Mr. Speaker, when we left the Fatherland we were guided by the bright light of liberty burning through the land. . . . The hearts of all German citizens beat with gratitude, love, and devotion to the Union. They are ready to lay down their lives in its defense." In Cincinnati, Gustav Tafel defined the coming storm as an epic dialectical clash of two mutually exclusive concepts, arguing, "Democracy is against the spread of slavery," and thus Germans should prepare, for "the battles must be fought! To it! They have taken up the sword, now get the rifles! Step into line! Attention! Forward march! Get set! Fire!"[56]

During Lincoln's triumphant stop in Cincinnati en route to Washington, eighteen German organizations sent members to greet the president-elect outside the Burnet House Hotel. Frederick H. Oberkline read from a prepared address, decreeing, "Sir, we the German free workingmen of Cincinnati avail ourselves this opportunity to assure you . . . of our sincere and heartfelt regard." Lincoln had earned German support as a champion "of free labor and free homesteads." Denouncing efforts to portray "the mass of workingmen [to be] in favor of compromises between the interests of free labor and slave labor," Oberkline assured the president, "We spurn such compromises." Shunning any bargaining or conciliation, he promised that "the German free workingmen, with others, will rise as one man at your call, ready to risk their lives in the effort to maintain the victory already won by freedom over slavery." Taking measure of his audience, Lincoln responded, "In regard to Germans and foreigners, I esteem them no better than other people, nor any worse. (Cries of 'good'!)" The *Belleviller Zeitung* praised Lincoln's speech in Cincinnati, and on April 11, 1861, the *Zeitung* avowed, "Finally the miserable time of uncertainty, whether or not our government would act manly and honorably, seems to have come to an end."[57]

CHAPTER 5

THE WEST'S MOST LOYAL UNIONISTS

UNION, EMANCIPATION, AND GERMAN SOLDIERS' MOTIVATIONS

Given their recent experience with *Kleinstaaterei*, the territorial fragmentation that plagued attempts at German national unity, the thought of facing yet another form of disunion underscored German American anxiety entering the winter of 1860.[1] Combating the nation's dissolution held a particularly deep significance for Germans directly confronting secession. More so than in other regions of the North, on the Middle Border, precariously positioned along the fracturing lines of secession, German soldiers and citizens possessed a distinct consciousness of the war's effects on their daily lives. As a result, for the majority of Germans in the region who supported the nation's perpetuity, slave owners and European aristocrats converged, and secession crystallized their belief that a war to save the Union required slavery's defeat.

The vast preponderance of German soldiers along both sides of the Ohio and Mississippi Valleys fought for the Union. While not all claimed profound ideological motivations, many conceived the war as an effort to preserve the nation and destroy the antidemocratic forces that appeared all too familiar. August Horstmann, a salesman from St. Louis who joined the Union ranks, explained to relatives, "Much the same as it is in Germany, the free and industrious people of the North are fighting against the lazy and haughty Junker spirit of the South. But down with the aristocracy . . . may industrious and free men revive the glorious soil of the South." But even if the motivation to fight was not rooted so explicitly or philosophically in a revolutionary past, Germans participating in the fight could still view it as symbolizing a universal cause. While stationed in southern Missouri in early 1862, Henry Voelkner received a letter from his parents confirming his brother Wilhelm had been killed in battle. He quickly responded, hoping to provide a modicum of comfort by assuring them, "[Wilhelm] has made a sacrifice for a worthy cause, which is fraught with humbug, but in general it remains a good cause . . . he gave his life to free downtrodden humanity."[2]

Enthusiastically entering the fray also represented an opportunity to demonstrate unquestionable loyalty. "It is high time that every one openly declares on which side he belongs," announced the *St. Charles Demokrat* in October 1861. "To wait until one is forced, or 'until we all have to,' is only a groundless excuse."[3] Such language left little room for compromise and instead demanded clear declarations at a time when most in the region were still cautious and preferred to remain neutral.[4] After Ernst Hoffmann graduated from St. Louis Medical College in 1861, the sectional fallout placed him in difficult circumstances. His American wife and her family were secessionists and were therefore "to the utmost opposed to [him] as a Republican." Risking personal relations, he decided the only way to prove his fealty was to join the Union army: "I mean and carry out what I advocate as a Republican and in order that I might be spared to listen to treasonable language which I despise from the bottom of my heart."[5]

While German men demonstrated their commitment by becoming soldiers, on the home front, German women took an active role in supporting the war effort. During the first months of the war, Josephine Kircher wrote to her husband about her efforts, along with other German women in Belleville, to collect donations for the many Union soldiers from the region. "I have been running around all day long," she explained. "It is an unpleasant thing, but I am glad to sacrifice myself for many reasons, because I definitely want [the war] to succeed, and for you, for all of you." Strong in her convictions, Josephine expected to confront Miss Bell Badge, who had attempted "to hang a secession flag out of the window," telling her husband, "We intend to do something about that."[6]

Enlisting exemplified German Americans' collective belief that they were particularly well suited to battle oppressive forces threatening their new homeland. In southern Indiana, the radical editor of the *Cincinnati Republikaner*, August Willich mustered together volunteers for the all-German Thirty-Second Indiana Infantry, promising the regiment would represent "the patriotic answer of the Germans of Indiana to the call of their government to take up arms to protect its republican institution." Willich wrote, "In this way the Germans will really prove that they are not foreigners and that they know how to protect their new republican homeland against the aristocracy of the South." As immigrants, evincing loyalty was paramount; for Germans, Willich and others believed, the continued contest against autocracy remained a driving force.[7]

By positioning themselves in opposition to slave owners, clandestine secession movements, and conditional loyalty to the Union at the outbreak of the Civil War, Germans on the Middle Border represented one of the strongest sources of unconditional Unionism in a region rife with uncertainties. Unlike native-born Unionists, German soldiers and citizens had ideological motivations that were in part rooted in a European experience, with familiar combatants and causes retrofitted to match the new American context. Seeing the continuation of Old World conflicts, Germans came to consider emancipation a natural outcome of that much larger struggle for freedom.[8] Delivering a speech meant to convey his reasons for joining the Union army, Friedrich Hecker, a hero of the German Revolution, declared it essential that the "Southern aristocracy be broken . . . for liberty to flourish."[9]

Although Dreissigers were of an older, more cautious generation than the outspoken Forty-Eighters, they too grasped the continuities between European struggles and the American Civil War. Friedrich "Papa" Münch, one of the most widely published and generally respected Germans in the West, seized on the indelible image of oligarchical "slave power" to drive home the parallels. Münch, recently elected as a Republican state senator in Missouri, implored Germans, "Don't lose your courage. The oppressed people of Europe lost their independence and freedom, the negro lost his person." He assured them, "Let my opponents, for the time being, decry my action and my endeavor as ideology . . . they too will learn the logic of fact, for this war can end only with complete extermination of slavery."[10] Though many would stop short of equating European struggles for liberty with the plight of African American slaves, Germans on the Middle Border largely understood the war, and to some degree emancipation, as the best means of striking down the repressive aristocratic forces afflicting the nation.

Such idealistic outpourings, though, obscured less altruistic convictions. Germans in the Ohio and Mississippi Valleys, at the geographic and ideological intersection of free and slave labor, were heavily invested in a nation of free white workers and free western lands. Moral convictions about the condition of black slaves were often absent. Primary considerations for overthrowing a landed aristocracy were to benefit a free labor economy, unseat obdurate proslavery politicians, and open the door for both laboring and middle-class white citizens. The German interpretation of Jefferson's independent republicanism thus secured, individuals could improve their lot, pursue *Bildung*, spread out across western lands, and collectively elevate the nation. Nowhere did German Americans conflate their own interest with the Union's preservation and slavery's destruction more than in the West, along the very seams that were ripping apart. With war ensured and calls for volunteers reverberating, Germans rushed to enlist, intending to defend the liberal nation-state and their place within it.

Though evidence of high participation in the Union army among German Americans can be seen from enlistment numbers, Civil War historians rarely give much consideration to their impact on the war or the politics surrounding it. By the war's end, some two hundred thousand Germans had served in the Union army, roughly one-tenth of total enlistments.[11] Yet as Susannah Ural makes clear, "Despite their numerical significance, as well as their influence on military and political strategies and their active role in the armies and navies engaged, [ethnic] groups have received relatively little attention from historians." Similarly, Christian Keller suggests that "German soldiers, who were collectively the largest ethnic group in the Federal service, have almost been forgotten."[12]

The dearth of scholarship investigating German soldiers' distinct perceptions of the war's meaning and causes has led to generalizations and few concrete conclusions. Seeking to understand German soldiers' motivations in the Union army, Walter D. Kamphoefner and Wolfgang Helbich sampled letters written by German soldiers and conclude, "Republican and egalitarian ideology manifest in the 1848 Revolution extended farther down the social scale than previous scholars have realized." Yet just a few pages later, they suggest that outside of German officers, an overall lack of ideological or patriotic enthusiasm pervaded, arguing, "Without a doubt German enlisted men in the Union army were strikingly less 'patriotic' than their American comrades." The explanation is that the average German soldier lacked personal ties to America and often enlisted as a result of economic necessity.[13]

Kamphoefner and Helbich's conclusions, however, are meant to address German soldiers broadly and therefore do not necessarily consider regional differences. Many German soldiers from the Middle Border, where slavery and secession appeared far more ominous than in distant Northern regions, expressed a real awareness of the war's likely consequences on their daily lives and had greater motivation to confront the crisis directly. Attempting to build support for emancipation in the war's first year, Friedrich Münch suggested that living in close proximity to slavery was problematic and argued that Germans in Missouri had always believed the institution would die out, inevitably overcome by free labor proponents. "But in reality," Münch explained, "we found ourselves under constant pressure, under the always present tutelage of the slave owners." Though speaking from a slave state, he also articulated the general anxieties of free soil and free labor Germans in free states who feared slavery's economic and political impact should it spread: "Not one can deny the humiliating truth that in this so-called free country we were not free people, [and] rather had to adapt to the slave owners' whims." As he promoted antislavery, Münch would continue to portray a stark dialectical relationship between freedom and slavery, in which true freedom for Germans could be had only after slavery's defeat.[14]

Given their regional distinctiveness—including proximity to slavery and secession—Germans on the Middle Border were able to construct unique arguments for the Union war. Though evidence suggests that German soldiers in the Northern armies often lacked clear ideological motivations, Germans from the border appear as outliers in Kamphoefner and Helbich's study. Though no regional breakdown is provided, of their sample, nearly 80 percent of letter writers from the border expressed political awareness and loyalty to the Union cause. In fact, the study's authors suggest that Germans "at the war's outset, especially in border states . . . were often among the most reliable and decisive Unionists." In contrast with Germans in northern Ohio, for example, those in Cincinnati enlisted in droves. On hearing the news of Fort Sumter's surrender, the Cincinnati Turners gathered, enraged by what they considered an act of treason. Germans flocked to sign up at the Arbeiterhalle (Workingmen's Hall) and the Loewengarten (Lion's Garden), and within four days Cincinnati met its initial quota. In the early months of the war, thousands of Germans in Covington crossed the Ohio River to join ethnic regiments forming in and around Cincinnati.[15]

The rush to enlist was also a product of ethnic pride and uniqueness, which Germans in the West confidently, and at times arrogantly, cited. Louisville's *Anzeiger* immodestly promised, "Whenever and wherever the Germans have participated in the holy war of justice against injustice, they have always proven their innate talent to be exceptional warriors."[16] Despite its disregard for Lincoln, the Democratic *Volksfreund* advertised a German mass meeting in Cincinnati on April 17 "to take the necessary steps toward forming a separate all-German regiment" to defend the Union. Invoking Germans' masculine and civic responsibility, Cincinnati judge Johann B. Stallo declared, "So long as the naturalized citizen has the same privileges as the native born, so, too, must he conduct himself like a man and fight and protect the Union and the Star Spangled Banner."[17] George Schneider of the Ninth Ohio asserted, "We Germans are second to none in loyalty and patriotism, for we love this country as we love a mother; we are ready to offer our blood and our treasure for her free and matchless institutions."[18]

When the war came, Germans on the Middle Border positioned themselves in direct confrontation with slavery and secession, and therefore engaged in highly personal conflicts. Unlike Germans in more northerly locales, those on the border had enemies in close proximity, enemies who were likewise cognizant of the threat Unionist Germans posed. As Stephen Engle demonstrates, Confederate sympathizers along the border "creat[ed] exaggerated stories, which portrayed [Germans] not simply as demeaning and disreputable but as demeaning and disreputable Germans fighting against the southern cause." The war along the border meant addressing immediate and personally consequential quarrels playing out not hundreds of miles away, but in one's daily experience.[19] It follows then that while Missouri's Germans "had far and above the highest level of Union army participation," Wisconsin, well removed from the border and slavery, although home to nearly double the total number of Germans in Missouri, provided only half as many soldiers.[20]

Along with opposing outright secession, German Unionists on the border detested any signs of wavering loyalty or conditional Unionism. Though the Lower North as a whole vigorously supported efforts to preserve the Union, conservative or conditional Unionism, most prominent in the southern regions of the Old Northwest, demanded compromise and rejected antislavery radicalism.[21] When conservative Unionists along the border began to dissent, Germans presented themselves as counterweight.[22] After learning of secessionist activity in St. Louis, Illinois Germans upriver in Quincy responded by raising a company of one hundred men, who were touted as "disciplined European soldiers" ready to put down the rebellion.[23]

German support for the war was not unanimous, but strong pro-Union sentiment existed even among conservative German Catholics.[24] East of St. Louis in Marion County, Illinois, a public meeting called in early 1861 discussed a potential separation from the Unionist northern region of the state. Simultaneously, though heavily Catholic and Democratic, Germans in the county met to denounce secession and volunteered at such a frenzied pace that one native-born onlooker believed they had "become more readily Americanized than any other foreigner."[25] In Dubois County, Indiana, the local Catholic German militia, called Father Kundek's Guards for the Catholic priest responsible for early settlement efforts, immediately joined the Twenty-Seventh Infantry. Christina Katterhenry, also in Dubois County, wrote to relatives in Germany regarding the war: "Many of the sons of acquaintances and relatives have gone to war. . . . The sons of my sister-in-law also had enough self-denial in regard to their lives to offer them, if need be, for the precious and freedom and honor of the Fatherland." "Because this is a free country," she explained, "they wish to fight [the war] through their own free will [*freiwillig*]."[26] Later in the war, facing attacks from Confederate guerrillas, Father J. Martin Seisl and other German Jesuit priests in Washington, Missouri, aided federal forces by acting as couriers while members of their congregation took up arms.[27]

Though not in slaveholding states, southern Indiana and Illinois Germans had varied motivations for enlisting. But their conception of the war as an ideological struggle, whether to preserve the nation, protect the interests of free white labor, or defeat aristocratic planters, was widespread. Asked by his wife to give up soldiering and return home, Albright Koehler, a druggist from central Illinois, expressed a less abstract and more material incentive for fighting: "Oh, I hope to earn something yon so I can make a [*sic*] honorable living with my dear wife and children." After witnessing the carnage of battle firsthand, he sent her a poem, lyrically reminding, "And always they will say gladly; They fell for the Union without fears."[28] Frederick Heuring, a chaplain with the Twenty-Fifth Regiment, Indiana Infantry, wrote that the South "has treated us very badly, because we will own no slaves but God will vindicate our cause." Before a likely battle outside of Springfield, Missouri, the chaplain prayed, "Oh Lord my God, crush out at once this viper of secession." In December 1861, the Forty-Third Illinois Infantry published a recruiting announcement for distribution in the Belleville region that urged, "When the one-half German St. Louis is threatened by the enemy from two sides . . . [the German must] rally to the flag of his country, the flag of freedom." After serving with the Twenty-Fourth Illinois, southern Illinois Germans Friedrich Braütigam, John Christian Wachter, Paul Ackerman, and Valentin Riegel reenlisted in the Eighty-Second Illinois in August 1862. When the new chaplain arrived, Braütigam applauded his "very liberal speech with not even the slightest religious reference. Theme [was] on the basis of true freedom."[29]

To be sure, not all German enlistees fought for higher ideals. Economic exigencies sometimes caused them to look at enlistment as opportunity, especially for newly arrived immigrants struggling to survive. Before Balzer Grebe joined the Fourteenth Illinois Infantry, he painted houses and his wife worked as a maid. After the couple bought a home and had a son, they went into debt following the economic crisis of 1857. With the war, Grebe enlisted for three months. Still facing financial hardship, he explained, "My wife and I decided that it was best that I go back into the military and that we should have faith and trust in the Lord." In southwestern Illinois, Amalie Rückels wrote that financial difficulties had forced two brothers-in-law and other local Germans to join the Union army. Left with few resources, Rückels worried about new uncertainties, including the potential that the men would never come home. "Oh, what would we poor women do then, as strangers in this country?" she wondered. "Around here there are hardly any men left."[30]

For many Germans, to fight meant a steady paycheck, which outweighed dislocation from home and family. A day laborer who had emigrated from Prussia in 1853, Theodor Heinrich Brandies lived for several years as a small farmer in Franklin County, Indiana, retreated to Cincinnati in search of work, and then returned to southern Indiana on the eve of the war. In 1862, when he became a voluntary substitute for Johann Pohlmann Jr., a twenty-year-old who stood to inherit a large, successful farm, Brandies was paid $800. In a letter he sent to his wife before he died of illness outside Vicksburg in 1863, he wrote, "This war is a humbug."[31]

Though the promise of wages or the excitement of leaving home enticed some enlistees, considerable numbers of German soldiers from the Middle Border ultimately perceived the war as a larger struggle for the Union. August Schramm and his brother joined a local home guard in southern Indiana in early 1861 and "drilled for the first time in the Union Hall." Schramm wrote in his diary, "There was 33 of us, all German. We had to drill for about an hour." He explained, "We want to do something for the Union to[o], if we are wanted." Eduard Ochsner, stationed in Bloomfield, Missouri, wrote to his brother that he had "joined the army of our fatherland . . . to defend our freedom." Likely responding to criticisms from those back home, Ochsner shot back, "I think you know I didn't go to make money or to leave my job, but I have joined the army to fight for freedom and justice." Stephen Werly, a deeply religious volunteer in the Twenty-First Missouri, wrote in his diary, "I Herewith make a vow, as I have decided to go with the soldiers to fight for the rights of the country . . . to help maintain and save the rights and the liberty of my country." German women, too, expressed a deep level of commitment. When presenting a flag to the Lyon's Fahnenwacht (Lyon's Color Guard), St. Louis women explained, "In keeping with old German custom, we women do not wish to remain mere onlookers when our men have dedicated themselves with joyful courage to the service of the Fatherland; so far as it is in our power, we too wish to take part in the struggle for freedom and fan the fire of enthusiasm into bright flames."[32]

Implicit in their belief in liberal nationalism, or Unionism, many Forty-Eighters and former revolutionaries interpreted sectional conflict as an ideological clash between free and slave labor, democracy and aristocracy. The war then offered the opportunity to overturn what they deemed to be an outmoded, feudal society reliant on coerced labor. The Thirty-Second Indiana, an all-German regiment led by the radical Forty-Eighter August Willich, was one of the most politically conscious regiments in the West. Many of its recruits were Turners from Cincinnati, Louisville, and Evansville, Indiana, who came to fight under the former Prussian military officer. As an editor for the *Cincinnati Republikaner*, Willich deplored the "slavocracy" of the South and portrayed the war's outbreak as a positive step toward its defeat. Though the *Cincinnati Daily Times* praised the Thirty-Second for its gallantry, the newspaper reminded, "Colonel Willich is, as most Cincinnatians will remember, an ultra Red Republican and most, if not all the members of his regiment partake of the same sentiments." Though an exaggeration, the point remained that those who fought with Willich shared to some degree his philosophical commitment.[33]

Fighting under an inspired commander attracted volunteers from northern Kentucky, a region inhospitable to federal army recruitment in 1861, to cross the Ohio. After joining the Thirty-Second, Germans from Louisville remained concerned for their home state, where teetering loyalty and proslavery advocates threatened to join the secessionist impulse. One soldier assured the *Anzeiger* in late 1861, "We Louisvillians would especially like to see if we come to Kentucky . . . although we have devoted our services to the whole union, and the good cause," he explained, "it would make us especially happy to give special protection to our fellow Louisville citizens, and keep the Rebel horde from its gates and be able to drive them out of Kentucky." While stationed in Tennessee, "Artaxerxes" wrote to the *Anzeiger*, "Were each individual not so totally convinced of the justice of his cause, indeed we could not long resist against these intoxicated and nearly mad Southerners." Fighting under August Willich, a commander who praised the abolitionist martyr John Brown and railed against the oppressive slave master, German Kentuckians in the Thirty-Second likewise conducted a war to free their state from such evils.[34]

Fighting for the Union cause took on different meanings, but from the beginning, German soldiers, especially those tied to a revolutionary past, anticipated that victory could be achieved only through the subordination of slave masters. At the beginning of the war, Emil Mallinckrodt expressed his belief that "a permanent restoration of the Union is no longer possible other than through the total and final abolition of slavery." That such a pronouncement seemed audacious, even radical, was not lost on Mallinckrodt, a Dreissiger once disappointed by a premature and unsupported revolution in Europe. This past failure led him to wonder about wartime abolition: "Whether the people are ready for such a rash, difficult measure, time will soon tell."[35]

In the West, implementing the end of slavery required overcoming conditional Unionists who sought solely to preserve the nation—the "Union as it was and the Constitution as it is."[36] From this perspective, the nation's unity was paramount, but slavery should remain intact where it existed and prohibited from western territories. This way, both white Northern workers and

Southern slave owners could coexist. One Unionist Democrat from southern Indiana proclaimed, "We intend to have in our State, as far as possible, a white population, and we do not intend to have our jails and penitentiaries filled with free blacks." In other words, African Americans would remain enslaved in the South, the nation's racial makeup untouched. In direct confrontation, Germans considered emancipation in part as a punishment not only for disloyal slave owners but also for those who maintained only conditional loyalty. Such sentiment failed to find wide reception among many native-born white people on either side of the border.[37]

When radical voices on the border did manage to push abolition forward, they found support almost solely from antislavery Germans. Northern Kentuckian Anton Herman Bullenhaar outlined the conflict's dimensions in simple terms: "The object of the war is the abolition of slavery. *Hurrah for the Union en the Sisechen gohn tor Helle* [and the Secesh gone to Hell]." As Missourian Karl Frick informed his parents, "It isn't a war where two powers fight to win a piece of land, instead it's about freedom or slavery, and as you can well imagine, dear mother, I support the cause of freedom." A few months later, he continued, "The main thing it's about is the Negro question, the black people who are certainly human beings, just black instead of white, but who are treated like animals and sold at will." George Hillgaertner, a Forty-Eighter and new editor of the *Anzeiger des Westens*, pursued emancipation as the most efficient war strategy, demanding "a short energetic war, a war that will bring freedom to Missouri." He then instructed his readers to send emancipation petitions to Congress.[38]

John C. Frémont's arrival in Missouri provided an impetus for antislavery Germans to treat abolition as a viable military strategy. The former Republican presidential candidate, named commander of the Department of the West in August, soon declared Missouri under martial law. Frémont also ordered slaves of known rebels freed. The *Anzeiger* cheered, "We are done once and for all with half measures, and that the suppression of rebellion at all costs is to proceed with fearful and bloody seriousness."[39] Missouri Germans applauded all attempts to punish rebellious secessionists, whom they blamed for leading the state into violent guerrilla warfare. Convinced of their cause, Missouri Germans embarked on a mission to undermine slave owners and were willing to contribute in whatever way possible. Capitalizing on such vehemence, Frémont, who did little to ingratiate himself among St. Louis's native-born Unionists, relied heavily on the city's antislavery Germans, who adopted an increasingly radical position.[40]

Frémont's enigmatic presence was enough to inspire hopes for a radical new strategy in the West. Following his arrival in St. Louis, returning German soldiers from the Fifth Missouri paraded through St. Louis's Tenth Ward. There a women's welcoming committee led by Frau Dr. Doehn greeted them. Addressing the soldiers and crowd, she proclaimed, "At this very moment the country that has become our new homeland is threatened by the enemy as at no other time and it demands that each of its sons serves with his whole strength, to hew a new path for liberty." But soldiers alone could not win the war, she insisted. "Not just men must shed their blood; women, too, must pay their tribute." Building momentum, Doehn pointed to Frémont's arrival as further evidence that German war efforts were sure to succeed. "Will not everyone reach for his sword with courage and enthusiasm when he knows a *Fremont* is within our walls?" she asked. "He knows how to value the Germans' contributions, he knows in them are the true sons of free America."[41] Few outside of these German allies supported the general's actions.

Montgomery Blair, Lincoln's postmaster general and one of Frémont's most important allies, complained to the president that Frémont had surrounded himself "with a German Staff, by distributing his money patronage among them [and] by flattering them with the idea of their controlling the politics of the country." Fearing he would lose the backing of conditional Unionists along the border, Lincoln quickly rescinded Frémont's emancipation order and within weeks removed the controversial commander. Though cognizant of their important role on the border, Lincoln likely knew that radical Germans would be outraged, but in the end they had nowhere else to turn.[42]

Infuriated by the proclamation's rescission, radicalized Germans began to protest the Lincoln administration's conservatism. Continued partisan warfare in Missouri fed German demands for fierce action against secessionists, but Frémont's dismissal indicated the opposite. The *Anzeiger des Westens* labeled the affair "an act of cowardice and baseness that no one can easily accept."[43] In Cincinnati, a protest meeting concluded that the loss of Frémont was "a sad blow to the Republic." German soldiers protested as well; some threatened mutiny, believing they had lost their leading advocate.[44] Henry Voelkner complained that the removal of Fremont "caused much consternation in the army; the Germans were most upset, while the Americans took it quite cool . . . some few even rejoiced." Voelkner recounted how "the officers, notably the Germans, made a demonstration to practically force Fremont to stay with the army," expressing their dissatisfaction. Fearing revolt, St. Louis's leading Republican Frank Blair confided to his brother, "The Germans here are rushing headlong into a revolution and we must use some means to check this tendency."[45]

Lincoln's dismissal of Frémont created dissension among radical Germans and committed Republicans. The symbiotic relationship between the region's

Republican Party and German voters had carried them from Thomas Hart Benton's defection in 1852 to prominence in state and city government in St. Louis. To abandon that alliance would likely reverse gains made by German Republicans in St. Louis and the region as a whole. In southern Illinois, Gustav Körner recognized what such a schism might portend. Körner labeled Frémont's sacking "outrageous" because it made it impossible to "disguise the fact the most energetic portion of our party in this region are now in opposition." As Körner saw it, the Republicans' problem was that radicalizing Germans threatened to drive off conservative Unionists from the fragile war coalition on the border. Though certain that emancipation, in some form, provided "the only remedy," he reassured Republican senator Lyman Trumbull, "I [have] always realized the extreme difficulty of its solution." Addressing the pervasive conservative racial attitudes in Missouri and southern Illinois, Körner determined, "We must care more now against a cry being raised against our party, that we are carrying on the war for universal emancipation." Körner knew that emancipation as a form of military necessity might be accepted by most southern Illinoisans, but universal abolition most likely would not. If radical Germans in St. Louis and in the Union army continued to push abolition, he feared a backlash to Republican rule.[46]

Despite Lincoln and western Republicans' attempts at moderation, radical Germans continued to drive abolition to the forefront. The German press in St. Louis became far more aggressive in its calls for emancipation. Though the *Anzeiger des Westens* remained loyal to Frank Blair and Lincoln, after editors Heinrich Börnstein and Charles Bernays were awarded diplomatic posts in Europe, its new editor, the radical George Hillgaertner, declared, "For us Germans, emancipation is a matter of life and death. If Missouri remains a slave state, then we will not remain here any longer. No one is fooled about that." The radical *Westliche Post* lampooned Blair's conservatism after he declared black colonization unnecessary "since the natural antipathy for the Negro is so great it will keep the races apart." "Where, then, do the Mulattoes come from?" inquired the *Westliche*. "All this exaggerated drivel about the inferiority of the Negro . . . is just so much fine sand strewn into the people's eyes." The *Hermanner Volksblatt* in central Missouri meanwhile congratulated the slaves "of our respectable neighbors on the other side of the [Missouri] River," after they had begun to "run away in masses."[47]

The guerrilla warfare that engulfed Missouri was in part a response to growing German radicalism. In turn, the escalating violence in Missouri served as a justification for heightened radicalism among Germans, leading to calls for a plan of abolition and a guarantee that victory would include slavery's defeat.

By May 1862, after losing a son at the Battle of Wilson's Creek, Republican state senator Friedrich Münch began outlining his vision for gradual, compensated abolition. He hoped to convince conditional Unionists that because the end of slavery was unavoidable, it was prudent to accept the situation.[48] Münch kicked off his crusade by first reaching out to Germans across the region, asking, "Do we want to allow the sad situation of Europe also to rise among us where the arrogant and intellectually decadent nobility rules over the millions?" Münch's call to arms positioned slavery as the pillar of an aristocratic class and the heart of the secession movement, and therefore, he said, "Shame upon us if we tolerate such disgrace a moment longer without opposing it with all our might."[49] One month later, with pressure building from the Emancipation Society of Missouri and its heavily German membership, a state emancipation convention was called in Jefferson City. A struggle between antislavery moderates who insisted on some form of compensation to slave owners and radicals who pursued immediate emancipation kept antislavery mired in debates and speeches. Though the convention's aims ultimately fell short, momentum for enacting a war of liberation continued to build.[50]

Flag of the First Missouri Volunteer Infantry listing five battle honors, including the August 10, 1861, Battle of Wilson's Creek near Springfield, Missouri. Many German Americans in the St. Louis Turner Society signed up for ninety days' service early in the war in the hopes of stifling rebellious activities, and they constituted the bulk of the first four Missouri volunteer regiments. Image courtesy of Wilson's Creek National Battlefield, with special thanks to Alan Chilton.

One of the strongest sources of support for abolition on the border came from German soldiers in the Union army. Already critical of slavery before enlisting, after experiencing slavery in the South they often became positive that abolition was essential to victory. Historians argue that Northern soldiers in the field soon became "practical abolitionists," widely accepting universal emancipation after recognizing its strategic value alongside the moral imperative.[51] Many conditional or conservative Unionists in the West, who did not understand slavery to be the driving force behind the war, expected the "peculiar institution" would remain intact where it existed. Because of the pervasive racial antipathy on the Middle Border, German soldiers who called for abolition not only in the rebellious South but also in the neutral Border States stood out as revolutionaries, as radicals.[52]

For many German soldiers, support for abolition came after experiencing slavery firsthand. Stationed near Helena, Arkansas, far from his home in Belleville, Illinois, Henry Kircher observed on September 2, 1862, "There are very many Negroes working here and many have been freed." Despite strong doubts in regard to black equality, he believed, "This is the only proper policy" for "as long as this does not occur throughout, the war will not take a successful turn." Though steeped in liberal Dreissiger traditions of the "Latin farmers," only after entering the South did he conclude, "Now I have witnessed the unnaturalness of slavery with my own eyes and with disgust." Based on his experiences, Kircher suspected that the South's dependency on slave labor meant that "all of the able-bodied men of the South might go against us in the battlefield before or until we emancipate the Negroes, and then they will have to go home." Kircher therefore endorsed emancipation as a vital war strategy.[53]

Growing antiwar sentiment in the border region led Germans to believe that emancipation and Union were synonymous. On September 10, 1862, Magnus Brucker, a Republican state congressman from Perry County, Indiana, serving as a physician in the Twenty-Third Indiana, received a letter from his wife informing him of open disloyalty in their hometown. A radical student during the 1848 uprisings, Brucker now believed he was engaged in a second revolution. His response assured his wife that "even if the southern-minded in Troy are cheering for the fall of the Union, it will not fall and must not fall." Brucker believed "the only way [to ensure victory] is to take away all their workforce, namely the Negroes, destroy everything they need to live, or use it ourselves."[54]

On September 22, 1862, President Lincoln announced the preliminary Emancipation Proclamation, freeing slaves in all areas of rebellion and launching a war of liberation. Before the announcement, Montgomery Blair warned of revolt on the Middle Border and Republicans' likely political defeat there.

As he predicted, following the proclamation, many dissenting soldiers from the region condemned a war to free slaves and threatened to throw down their rifles. A collection of Illinois Democrats met in Springfield in late 1862 and issued a string of resolutions that called for peace, submitting that "further prosecution of the present war cannot result in the restoration of the Union and the preservation of the constitution as our fathers made it, unless the President's emancipation proclamation is withdrawn."[55]

Though far from united in their reaction to emancipation, Germans widely embraced the act as the final indispensable step to defeating the slave South. The *Anzeiger des Westens* believed Lincoln had turned "every soldier in this army into an emancipator, into a soldier for freedom."[56] Inspired, attendees at a German meeting in Femme Osage, Missouri, stated their "demand of our candidates a public declaration through the press that with all their strength they will support and advocate 'Emancipation,' and especially Emancipation in our state."[57]

More broadly, German soldiers from the border celebrated emancipation. Adolf Engelmann described a Unionist meeting in Bolivar, Tennessee, held to elect a representative to oppose the proclamation and enforce the Fugitive Slave Law. Engelmann's incredulous response: "I really had not thought that the people here were so foolish."[58] In his letter home, southern Illinoisan Friedrich Braütigam of the Eighty-Second Illinois described the moment when "[Friedrich] Hecker read President Lincoln's Proclamation to emancipate the slaves at the battalion drill this morning. It was accepted with great jubilation." The next day, he reported that the nearby military hospital was "on the farm of a secesh whose son is serving as a Major in Stuart's Raiders. His 10 Negroes quit their duties as a result of Lincoln's Emancipation Proclamation." Braütigam confirmed that this act was met with great approval and admiration from the regiment.[59] Karl Frick believed "the president has taken strong steps to crush the rebellion with all his might" and "will certainly deal the deathblow. . . . For slavery is the sole cause of this disastrous war."[60] Frederick Heuring, a pastor from Evansville serving as chaplain with the Twenty-Fifth Indiana, cheered when "the negroes of our landlord [the plantation where his regiment was camped] go off, and all the tears and entreaties of their mistress combined with the threats of their master are not sufficient enough to keep them."[61]

Although Missouri was exempted from the Emancipation Proclamation, its descent into guerrilla warfare was only amplified by the federal government's reliance on German militia and radical German leaders who pushed for emancipation. After many radicals trumpeted that their demands for liberty had moved history toward a revolutionary moment, secessionist and conditional

Unionists alike feared abolition might soon be imposed by foreign mercenaries in their own state. Such fears were soon substantiated when Germans in Augusta gathered to celebrate emancipation, announcing, "It is the undeniable fact that the powerful transformation in Missouri is to be credited primarily to the untiring efforts of the Germans . . . who oppose the institution of slavery not only because of the economic and political reasons but fight it more so because it stands in direct contrast to their feelings of justice and morality." The *St. Charles Demokrat* rejoiced over news that "the Blacks in Warren County have emancipated themselves." Reporting that a slave fled to a German militia, the editor celebrated that "there the black, two-legged piece of property was made into a human." Weeks later, with the support of the German militia, the former slave returned to his master to retrieve members of his family. Once there, the "master hits his former slave in the face; he, not lazy, returns the compliment and beats the master up until he remains laying weakly on the ground."[62] One Missouri slave remembered that after several slaves started waving switches to keep the flies away from some German soldiers as they ate, the Germans said, "We don't need that . . . Come on and eat with us."[63]

The president's proclamation also revealed that although Germans on the border widely praised the move, not all subscribed to abolition or supported radical war measures. Though support for emancipation was abundant among antislavery Germans in urban centers such as St. Louis, Evansville, and Cincinnati and smaller cities such as Belleville, Illinois, and Cape Girardeau and Hermann, Missouri, some rural racially conservative Germans offered far less enthusiasm. In the opinion of William Hofmann, a war in defense of the Union superseded any act of emancipation. Writing from southern Indiana, where rural German enlistments lagged, Hofmann continued to support the war but believed it "would long be at an end if the principle 'The constitution as it is and the Union as it was' would be maintained, as this sissy Lincoln promised upon his entrance into his official position." Instead, he lamented, "the whole war has degenerated itself into an Abolitionists war and all will be risked not for the restoration of the Union, but for the freeing of the slaves."[64]

Despite support for a radical war policy, in a region where racial subordination prevailed, some Germans expressed clear doubts over emancipation's consequences. Even in urban centers, a portion of the German population balked, fearing that the proclamation would lead to total abolition and black migrants fleeing the South heading straight to their city. In Cincinnati, a riot broke out in July 1862 along the riverfront, where black workers had increasingly found employment for lower wages. White workers struck back with violence and intimidation. The *Cincinnati Volksfreund* denounced the mob and pointed to the leading role played by Irish workers, but the German Democratic newspaper asked the city's Republicans, "Are you really serious with the idea of making the Negro our equal?" A month later, the *Volksfreund* accused German Republicans of fighting for "the Union . . . only if all the Blacks are free in all the slavery states." "We also abhor slavery," the paper assured its audience, but questioned, "will you set [slaves] free by legislating some decree?" Instead, skeptical of the millions of slaves who might suddenly be freed, the paper asked not for a liberation, but for restoration. "What we want foremost is the Union, the whole, the great, the all proud Union."[65]

Though outspoken in their concerns and doubts regarding abolition, conservatives represented the minority position among Germans on the border. In Illinois, the Democratic *Belleviller Volksblatt* believed that abolitionists sought to elevate black people over white people, envisioning a society turned upside down. The newspaper insisted, "The question has to emerge, who in the various states should be entrusted with the civilization and progress of the country. Should it be the white working man or the Negro?" The answer seemed obvious. "It is not the question of what the Negro should be, but rather what he is. Not what utopian dreamers and fanatics would like to do in order to experiment with the Negro at the cost of the white man, but rather what the security of the white man requires."[66] While emphatic, this opinion was not well received locally, and repercussions soon followed.

By this point, Louis Houck edited the *Volksblatt*. Houck once served as an apprentice to Eduard Mühl at the *Hermanner Wochenblätt* in Hermann, Missouri, where he listened to Mühl and Friedrich Münch articulate the rationalist critique of slavery in Missouri. Houck often disagreed and eventually returned to Illinois. In 1859, he was offered financial support from Illinois's Speaker of the House, William Ralls Morrison, to continue printing the struggling Democratic *Volksblatt*. Houck accepted and harangued Lincoln for his radical abolitionism in 1860. When the war began, Houck called for compromise while claiming to be an "unconditional Unionist." Very quickly Houck, by his own account, "became very unpopular," was labeled a Copperhead, had his office was ransacked, and felt it necessary to buy a revolver. On May 19, 1864, after he persisted in denouncing Lincoln and all forms of emancipation, the *Volksblatt*'s offices were totally destroyed by German soldiers from Belleville who had had enough. Soon after, Houck lost financial support, without which a German Democratic newspaper in Belleville could not survive. Defeated, Houck sold out and headed south to Cairo, Illinois.[67]

In German communities, where Lincoln's proclamation was widely celebrated, the act symbolized a purposeful step toward a new war, injected with deeper significance that aligned with the liberalism that had swept Europe decades prior. After being exchanged from a Confederate prison, August Willich returned to Cincinnati and delivered a speech to a jubilant audience, saying, "At the beginning of the war the views about its significance were very different, and when the war began it was viewed merely as a battle about nationality; it also turns out, however, that it is in the interest of all humanity." While in prison, Willich found that "the only ones who accepted us, cooked for us, or did us favors at every opportunity, were the slaves who saw Northerners as their liberators. Although their understanding of freedom is very vague, they only know it has to provide a happier situation than slavery." Though still skeptical of the slaves' ability to recognize liberty, he believed that these deeper currents drove the war forward.[68]

Though he would succumb to his wounds months after completing a letter home to friends and family, Georg Bauer expressed his belief that to achieve true victory, there would be "no more slaves, and freedom for all."[69] Adolf Engelmann had never placed black liberation at the center of the war, but it appeared clear that emancipation represented a needed transformation, both in terms of military strategy and philosophically. He argued, "The blacks are a factor that up to now have been a help to the South. Now in case of a revolution in the North that will be all changed. And from the ruins of the old laws, the Abstract Right will need to be planted. The downfall of the old will be frightful but the victory of the Right will be most brilliant."[70]

That so many German immigrants would embrace the "downfall of the old" in a region that had desperately sought compromise and peace in an effort to avoid such radical change would have major consequences. For native-born citizens on the Middle Border who decried abolition, adopted antifederal positions, and even supported outright secession, Germans increasingly personified radicalism and an oppressive government's most visible proxy. Nowhere were these animosities more evident than in Missouri, where deep-rooted tensions came rushing to the surface, pitting German Unionists intent on eradicating slavery once and for all against secessionist guerrilla fighters determined to expel what they considered to be a foreign army invading their land.

CHAPTER 6

REBEL BUSHWHACKERS AND THE "DAMNED DUTCH"

RADICAL GERMANS AND THE DEEPER ROOTS OF MISSOURI'S GUERRILLA WAR

By summer 1863, Sam Hildebrand was perhaps the most notorious guerrilla fighter in southeastern Missouri. The *Perryville Union* suggested, "It would be an exceedingly good thing if this rascal could be caught and hung. No man deserves it more." For the war's duration, his name appeared regularly in military reports and newspaper accounts deploring the spiraling violence. Although those loyal to the Union had much to fear, Hildebrand's wrath seemed curiously concentrated on one segment of the population: German immigrants, or the "Dutch," "Damned Dutch," or "Black Dutch," as Hildebrand and other noted guerrillas and native-born white people derisively referred to them.[1]

Indeed, throughout his colorful postwar memoir, Hildebrand often revealed his pointed enmity for Germans. In one instance, in August 1863, he and a small band of riders set out for the town of Hamburg, hoping to "take in three or four Dutchmen who had given the relatives of my two men a great deal of trouble." Deceptively donning the Union blue, Hildebrand coaxed one German to abandon his initial fear and leave the protection of his home. On realizing the grave error, "the whole family came out, placed themselves in a group near us and implored in broken English to spare their father." Despite the pleas, Hildebrand took the man a short distance away and "hung him to a lean tree." In justification, Hildebrand cited a number of instances in which he believed Germans had victimized his own family, a fact compounded by the realization that "during the whole war the Dutch went further, tried harder and risked more for my capture than any other people." For Hildebrand, his family and his culture were under attack, suffering at the hands of immigrant outsiders.[2]

Consistent with traditional interpretations of Missouri's guerrilla war, Hildebrand's actions fit a pattern of personalized, retributive violence that largely lacked broader meaning or ideology.[3] Yet plumbing the depths of Missouri's guerrilla war reveals a cultural, economic, and ideological conflict with roots stretching decades before 1861, including German immigrants' first arrival in Missouri. Throughout the sectional crisis, Germans elevated their criticisms, portraying slave labor as anathema to a free society. By forming a powerful voting bloc in St. Louis and several river counties, they threatened to alter the state's political dynamic and uproot its institutions. This emboldened political activism fed the perception that Germans represented Northern fanatic abolitionism and were a horde of foreign mercenaries armed by an oppressive federal government. Yet rarely is German liberalism's radical antislavery ascendance factored into interpretations of Missouri's guerrilla warfare.

In German liberalism's vision of western progress, slavery was an ugly contradiction and a historical wrong that needed correction. Sectional politics and the threat that secession posed to the Union radicalized antislavery Germans along the Middle Border. This was especially true in Missouri, where they saw the chance to upend traditional powers on the state and local levels and open avenues to German leadership. Militarily, Germans made up 40 percent of Missouri's Union enlistments and played a decisive and controversial role in securing the state's loyalties in the war's early months. Sam Hildebrand was certainly not the only guerrilla who saw Germans as illicit invaders, culturally, politically, and now militarily.[4]

Like many other American families from the slave states living in the Big River Mills settlement in St. Francois County, the Hildebrands were subsistence farmers with a reliance on hogs. Traditionally, this meant letting livestock forage with open fencing and crop enclosures, with a crude sense of ownership practiced and accepted by all involved.[5] But this local system was suddenly challenged during the late 1830s, after several German immigrant families settled nearby. Hildebrand was just a child when the first Germans appeared, but the resentment persisted, and he later lamented that "they were very numerous and constituted about two-thirds of the population."[6] Though Hildebrand exaggerated Germans' prominence in his community, tempers flared when Germans "set up 'wild hog claims,' declaring that some of their hogs had also run wild." According to Hildebrand, "This led to disputes and quarrels, and some 'fist and skull fighting,' in which my brothers and myself soon won the reputation of bullies." Disagreements turned into lawsuits that did not go the Hildebrands' way. In the end, "the Dutch out swore us and we soon found the Hildebrand family branded by them with the very unjust epithet of hog thieves."[7]

But if St. Francois County in the 1840s seemed suddenly foreign and unsympathetic to the Hildebrands, others remained within the community who could provide support and empathy. In 1950, Henry C. Thompson, a journalist and historian, published the first study of Sam Hildebrand and concluded that after coming out on the losing end of litigation, the family looked to the "older members of the community . . . true friends who believed in their integrity." These families were the first settlers in Missouri and "had large farms that necessitated the use of negroes to work them."[8] Though the Hildebrands never rose to the ranks of the slaveholding elite, they nevertheless remained among the yeoman class and by 1850 owned a slave woman and her young daughter. When the troubles with the newcomers began, the Hildebrands relied on their relations with those older families with whom they shared a similar worldview. Well before 1861, Hildebrand's loyalty connected him to the social network of slaveholding families who offered support.[9]

Though guerrillas were long peripheral to Civil War scholarship, historians began to peel back the top layers of irregular warfare, positing that behind the personalized provocations, grudges, and jealousies, a deeper logic and purpose motivated these gray ghosts.[10] For the outlaw Jesse James, a fiery antiabolitionist father, a web of kin connections with slave ownership, and his family's hard treatment by federal troops provided motivation for James and his brother to take to the brush during the Civil War. Much as with Hildebrand, the Jameses' personal war was spurred not by reckless youth, but by a far more deadly mix of vengeance and antiemancipation politics.[11]

More recently, innovative scholarship on guerrilla fighters attaches clearer ideological motivations. Rather than being thieves or bandits who lacked ideology, guerrillas in western Missouri were mostly young men who overwhelmingly emerged from slaveholding families and were therefore the ones with the most to lose should slavery be abolished. Failed financial scheming on the part of Missouri's pro-Confederate leaders in anticipation of secession resulted in severe indebtedness and loss of property among leading slave-owning families. Forced to sell off large pieces of real estate and facing financial ruin, many from these families rode as guerrillas and "engaged in more violence than did individual guerrillas in other states." In addition to defending hearth and home, irregular warfare served to uphold Southern notions of manhood, including slaveholding.[12] Those who took up the Black Flag did so to protect home, familial relations, and slave property; to have done otherwise was understood as a form of emasculation and dishonor. The perceived threat German radicalism posed was therefore a powerful reason to fight as a guerrilla.[13] And thus when federal forces began to occupy Missouri, German soldiers most visibly represented a foreign invasion of the locals' homes and cultural traditions.[14]

As he rode off to join guerrilla outfits on the Arkansas border, Sam Hildebrand blamed outsiders for fracturing his community and dislodging his family. In early 1861, he and his brother Frank stood accused of stealing horses from Union families. Although Sam escaped, Frank was caught and hanged, and German soldiers burned their mother's home and killed their uncle and younger brother, both accused of guerrilla activity. Hildebrand's revenge stemmed from wrongs committed against him by Union men, most notably Germans. On a deeper level, Hildebrand was fighting to preserve an older version of Missouri that had existed before the arrival of German immigrants and German soldiers donning blue uniforms. In fact, he was still fighting over hogs, carrying his family's resentment from their first conflict with German neighbors into his battle with antislavery Germans invading his home and destroying his community. The two collided when Hildebrand encountered a German farmer near his home: "I talked all the Dutch language to him that I knew, and after giving him distinctly to understand that 'hog killing time' had come, I shot him."[15]

From the German perspective, sectional discord and partisan extremism in 1861—including guerrilla activity—was evidence that the liberal nation was under assault and radical preventive measures were needed. With Lincoln and his allies in Missouri desperately attempting to hold this border slave state, Germans were suddenly thrust into a leading role as the state's most reliably antislavery and unconditional Unionist constituency. Opportunistically, they claimed a new authoritative position in Missouri, openly challenging the political elite, who were just as reliably proslavery and often slave owners themselves.[16]

As evidence of antebellum anti-German rhetoric, proslavery stalwart and future governor Claiborne Fox Jackson in 1857 suggested that "Germans seeking homes in Missouri should be met at the threshold, knocked on the head, and driven back."[17] Months later, on Election Day, after the German Democratic defection to the local Republican Party in St. Charles County was followed by German emancipation meetings, Peter H. Fulkson, a leading slaveholder, shot at two Germans, John F. Schroer and George H. Tupker. According to courtroom testimony from twenty witnesses, Fulkson fired "with intent to kill." All charges were dropped.[18]

Wie unfere Truppen in Missouri fur ihre Hungrigen Bferbe forgen (How our troops in Missouri secure food for their hungry horses). During Missouri's guerrilla war, German soldiers commandeered alleged Southern sympathizers' resources to maintain the war effort and punish disloyalty. Courtesy of the Missouri Historical Society, St. Louis; http://collections.mohistory.org/resource/156152.

In 1859, Friedrich Münch, the experienced Dreissiger, published a proimmigration response to Jackson and rising anti-German sentiment titled *The State of Missouri*. In it, he countered Jackson's hostile xenophobia by assuring his fellow countrymen, "There is still space enough for enormous numbers of German immigrants, and if these arrive, Missouri could . . . be made the most nearly German state of the entire Union." With slavery increasingly under attack, the views of men like Jackson, Münch surmised, faced certain extinction. In fact, Münch predicted, "Missouri will be the first to emancipate itself as soon as the national government has been torn from the hands of the 'slavokratie.'"[19]

Entwining slave masters with the specter of aristocratic rule made for a powerful message to alienated Germans, rekindling memories of revolution and the continued desire to foster liberal progress. Therefore, given their revolutionary heritage, Münch described a clear-cut mission for the proclaimed guardians of freedom: "It seems to be the task assigned the Germans in Missouri to unrest one of the largest, most beautiful states blessed by nature with inexhaustible natural resources from the destructive bonds of slavery, and for this we still need thousands of companions in arms." By 1861, such contrasting vitriol was not simply a product of Republican ascendance or Southern Fire-Eaters' secessionist rhetoric. Rather, its origins lay in a long-standing incongruity between conflicting visions for Missouri, the West, and the nation.[20]

The opening decades of the nineteenth century saw native-born migrants from the slave states make their way to Missouri, a frontier territory.[21] Not unlike German immigrants, these settlers believed the West offered the best chance to expand opportunities; unlike Germans, some brought with them their most valuable assets—their slaves. In 1816, the *Missouri Gazette and Advertiser* reported, "A stranger would imagine that Virginia, Kentucky, Tennessee and the Carolinas' [*sic*] had made an agreement to introduce us as soon as possible to the bosom of the American family. Every ferry on the river is daily occupied in passing families, carriages, wagons, Negroes, carts, &c. &c."[22] By bringing their slaves, these migrants expected western expansion would protect the rights of slave masters.

When the Compromise of 1820 admitted the then territory into the Union, Missouri became the northernmost and westernmost state to permit slavery. In addition, the compromise decreed that with regard to future western expansion, slavery would not be allowed north of the 36° 30′ line of latitude—not coincidentally, Missouri's southern border. The few dissenters who challenged the institution during the march toward statehood were characterized as interlopers and traitors. Though the rest of the nation fiercely debated the addition of a slave state on the frontier, few within the new state considered that Missouri might rid itself of slavery in the future.[23]

Beginning in the 1830s, the liberal nationalism and emphasis on individual freedoms articulated by German Dreissigers posed an ideological challenge to slavery and cultural traditions. Their sudden and conspicuous influx unsurprisingly bred concern over who exactly these foreigners were and what their arrival might mean. Already in 1834, the *Columbia Missouri Intelligencer* reported, "In the counties of St. Charles and Warren, we observe that a new population consisting chiefly of German emigrants, are fast displacing the older settlers. In some large neighborhoods there remain but few of those who resided there a year or two ago." The demographic shift was significant enough to make the newspaper take notice and consider the implications. "Thus far we believe great harmony has prevailed between them and their neighbors, the American citizens," the paper explained. But it admitted, "There is, however, a degree of jealousy existing in the minds of many, arising from the peculiarity of their foreign manners and customs." Twenty years later, in 1857, the German-language *St. Charles Demokrat* turned the tables, explaining that in central Missouri, "The farms are more like plantations, and all are inhabited and worked by Virginians, who almost all own Negroes [and]. . . . seem to resist stubbornly the 'invasion of foreign elements.'"[24]

The struggle to harmonize Germans and Americans frequently played out on the local level as power and influence shifted along with changing demographics. Initially a colony of the German Philadelphia Immigration Society, the town of Hermann, Missouri, grew quickly after its founding and settlement in the late 1830s. The new immigrants were so numerous that less than a decade after their arrival, led by the efforts of the outspoken rationalist and antislavery newspaper editor Eduard Mühl, they successfully relocated the Gasconade County seat to Hermann. This usurpation, Gert Göbel recounted, "aroused the anger of many Americans against the Germans and led to some bloody quarrels," though "the Germans . . . held their ground and did not let themselves be intimidated."[25] Such strong-arm tactics were a harbinger to Americans in Gasconade County that change was under way. As Göbel outlined, while generally amicable relations prevailed between Germans and Americans, "there existed in some localities old feuds, which sometimes lay smoldering under the ashes for a long time. When some occasion gave rise to an outbreak, they resulted in bloody quarrels."[26]

Along the wide Missouri and Mississippi River bottomlands, long-standing animosity between Germans and American neighbors indicated that later conflict emerged within a historical context. In the 1830s, in reaction to local nativist activities, a German convention in Cape Girardeau met to appoint the Committee of Vigilance and Correspondence to "watch the proceedings of Native Americans."[27] After quickly demonstrating political awareness in the 1830s, Germans in the county continued to be active over the next two decades, so much so that in 1855, amid nativist fervor sweeping the nation, the *Eagle*, a Cape Girardeau newspaper, printed an editorial that attacked a local group of "anti-Americans." As the article described, "The anti-Americans have fallen desperately in love with the idea of universal free suffrage. They affect not to understand why a man's fitness to vote or hold office should be estimated by his place of birth. They condemn this principle as a feature of an aristocracy unworthy of free government, and one which our Fathers often expressed a hope would never be tolerated. We do not know who are meant by 'our fathers,' unless it is the fathers of Germans."[28] Not long after, nearby Mississippi and Bollinger Counties passed restrictive ordinances that German peddlers be arrested on sight.[29]

By 1860, in Cape Girardeau, the largest city in southeast Missouri, 56 percent of the heads of households had been born in Germany and staunchly supported the Union. The city's unabashedly secessionist paper, the *Democrat*, found such a stance untenable. In an editorial titled "German Population," the writer explicitly warned, "For some time past we have heard of ominous mutterings throughout the county against all those Germans of this city who are Black Republicans, and heard repeated threats to expel them by mob force." Describing them as "Black Republicans" signified the belief that these Germans were the most dangerous of foes—abolitionists. "If the Black Republican Germans, after having been admitted to our shores on equal terms with us . . . knowing in advance what are institutions are—repay us with dirty ingratitude by opposing us . . . why let them?" Finally, the writer recommended, "Let us secede first; it will then be soon enough to call them to question, and if they cannot bear our institutions, no one will object to their peaceful departure." Within a few months, the situation was quite the reverse. Cape Girardeau County became a Union stronghold, anchored by the heavily German city of Cape Girardeau, while local secessionists found themselves forced into irregular warfare in rural parts of the occupied county.[30]

During the early months of the war in Jackson, in Cape Girardeau County, Rev. Joseph Maple witnessed the deteriorating relations between the occupying Union army and residents after German soldiers plundered rumored secessionists' homes.[31] Although a Unionist, Maple denounced the inspections, specifically the behavior of the "infidel barbarous-alien Dutch." Maple believed the Germans were "demons in human form, under the garb of soldiers, professing to be better representatives of American Liberty than Americans themselves." On one occasion, Maple reported that soldiers had so frightened two young girls that they were "thrown into paroxysms and from that into fever." The oldest died a few days later. The event led Maple and many others to conclude that the girl was "frightened to death by a horde of vandals, who joined the army, only that they might have a chance to steal." "Ruffians," Maple concluded, "whose patriotism has been aroused by the promise of fifteen dollars a month."[32]

Less than two weeks after the episode, one hundred riders stampeded into town and promptly pulled down the American flag flying over the courthouse.

They then headed toward a neighboring German settlement along the Whitewater River. As Maple reported the next day, "We still hear of suffern [*sic*] among the Germans west of Jackson." The body of a German soldier, taken prisoner in a skirmish, was discovered in the nearby woods. The man had clearly been executed, "shot below the forehead just between the eyes and stabbed in three places." The soldier belonged to the federal regiment that weeks before had searched suspected secessionists' homes. The soldier's death came as no surprise—the riders had loudly "sworn vengeance." A month later, seven German soldiers' skeletons were found in the woods.[33]

Following Union occupation in Cape Girardeau, guerrillas retaliated. One Union officer noted with alarm that the guerrillas often focused on German families. He reported, "A rebel force was ravaging the White Water settlement in Cape Girardeau County, murdering the Germans and despoiling them of their possessions, horses and other property."[34] Just to the south, in Scott County, Captain Charles Hinrichs formed Company L, Tenth Missouri Cavalry, with twenty-seven recruits from the German community in New Hamburg.[35] Shortly after, M. Jeff Thompson, known as the "Swamp Fox," explained that "the temptation to have a brush before leaving was too great, and [we] charged into the town of Hamburg scattering the Dutch in all directions."[36]

In the agriculturally rich and most slave-dependent central region of the state, Germans seemed especially alien not only because of their culture but also by their nonreliance on slave labor. In Lafayette County, immigrant farmers adopted hemp, a highly profitable cash crop.[37] In 1844, Johann Bruns harvested his first eight acres, and by 1849, nine out of ten German farmers in Lafayette County produced hemp, averaging over $100 in profit. But unlike their American neighbors, these German farmers planted and harvested this perceived "plantation crop" without slaves. And while they could never match the output of hemp growers using slave labor, they competed with them.[38]

Describing his childhood in Lafayette County, William Walkenhorst, a son of German immigrants, revealed that Germans were hyperconscious of and sensitive to the state's cultural divisions stemming from slavery. Even in slave-rich counties like Lafayette, slavery was characterized by small holdings rather than large plantations with hundreds of slaves. Yet Walkenhorst focused his remembrance primarily on the elite and very small planter class. "Lafayette County, one of the richest in the state, was settling up, perhaps, as fast as any other," he wrote, but the county's wealth was in part tied to slave owners who "owned large farms and from half a dozen to 20 or more slaves—men, women and children," the majority of whom, he noted, "were mulattoes." As far as the Germans were concerned, this represented an aristocracy.[39]

Such a seemingly unfair advantage engendered hostility toward slave owners, a sentiment Germans did not hide. Walkenhorst wrote bluntly, "One of the reasons why [slave owners] did not like the Germans was because most of them were antislavery." Conversely, the statement just as easily read that Missouri's Germans did not like the native-born because they supported slavery. Germans argued that the concentration of wealth echoed a European past, and Walkenhorst highlighted the separation this provoked: "These [slave-owning] farmers lived in fine houses built of stone or brick. They rode in fine carriages and dressed well. . . . Of course, all of the manual labor was performed by the slaves." By contrast, "Germans without wealth . . . came into possession of their homes by hard work and strict economy." Walkenhorst expressed disbelief that "slave-owner farmers considered themselves the real Americans. They did not mix with the Germans. . . . When they talked about those who were not of their class they called them the 'Dutch.'" For Walkenhorst, slave labor afforded symbols of wealth, which Germans identified as proof that slave owners enjoyed inequitable advantages.[40] However, just as few Germans in Missouri were outright abolitionists, few slave owners belonged to the planter class, yet both groups recognized primarily the other's extremes.

The Civil War brought to the surface such cultural and economic resentments in Lafayette County. In late 1860, the Lexington Turnverein, the German gymnastic and educational organization that embraced Unionism and antislavery, applied for incorporation but was opposed by state senator James T. V. Thompson, one of the largest slaveholders in the county and state, who reasoned, "It was intended to incorporate a set of infidel Dutch, who did not believe either in heaven or hell, or the devil." The *Lexington Weekly Express* reported that Thompson "was informed that there was more than gymnastics in it."[41] Months later, when local secessionists proclaimed their desire to leave the Union, Germans recognized an opportunity to turn the tables and immediately began to organize. Violence broke out on May 2, 1861, after a pro-Union rally led and attended by several hundred Germans was disrupted by the arrival of armed men intent on preventing any discussion of ending slavery. A correspondent for the *Westliche Post* reported, "All hatred is concentrated on the 'Dutch.' . . . Many have already made themselves ready to depart."[42] After the Missouri State Guard searched and effectively shuttered the Turner Hall in neighboring Benton County, Germans gathered to form their own protective militia. Within two weeks the camp fell under attack in the early morning hours, leaving over thirty men dead.[43]

Soon after, the German Home Guard in Lafayette County retaliated, pursuing a local man named Grissom accused of robbing Meineke's general store.

German soldiers recovered the stolen goods and dragged the man from his home while his wife and newborn child pleaded in vain. They took him a short distance and shot him, leaving the body covered by brush, where it sat for a month until his brother, a local guerrilla, stumbled on it.[44] Following Grissom's murder, intensified raids targeted Germans in Lafayette County, marked by four German civilians' execution.[45] Months later, a small gathering of German families was interrupted by a guerrilla raid. When Marie Blitz asked what would become of her husband, a preacher, one of the guerrillas responded, "We'll do to you what you do to us." Before dawn, three of the Germans were pulled off their horses and shot. In what must have felt like divine intervention, Pastor Blitz was released unharmed. Marie Blitz later wrote to her sister, "Oh, these were not humans; these were devils in human form," while her husband described his captors as having "neither Christian nor human feeling."[46]

Even in St. Louis, German Unionism stood in stark contrast to secessionist elements in and around the city.[47] In early 1860, Frederick Behlendorff left New Orleans, a city suddenly hostile toward Germans. After his employer accused him "of being an abolitionist and a traitor to the South," he returned to Missouri only to find a similar situation, determining that "one half of the population of St. Louis were determined secessionists." He observed, "Finely dressed ladies would even loudly insult us by shouting the vilest names from the porches and windows of houses in the finest residence portion of the city." For stonecutter John Buegel, the secession crisis presented a chance to rebuff those in the city who, he believed, had long abused Germans, "since we Germans at that time were looked upon as belonging to an unworthy nation," he explained, "and Americans, old and young, looked upon us with contempt and disdain."[48]

The bitterness Germans in St. Louis expressed reached new heights on Sunday, April 14, 1861, after a committee appointed by Missouri's governor Claiborne Fox Jackson took control of city police. One immediate act sent police into German saloons, beer gardens, concert halls, and even the opera house, shutting off the taps and effectively cutting off Germans from their lager beer on Sundays. Soon after, English became the only official language of state business, while public schools, a point of pride for Germans who preached *Bildung* and edification, lost funding in favor of mustering Jackson's militia.[49]

Though elected as a pro-Union Douglas Democrat, Jackson aspired to lead his state into the open arms of the Confederacy. But in February 1861, during a special convention to decide Missouri's future, secession was overwhelmingly voted down. Undeterred, Jackson clandestinely corresponded with Confederate president Jefferson Davis to discuss a military coup that included seizing the federal arsenal in St. Louis.[50] The largest in any slave state, the arsenal held significant stores and weapon-making machinery—all materials essential to Southern armies. From a strategic position, as the gatekeeper to both western lands and the mighty Mississippi River, St. Louis stood as the most important city in the West; it was also the most densely German.[51]

On May 7, 1861, Governor Jackson ordered state militia to make camp in Lindell Grove, just outside St. Louis. Poised on the city's perimeter, militiamen christened their temporary lodgings Camp Jackson and proceeded to name its streets after Confederate generals. Such activity raised suspicions, especially among the city's Germans.[52] Since the 1860 election, German militias, including the Turners, were highly active, emboldened by William H. Seward's speech in St. Louis in which he claimed, "Wherever the Germans come, it is their mission to create a way for freedom. . . . So let us happily permit Missouri to be Germanized."[53] Outraged, state militiaman accused the Germans of being "offensive to the greatest degree, frequently parading the streets at night in torchlight. . . . They had their military uniform, a military organization, and were thoroughly drilled in military tactics." Conversely, Germans believed Southern sympathizers were equally active and dangerous, pointing to a resolution passed by "Ninth Ward Washington Minute Men" in December 1860 proclaiming that "we are Southern men and that we wish to uphold and defend our interests and institutions with our lives, to the exclusion of all others."[54]

Believing Camp Jackson's militia harbored similar sentiments, the city's Republican leaders worked with Captain Nathaniel Lyon, an ardent Connecticut-born Unionist then in command of federal regulars at the arsenal, to enlist volunteers. Of the eight thousand who answered the call, roughly 90 percent were German. John Buegel, who hastily mustered into service, outlined, "It was known to all of us . . . that the southerners [state militia] intended to attack the arsenal, take away the available war material, and drown the hated Dutch, one and all, in the Mississippi." Though state militia paraded in a small peaceful field on the western edge of the city for an audience of picnicking families and enthusiastic spectators, the Germans continued to organize, believing they had uncovered a threat not only to St. Louis but also to their own well-being.[55]

On the morning of May 10, orders came down to march on Camp Jackson. John Buegel carried a simple objective: "The main thing was to teach the German-haters a never-to-be-forgotten lesson."[56] In the late afternoon, federal soldiers surrounded Camp Jackson and forced its peaceful surrender; not a single shot was fired.[57] Soon afterward, violence erupted. What seemed to most enrage the growing crowd watching the surrender was the fact that the federal soldiers were nearly all German. Democratic newspaper editor Daniel Grissom offered that many in the crowd were "under the impression that they were called upon to help save their friends from massacre by the Germans." After the surrender, the onlookers' "American spirit was intensely excited at seeing [surrendered state militia] disarmed and held captive by the 'Dutch.'"[58]

As the incensed crowd pressed forward, the intensity reached a crescendo. When the initial volleys of gunfire were heard, it was unclear who fired first. As news spread, Sarah Hill described her neighbor, who "rushed in wildly excited, crying, 'The Black Dutch! The Black Dutch are killing them all! They are shooting women and children in cold blood!'" By late afternoon, Lindell Grove lay littered with over one hundred wounded and twenty-eight dead civilians.[59]

In the aftermath, it was evident that the city was transformed. Reflecting on the sudden developments, Robert J. Rombauer observed, "On April 20, there were less than 500 regulars (federal troops) at the St. Louis Arsenal [while] a much stronger body of secessionist remained in the city. On May 11, the secessionist were captured and 10,000 Union men, mainly Germans, were in command." "They were simply prisoners," John Buegel triumphantly wrote in his diary about the state militia, "and the Dutch, as we were generally called, were masters of the situation."[60] Radical German editor Heinrich Börnstein reveled in the new reality: "Only yesterday the secessionist had been masters of the government and legislation of the state and city." But now, he seemed to imply, new masters had emerged.[61]

For Germans in St. Louis and throughout the Middle Border, their decisive action saved the city for the Union. One volunteer saw events as a revolutionary awakening, believing, "We felt ourselves set back into the days of 1848 and 1849, and the dried-up milk of enthusiasm seemed in fact to flow again." On Camp Jackson's second anniversary, Germans in St. Louis held a celebration in which over eight thousand participated.[62] Wilhelm Kaufmann later labeled the event "The Saving of St. Louis," contending, "The salvation of St. Louis by the Germans must be seen as one of the most significant and wide-ranging of all Union victories during the entire Civil War." Though lacking in humility, such statements were not without substance. Steven Rowan argues that "nowhere else in American history has a single group of foreigners or a single cohort of leaders made such a difference in the course of a region as in St. Louis between April and June 1861."[63]

Though Germans touted their victory, many native-born onlookers saw the Camp Jackson "massacre" as German radicalism's opening volley, an explicit threat to the state's cultural and racial authority. In Tennessee, the *Fayetteville Observer* reported that Southern businessmen left St. Louis "on account of the odium attached to them by the hireling *Dutch*" and opined, "The present war is establishing the fact beyond question that the *Dutch*—or, as they call themselves, the 'Germans,' as a class . . . are the meanest, filthiest, most inhuman, brutal, nigger-loving, amalgamating soldiers in America."[64]

In Missouri, many conditional Unionists became convinced that they, like the South, were under attack.[65] The following morning, in the *Missouri Republican*, the city's Democratic mouthpiece, the headline rang out, "German mercenaries Murder American Citizens."[66] Uriel Wright, who a few months earlier had voted against Missouri's secession movement, proclaimed, "If Unionism means such atrocious deeds as I have witnessed in St. Louis, I am no longer a Union man." Alice Cayton wrote to her brother complaining that recent events were "enough to make every true American heart swell with indignation against the Germans.[67] As federal soldiers marched across the state, anger aimed at the "Black Dutch" swelled. Germans soldiers became seen as a repressive, foreign government imposing its will.

Though Lincoln and Republicans readily used German enlistees to stay the course in Missouri, Germans' apparent adoption of radical antislavery and hard-line warfare persuaded many to join guerrilla bands in opposition. In early 1862, after an inundation of complaints, Henry W. Halleck, federal commander of the Department of the Missouri, reported to the War Department that "wherever [German general Franz Sigel and his German soldiers] go, they turn all Union people into bitter enemies." Indeed, Martin Öfele argues that the activities of Germans in St. Louis "drove into the arms of the secessionists numerous lukewarm Unionist Americans." Whether as Missouri's saviors or a conquering army, the German soldiers' high level of participation and unwavering convictions profoundly shaped the war's contours.[68]

Yet because guerrillas have so often been depicted as romantic outlaws or devious cutthroats, their violent acts overshadow their enemy's. Germans in particular are usually blended into generic, faceless Unionists or abolitionists in most accounts of Missouri's Civil War. But in truth, German soldiers, beginning at Camp Jackson, matched the guerrillas step for step in their commitment to making hard-line warfare. One Union officer in Washington, Missouri, complained, "My command is made up largely of Germans, and it has been very hard to restrain them from depredations on people known as Southern sympathizers."[69] Colonel Conrad Weinrich, a radical German Republican, reported that while patrolling central Missouri in November 1862, "We had our food and drink provided by the *Sisesch* . . . and when they didn't want to cook for us, we threatened to take everything away from them."[70] The decidedly Southern-leaning *Plaindealer* in Sainte Genevieve, Missouri, complained of "Teutons" riding through town with American flags and harassing local residents, which the paper attributed to "whiskey and beer . . . without a doubt the principle and inspiring cause."[71]

In fact, Germans in Missouri pursued a far more ideological cause than "whiskey and beer": dismantling slavery. General John C. Frémont's rejection and dismissal following his early attempt at emancipation in Missouri emboldened and radicalized antislavery Germans. Friedrich Münch offered a rationale for participation in the war and the antislavery cause in early 1862. Münch began by admitting that the Dreissiger immigrants, himself included, "knew that we were going to a slave state, but we did not attribute very great importance to that fact . . . we ourselves wanted nothing to do with slavery, but we also expected that we would not be burdened by it." "I readily confess, as will thousands of others," he continued, "that in this last expectation we deceived ourselves . . . slavery and true freedom can not, in fact, exist next to each other." As a former European revolutionary and longtime opponent of slavery, Münch seized on the building antislavery momentum, reminding his fellow Germans, "Many of us have had hungry slaves come to our door. . . . Or we were witnesses to real kidnappings, the dreadful show where parents, children and spouses were torn apart in the midst of the raw jokes of traders in human flesh. Could the feeling of a single one among us have been so hardened that he no longer was moved by such things?"[72]

After Lincoln announced his preliminary Emancipation Proclamation, Germans in Missouri demanded action in their state as well. Münch and other German politicians initially called for gradual and even compensated emancipation, but after conservative Unionists rejected these proposals, the march to a fuller radicalism quickened its pace. At a German mass meeting in St. Louis's Turner Hall in January 1863, a call for immediate emancipation echoed out to a jubilant audience. St. Louis's Freiheits-Verein (Freedom Association) proposed "to remove Secessionists from the city council and to get good Republicans in their place."[73] Münch called for Germans to "rescue from perdition this state we have chosen as our homeland," and even more significantly, to fight for "Negro equality."[74]

Animated by Lincoln's move toward emancipation, Missouri's Germans turned to radical antislavery as a means to defeat secessionist sympathizers and guerrillas. In Saint Charles County, slave owners in Darst Bottoms felt the brunt of German antislavery. William Cocheau, one of the largest slave owners in the bottomlands, attempted to retrieve a runaway slave in October

1863 from a Union military camp. But before he could return with his human property, a local German militia confronted Cocheau and, under likely duress, he finally "agreed that the Negro should be taken back to where he was captured and be permitted to choose between freedom and slavery." Not long after, the militia led the slave-turned-freedman back into the town of Augusta to "loud hurrahs from old and young." The German *St. Charles Demokrat* opined, "Americans say, 'Help yourself' when meat is offered at their table; we say 'help yourself' when securing the basic human-civil rights which despotic caprice withholds from us." Although before the war, L. H. Howell, "one of the largest land and slave holders in that part of the country," had reigned over Darst Bottoms, by December 1863 his entire property was auctioned off, purchased by a German neighbor for $6,000.[75]

Just as the war moved down a new radical path, Germans in Missouri were in the vanguard of a new regime. In October 1862, Germans in Femme Osage demanded, "our candidates make a public declaration through the press that with all their strength they will support and advocate 'Emancipation,' and especially Emancipation in our state."[76] A month later, the *Westliche Post* noted, "We now have a register of German names among the *patribus conscriptis* who clearly represent the emancipating and progressive principles."[77] Removing slave-owning politicians from power accomplished the goal of abolishing slave labor, but it also created a vacuum, allowing Germans to fill the void and seize political offices in large numbers. The *St. Charles Demokrat* fully supported disqualifying from voting any individual guilty of disloyalty, regardless of whether they agreed to officially pledge loyalty required for enfranchisement: "We consider everyone who now swears the Loyalty Oath but previously supported the rebellion, openly or secretly, to still be traitors in their hearts, even if the Loyalty Oath is sworn a thousand times."[78]

Because they played a large and vocal role in pushing Missouri toward emancipation, Germans became prime targets for guerrilla reprisals. After Abraham Lincoln formally announced emancipation as a federal war policy in 1862, guerrilla activity in Missouri began to intensify. Christopher Phillips argues that this was not a coincidence and that this chronology is critical in tracing guerrilla participation. Phillips cites data culled from the Union Provost Marshal Papers in Missouri to demonstrate that provost reports for guerrilla or bushwhacker activity overwhelmingly occurred in the three months following Lincoln's preliminary Emancipation Proclamation announcement in 1862 and during the spring and summer of 1863. On September 22, 1863, Confederate general Joe Shelby began his raid into southern Missouri. The date marked the one-year anniversary of Lincoln's preliminary Emancipation Proclamation.[79]

When guerrillas began to strike back at radical federal policies, they often sought German targets, indicating their belief that Germans had a significant hand in driving the radical war forward. Beginning with their support for John C. Frémont's attempt to confiscate slaves and threat to execute guerrillas, antislavery Germans confirmed guerrillas' worst fears as an empowered invasive force.[80] After first entering Missouri, Confederate cavalry commander Joseph O. Shelby was dismayed to find that "every house belonging to a Southern family has been burned, and the family as effectually destroyed." Shelby's riders struck back, targeting African Americans and Germans, "Missouri's most consistent antislavery constituency."[81]

In an effort to break the Union army's ever-tightening grip, Confederate general Sterling Price launched a last-ditch effort to retake Missouri, invading the state in 1864. Price blamed "Hessians," an obvious reference to the role German mercenaries played in the American Revolution, and abolitionist "Jay-Hawkers," perhaps the only more contemptuous epithet, for carrying out the "causeless despotism" of the federal government.[82] The two faces of radicalism now entwined, Confederates sought to expel those who had fully adopted both as their most visible enemies: Germans. The *St. Louis Democrat* reported that most victims "added to the crime of Unionism that of being German."[83] One member of the invading force revealed his personal intention to "kill and burn out the Dutch."[84]

Guerrilla bands loosely attached to Price's troops made good on ambitions to seek out Germans. Anticipating the worst and hoping to provide at least a semblance of forewarning against guerrilla attacks, Germans in one township in Lexington County installed a warning system. When cow horns echoed across the valley one afternoon, local Germans raced to form an ad hoc militia, supported by a nearby German Home Guard unit. They soon found themselves completely overwhelmed. Louis Meyer described the brief engagement's aftermath in shocking detail: "When the smoke cleared away, it was found that there were 25 Germans killed and none left wounded. Every man's skull was broken with the butt end of their guns."[85]

Price's invasion was carried out under the auspices of military strategy, but it also offered irregular or guerrilla troops the chance to strike back at Unionists who had seized control, including Germans. Following the path of Price's troops, guerrillas often went out of their way to target Germans specifically. In Newtonia, Union militia quickly submitted to the overpowering Confederate force. After accepting the surrender, the Confederates shot and scalped Robert H. Christenson, the young German commander, and removed his left hand. Though Price's invasion ultimately failed, it gave guerrillas the chance to push back against the federal occupation. In turn, this last major guerrilla attack devastated communities across the state, while gruesome personal attacks like the one committed in Newtonia set the stage for continued bitterness on both sides in the postwar years.[86] In fact, memories of wartime transgressions remained so salient that upon America's entrance into World War I, one former guerrilla believed the time for retribution had finally come. "Of all the troops that did things to cause bitter memories in western Missouri during the Civil War," he announced, "none left so many monuments of hate as the Germans. We'd like to take a crack at the Germans for that reason."[87]

For guerrilla fighters in Missouri, Germans symbolized not only an enemy but also a cultural and then military invasion. For decades, Germans most visibly represented a growing danger to the traditions and practices that Missourians with Southern origins held dear, particularly slavery. As sectional politics and secession compelled Germans to embrace a radical antislavery position, they became inextricably tied to abolitionism and Black Republicanism. One guerrilla leader held Germans in such contempt that he placed them on equal terms with black soldiers, proclaiming, "We can't stand the dutch and negroes both."[88]

By preserving the liberal nation, deposing slave-owning politicians, and embracing radical antislavery, many Germans believed they would secure their place in a transformed Missouri. In 1862, during a speech delivered in Augusta, Georg Münch, brother to the renowned Friedrich Münch, who had just begun his campaign to end slavery in Missouri, emphasized the early years following immigration. He recalled how Americans "with a shrug of the shoulders, indeed with disrespect, looked down on the German 'dirt grubbers,' and how one demanded that the German kiss the hand which had just been lifted in haughty arrogance to hit him." The resentment still remained with Münch. With obvious alacrity, he boasted, "But the times have changed."[89] Indeed, in Missouri and throughout the Middle Border, Germans had asserted themselves as radicals in the war to transform the nation. Believing they had a central role to play, the self-proclaimed saviors of Missouri embarked on a mission to save the borderlands for the Union.

CHAPTER 7

THE RADICAL TURN

ABOLITION AND THE CRISIS OF GERMAN LIBERALISM

Beginning in the late 1850s, intensified sectional debate loosely united the parallel causes of liberal nationalism, free soil, free labor, *Bildung*, and Manifest Destiny. In 1860, as slavery encroached on western territories, antislavery Germans, no longer able to abide the Democratic Party's ties to the "peculiar institution," helped vault Republicans into power in key cities and towns on the Middle Border. But ultimately it was secession and civil war that persuaded many Germans to intertwine Union, or liberal nationalism, with an antislavery impetus to implement a "hard" or punishing war against proslavery and slaveholding civilians.[1]

Beginning in early 1862, wartime Germans pursued radical aims through forceful and violent means.[2] This translated to removing forces impeding liberal progress—namely, conservative Unionists and secessionists who refused to accept emancipation. Implicit in Germans' message was the belief that they understood republicanism far better than those political leaders who pursued either disunion or slavery's perpetuation. Conceiving their role as proponents of true liberal democracy challenging a conservative aristocracy, many Germans justified their extremism as a necessary step toward a new progressive synthesis. This radical turn was most visible in Missouri, where Germans moved to crush guerrilla resistance and supplant leading slave-owning politicians. But unconditional Unionism and support for hard-line war strategies carried over throughout the region as Germans encountered waning enthusiasm for a war tied to universal emancipation and general disaffection with emergent Radical Republican rule. Defying this racially conservative, conditionally loyal current, Germans were consequently identified as extremists—the most visible representatives of the perceived repression radiating from Washington, D.C.[3]

Responding to the rising conservative reaction on the Middle Border, many Germans fortified their support for the war, abolition, and the Radical Republican program while rejecting the burgeoning antiwar movement north of the Ohio. Augusta Kircher wrote to her soldiering son that if Germans failed to "step on the head of the snake of treason, then . . . we will be lost and the tyrants hold the flag high over the murdered freedom!" In her estimation, no middle ground remained, only antislavery patriots and proslavery traitors.[4] By drawing clear lines in the sand, Germans distanced themselves from the region's dominant political and racial mentalities.

German radicalism on the Middle Border found its greatest expression after decades of maintaining a fairly muted position in American politics. Overwhelmingly identifying with Jefferson-Jacksonian republicanism, Germans nearly unequivocally denounced slavery on ideological grounds but for practical purposes largely accepted the institution's constitutional protections and ingrained place in the region's socioeconomic makeup. Only when slavery threatened western progress along with free soil and free labor policies did they insert themselves into the debates, interpreting sectional conflict as the product of an aristocratic class that had egregiously limited idyllic Jeffersonian individualism, or *Bildung*. Still, while the Republican Party introduced the platform from which the paradox of slave labor in a free society could be exposed and in some way rectified, even in 1860 few Germans advocated immediate, universal emancipation.

Secession, crumbling loyalty, and guerrilla warfare's crescendo along an increasingly tenuous border convinced many Germans that saving the liberal nation required slavery's immediate destruction. Germans justified emancipation because it expanded individual freedom and opportunity not strictly for slaves but also for the ever-expanding white middle class, despite proslavery moderates' and conservatives' arguments defending constitutional rights to property. Germans' liberal tradition led them to conclude that the slave-owning class harmed democracy and *Bildung*, or individual self-betterment, so they philosophically opposed slave masters' accumulation of wealth and property on the backs of a permanent laboring class. Ultimately, the secession crisis persuaded liberals to temporarily adopt the radical argument that emancipation acted as a needed redistribution of concentrated property and power.

The move to join the Radical Republicans came with great risk. When fellow white Unionists recoiled from the consequences of black emancipation and citizenship, radical Germans insisted on unfaltering loyalty and unassailable patriotism. This strengthened their position within the Republican Party but simultaneously contributed to their alienation regionally. Between the 1860 and 1864 elections, Germans rode the Republican wave, building on the perception that their vote was necessary to swing elections and their guns were necessary to preserve loyalty. This newfound relevance opened new paths to political opportunity. The *Westliche Post* noted that in the past, "by 'wheeling and dealing' it formerly was possible here and there in St. Louis County to send one or two German into the House of Representatives." Given the Republican Party's reliance on German political and military support on the Middle Border, "we now have a register of German names among the *patribus conscriptis* [elected officials] who clearly represent the emancipating and progressive principles." This clear association with the "emancipating and progressive principles" would have consequences in a region largely averse to such radical aims.[5]

The strengthening German and Republican alliance bred confrontation, and as Germans advanced emancipation, they met resistance not only from outright secessionists but also from conservative Unionists. Not long after preliminary emancipation was announced in September 1862, Missouri's conservative Unionists began to fear slavery's inevitable end in their own state. In November, Missouri militia general Odon Guitar dissolved Arnold Krekel's German state militia after the unit scorched through secessionist Callaway County, commandeering horses and liberally confiscating slaves as contraband. Months before, Krekel's troops had defeated a guerrilla outfit, and afterward he cited the help of "a negro boy [who] gave valuable information in conducting the command," saying, "I would ask for permission to retain him until the war is over, as he cannot safely return."[6] Guitar ordered that the militia surrender all arms, and according to the incredulous *St. Charles Demokrat*, "The contraband Negroes, about 20 in number, were caught with help of the accompanying [non-German] State Militia, bound and muzzled, and handed over to their masters." In response, the radical German newspaper asked, "Has the Fight against Germanism Begun?" Suspicion that conservative Unionists had jettisoned the war's liberating mission undergirded the question. Tellingly, the *Demokrat* now associated Germanism with liberating slaves and conducting a punishing war on their masters.[7]

Conditional Unionists' resistance to a radical war infuriated many Germans and pushed them farther away from the moderate middle. Writing to his son serving in the Union army, Leonhard Tafel saw the logic in attempting moderation and avoiding extremism, "But when it concerns the common good? There can be no neutrality."[8] In Europe during the 1820s, Leonhard Tafel had belonged to a youth league consisting of student radicals "whose object was to bring about the unity of Germany and freer institutions." Describing the *Zeitgeist* that had so inspired him as a young man, Tafel wrote, "I dreamed, at the time, as so many others did, of the unity of Germany and of Liberal institutions and would have made every sacrifice for their realization." But his activities led to arrest and disappointment and eventually escape. In Cincinnati, his sons continued the family tradition, establishing the first Turnverein in America and organizing antislavery Germans in southwestern Ohio to support the Republican Party. Though too old to join the Union army with his two sons, Tafel nevertheless remained a fiery observer, continuing to pursue his collegiate ideals despite their radical nature.[9]

Viewing the Civil War through the lens of past European revolutions imbued German Americans with a sense of duty and prominence. Often citing an innate cultural predisposition to pursue enlightened endeavors, Germans approached the war as if it represented a natural step toward progress. In America, they continued to act in the spirit of 1848 but believed Americans largely lacked philosophical grounding and military training. As proof, they often emphasized the fact that so many in the North, particularly on the Middle Border, seemed unwilling to throw themselves unconditionally into the war effort. Fighting in the Eighty-Second Illinois, Rudolph Mueller wrote, "What a miserable nation of shopkeepers these citizens of the Republic, who lack almost all the characteristics of genuine republicans, and which after three years of bloody war hasn't learned yet that peace can be achieved only by decisiveness and rapid development of its entire strength and power."[10] What Mueller and other Germans refused to accept was that many native-born Americans on the Middle Border desired Union but were hesitant to engage in a radical war that threatened their conservative racial mentalities.

The conservative counterattack on the Middle Border in reaction to emancipation signified a clear rejection of the war's radical end game, and this conspicuously left radical Germans isolated. While many of their native-born neighbors questioned the war, Germans combatively reiterated calls for abolition and severe punishment for disloyalty, both in the South and in their own Northern communities. In Missouri, federal occupation, in large part reliant on Germans, led to violence and guerrilla warfare, but antiabolition and even antiwar sentiment was expressed throughout the region. As early as 1862, Democrats campaigning on a conservative platform that opposed Radical Republicanism recaptured the majority of voters in large swaths of the lower North. At the same time, soldiers from southern Illinois and Indiana displayed an unwillingness to fight and die for black freedom. Though a war of liberation gradually gained acceptance, widespread resistance nevertheless remained pervasive in communities along the border. Many in the Ohio Valley, stretching from Cincinnati to Charleston, Missouri, only warily accepted emancipation as a practical wartime measure yet still abhorred black civil rights and feared a mass exodus of former slaves out of the South and into their own communities.[11]

On both the slave and free sides of the Ohio and Mississippi Valleys, emancipation translated to betrayal by a president from their region who had promised to leave slavery untouched where it existed. Anne Marshall contends that before the Emancipation Proclamation, "many border southerners offered their loyalty to the Union with the expectation that the United States government, instead of destroying slavery, would be the best *protector* of the institution." Following the act, it seemed abolition would creep into all corners of the Union. Nearly in unison, Kentuckians rose up to denounce emancipation, effectively abandoning the conservative Unionist position.[12]

Though it was a free state, many in southern Illinois's "Little Egypt" strongly opposed Lincoln's Emancipation Proclamation and discouraged African Americans, often violently, from settling in the state. In the 1862 elections, Illinois Democrats regained control of the state legislature. That same year, Illinois pushed forward two "black codes" to prevent black settlement and voting rights. Fearing a revolt in southern Illinois, a Chicago newspaper asked, "Is Illinois to be plunged into the same condition of war and desolation as Missouri, Kentucky and Tennessee?" On cue, state Democrats condemned Lincoln's proclamation and outlined a plan to peacefully end the war. In response, Union supporters gathered in Springfield. There, Illinois Germans applauded Heinrich Goedeking, former mayor of Belleville, who implored his audience to strike back at the burgeoning antiwar movement.[13]

Emancipation might have received widespread support among Germans, but over the course of the war, southern Illinois only became more hostile to African American settlement. While stationed in Little Rock, Arkansas, Adolf Engelmann wrote to his wife about possibly sending Andy, an escaped slave working as his paid servant, back to St. Clair County, Illinois. "I spoke to Andy, promising him $15.00 a month if he would go to Illinois with the veterans and work on the farm," informed Engelmann. "I told him to get married and we would pay his wife $6.00 and give them a cabin to live in. He seems to like the idea." Revealing his own prejudices, Engelmann added, "For a negro, Andy is industrious and honest." What worried him, though, was not Andy's capabilities but the reception a free black man might receive, asking, "Have we still got 'Copperheads' in the vicinity who would drive poor Andy out of the country?" One month later, aware that disloyal and vehemently antiblack Copperheads were pervasive in southern Illinois, Engelmann concluded that too many "would take exception to a negro and since there are always some copperheads left to make trouble, I better keep Andy here. While we do not obey our Illinois 'Blacklaws' nevertheless we fear them."[14]

As in Illinois, the clear victory for Indiana's Democrats in 1862 "was a repudiation of Republicanism."[15] The Democratic *Evansville Enquirer* denounced abolition and black equality, citing the likelihood that Southern black people would soon invade the city. One native-born soldier from southern Indiana predicted that abolitionists would begin to "take other peoples' properties." Determined, he resolved, "If I fight at all, I will be found to fight for principal and not for a damned negro."[16] As these attitudes evolved, the popularity of conservative leaders such as Clement L. Vallandigham and other Copperheads gave rise to secret societies like the Knights of the Golden Circle and the Order of American Knights. Such groups were in abundance in Cincinnati; New Albany, Indiana; Cairo, Illinois; and throughout the Middle Border.[17]

Conversely, radical Germans in the region demanded emancipation, which placed them in direct opposition to the antiwar movement. Regarding Peace Democrats and Copperheads, in southern Ohio, the Cincinnati Arbeiterverein (Workers Association) concluded they were "deserving [of] the contempt of every loyal citizen." One German soldier in the Seventh Indiana informed his brother, "I am in favor of a vigorous prosecution of the war and I am in favor of keeping Vallandigham out of the 'United' States. If it had not been for Val the war would have been over before this time, he is an agent of the southern confederacy."[18] August Mersy, a former cashier in Belleville, Illinois, who had once fought in the revolutionary armies in Baden, despised "half & half" generals who identified with the Democratic Party. Mersy believed that Illinois's Republican governor Richard Yates "had the power to change [the state legislature] around like a European ruler" and "rid the body of antiwar Democrats."[19] That a former democratic revolutionary would encourage dictatorial action indicates just how far many Germans were willing to go to stamp out disloyalty.

Dissent on the home front caused concerned German soldiers to turn their attention to the battles being waged in the towns and cities they had left behind. Writing from Atlanta, Magnus Brucker, a Republican state representative fighting with the Twenty-Third Indiana, instructed his wife to disregard any disparaging comments directed toward him back home in Troy, Indiana. Though the invectives ran the gamut, including "a black Republican, abolitionist, Lincolnist or Yankee Vandal," he told her, "I am satisfied with myself and do my duty as [a] citizen of this republic." In Brucker's opinion, "Would it not be for the cowardly traitors in the North, the revolution would long be suppressed."[20] Like many Germans in St. Clair County, Illinois, Friedrich Braütigam joined the Eighty-Second Illinois under the command of Friedrich Hecker. When the regiment received word "regarding the traitorous Democratic legislative majority in Springfield, Illinois," Braütigam reported, "it was accepted rather coolly by our troops."[21] Following the preliminary Emancipation Proclamation, Adolf Engelmann asked for "above all, 'no treason by those at home.'" "Let those at home but do their share in this great work," Engelmann insisted, "and the Western soldiers will do the balance." Soon after, the negative response to emancipation in southern Illinois and the resurgence of the Democrats disappointed Engelmann. Frustrated, he assured his wife, "The Army is utterly opposed to the views of the Northern Democrats as to the negroes. The action of the Democrats is viewed here as being hostile to the Union."[22]

When those opposing the war took bold action, Germans shouted them down. During a Union meeting in Evansville, Indiana, Butternuts interrupted the speaker because, as the *Evansville Daily Journal* explained, his pro-Union views "have not heretofore been popular in this community." Turning the tables on the white Unionist, an agitated audience cried out, "'Stop the d——n nigger' . . . and the usual amount of slang phrases which constitute the stock in trade of the Butternuts." Tempers flaring, a riot nearly broke out until Frederick Heuring, a German chaplain in the Twenty-Fifth Indiana, stood up on a chair and, "in a clear, ringing voice and with flashing eye, exclaimed, 'I have fought the rebels at Fort Donelson; I have fought the Rebels on the bloody field of Shiloh; I have faced death at the cannon's mouth, and while I did not expect to find rebels in the Court House of Evansville, I am prepared to fight rebels right here, and lay down my life for the sacred right of free speech.'" Having encountered fugitive slaves outside Memphis, Heuring wrote in his journal, "The poor things, are in a dreadful condition, with no one to care for them" and blamed their circumstances on "unmerciful owners on the one hand, and the Democratic Hell-hounds on the other."[23]

As Democrats on the Middle Border attempted to move abolition to the periphery, many Germans only deepened their commitment to a radical war designed to set emancipation at the war's very center. Magnus Brucker reiterated that "slavery in all parts of the United States must be forbidden to end any further conflict, and to open the country for free labor, and to keep it free for our children's children." He steadfastly believed that emancipation "alone will sanctify the war, and this goal we shall reach."[24] Fighting with the

Second Missouri, Karl Fülle wrote letters home that were filled with the horrors of war, yet he maintained that "the battles of the country must be fought, [even] if it comes to the extreme, if otherwise the country will be saved. May the goddess of liberty give our weak army fresh strength." In February 1863, one month after the Emancipation Proclamation, Fülle declared that despite a "large measure of betrayers and oafs," in the Union army "resides the spirit of freedom." He was determined then that there could be "no lazy peace, no, first the last rebel must either lay his weapon or be shot."[25]

What most radicalized the Germans' position was merging Union and abolition into a single cause. In doing so, they broke the shackles of the region's traditional racial conservatism. Outlining the war to relatives in Germany, Karl Frick made clear that "Germans, almost without exception, support the legitimate government and fight for its honor." He was equally adamant that "the Americans who are slaveholders are the enemies of the government, they don't want to set their slaves free and just want to exploit other humans, that is blacks, because they don't regard them as human beings but as animals." Frick now saw clearly that the war, as Lincoln would soon articulate, was dedicated to a new birth of freedom. "[Slavery] is what our government can't stand to see any more. . . . After all, all men are born equal. And that is the cause of this terrible war." Beyond the emancipation of slaves, Frick believed the war would secure a new measure of humanity.[26]

In achieving freedom, some Germans adopted the radical position that African Americans be allowed to take up arms against their former masters. After his medical discharge from the Eighty-Second Illinois in late 1863, Friedrich Braütigam, a Republican and strong supporter of emancipation, returned to St. Clair County to find heated resistance to recently arrived Southern black migrants. Yet when he met with other local Germans, they engaged in "a lively conversation which mostly was in regard to the all-absorbing Negro issue" and supported black men joining the ranks, which they believed would both quell antiblack sentiment and help win the war. The war had embraced emancipation, and the Germans believed, "The negroes should fight for their civil rights on the battlefield where our white brothers are fighting and bleeding for the freedom of the slaves." Sitting there listening, Braütigam felt "completely compelled to go along with this viewpoint with all my heart and conviction."[27]

But while Germans often were in the forefront of wartime radicalism, few completely accepted full racial equality or total integration. Touting abolition as a military necessity was not the same as elevating former slaves to equal status. A son of "Latin farmers," highly educated, and surrounded by liberal German intellectuals in Belleville, Henry Kircher had entered the war determined to preserve the nation and believed defeating slavery was paramount to victory. Yet even if Kircher's liberal ideology led him to denounce slavery, he nevertheless felt that African Americans remained inferior to some degree and that this prevented total equality.[28] He wrote to his father that following emancipation, he and his comrades were "all healthy and alert and terribly eager for battle," yet struggled with serving alongside black soldiers. "I, like most, don't like the idea of fighting side by side with a negro though. That's asking a little too much." He supported the army's use of free black labor, "But to see him fighting with weapons in his hand at my better side . . . no sir." After his father conveyed disappointment, Kircher clarified his stance: "You mustn't get me wrong when I say I wouldn't like to fight with a black. By that I am only saying that I wouldn't like to be a slave boss, a slave driver, and fight at his side, mix my blood with his." Softening the blow, he explained that he was "not far enough advanced in civilization" that he didn't "know the difference between white and black anymore." Freedom was just and necessary, but it did not translate to racial egalitarianism in Kircher's worldview. It wasn't, then, that Kircher opposed black soldiers, and he was quick to remind his father that at the beginning of the war, he had suggested the logic of just such a move, but only "if it is carried out as proposed, that the black regiments don't come into contact with any white ones." "What is a white who forgets that he stands above the African?" he asked, foreshadowing German liberalism's limitations.[29]

When Germans did question radical politics, they expressed a fear that Radical Republicans intended to elevate racial equality and black civil rights above all other, in their view more pressing, concerns. Though he supported the war and voted for Lincoln in 1860, Bernhard van Dreveldt of Waterloo, Illinois, questioned what he felt was an extreme direction taken by Radical Republicans. He predicted that if Lincoln remained in power, "there will be no end in sight, and everything will be done for the Negroes." In fact, Dreveldt was concerned that "in the end, it may go so far that the blacks get the vote while the whites are denied theirs."[30]

Facing an onslaught from relatives condemning his rationale, Dreveldt found it necessary to respond to the criticism. "I just don't understand where you get the idea that I am proslavery and belong to a party that you would want to see disappear?" he asked. He clarified, "I am neither proslavery nor a secessionist, and that is it." Still, he was adamant that "it does not follow that I am therefore an abolitionists or even one of the radicals." Instead, he delicately explained, "I am nothing more than a conservative who wants to conserve the Union and institutions of this country." Though Dreveldt identified as antislavery, a Republican voter, and German, none of these kept him from feeling uncomfortable with what he viewed would be a world turned upside down, with black over white.[31]

In addition to black enlistment, conscription further challenged German enthusiasm for the war. On emancipation's heels, Congress passed the Enrollment Act, which signaled an impending federal military draft reminiscent of conscripted European military service. The substitute policy, allowing draftees to avoid the war by buying others' service, white or black, added to despotic characterizations of the federal government. The *Belleviller Volksblatt*, a Democratic German-language paper, emphasized the senseless sacrifice of working-class white people forced to fight a war on behalf of Southern black people. "The white poor man is led into the field as cannon fodder," the *Volksblatt* argued. More important, poor white people were often unwilling participants. "Above him, one does not swing a whip but a saber. For he is a drafted person and a poor devil." The *Volksblatt* likened the draft to "white slavery" and sardonically noted, "This is not a concern to the abolitionist press. O you Republican hypocrites and deceivers of people."[32]

Although they represented a minority view among Germans on the Middle Border, conservative Germans made their complaints against radicalism well known, arguing that the interests of slaves had mistakenly been placed above all else. The *Belleviller Volksblatt* was founded to counter the increasingly radical tone of the Republican *Belleviller Zeitung*, and though it wrote for a smaller audience, its scathing editorials battled the intensified radicalism of the Republicans. The *Volksblatt* agreed with liberal democracy's core principles, fully in harmony with the belief that "freedom is the inheritance of every man and that all human slavery is unjust." But the paper's editor, Louis Houck, inserted a caveat, arguing, "The Southern system is not slavery; but is an economic social-system which exists between two different races and is based on the interests of both races." By this logic, Southern slaves were not so much literal slaves as they were well-cared-for servants who benefited from the arrangement. Thus, the *Volksblatt* concluded, "this system, whether right or wrong, cannot be destroyed by force," or all would suffer. In May 1864, the *Belleviller Volksblatt*'s offices were destroyed by soldiers from the Ninth Illinois, a regiment with six German companies from Belleville and St. Clair County. The paper failed to print a page for the rest of 1864 after financial support from state Democrats disappeared. Clearly, conservative sentiment toward the war existed among Germans, however tenuous and impermanent.[33]

Offering caution, conservative Germans often pointed to the dangers tied to universal emancipation, which they attributed to Radical Republicans and a weak president. Cincinnati's Democratic *Volksfreund* persisted in its criticism of Lincoln and the Republican Party's handling of the war, warning that black migrants would soon stream across the Ohio.[34] Frederick Blum, a German elected chairman of Cincinnati's Democratic executive committee, called on "all citizens who are in favor of strong and quick leadership in the current brother-murdering war, and for the purpose of the reunification of the Union as it was, the constitution as it is, and for a strict execution of the laws."[35] In southern Indiana, Wilhelm Hoffmann also decried Radical Republicans, whom he blamed for pushing the war in an extreme direction. Hoffmann expressed the most disappointment in the commander in chief, complaining, "This President Lincoln, forgetting his duties, permits himself to be led to and fro by his radical clique."[36]

But while conservative Germans derided President Lincoln, his biggest critics were in fact radical Germans who believed he was overly cautious and blamed the war's longevity on shortsighted restraint. The Emancipation Proclamation, in their eyes, had not gone far enough—Missouri and Kentucky remained slave states, and no plan of universal emancipation appeared eminent.[37] During Missouri's state convention in June 1863, both the *Westliche Post* and the *Neue Zeit* demanded immediate emancipation. Instead, the convention took a more conservative path, outlining a plan of gradual emancipation beginning on July 4, 1870, combined with a period of apprenticeship. Though some moderate German Republicans quietly supported the plan, radical Germans expressed outrage.[38]

Frustrated with Lincoln's hesitations, radical Germans saw the 1864 election as an opportunity to potentially find a worthier substitute. Emil Mallinckrodt lamented, "In Lincoln we unfortunately have the most miserable President possible in these agitated times." What troubled Mallinckrodt most was Lincoln's constant attempts at diplomacy. "He is a weakling . . . [who] wants to do right by all parties and every individual and thereby ruins everything."[39] Gustav Körner, perhaps Lincoln's closest German ally, recognized that in St. Louis and Belleville, "so many Germans were found in opposition to Lincoln." He explained that German leadership was the "most radical on the slavery question, and Lincoln was too slow for them."[40]

In their quest for Lincoln's suitable replacement, radicalized Germans once again placed their hopes in John C. Frémont. The *Westliche Post*, now one of the most popular and also most radical German-language newspapers in the West, endorsed the controversial former general and onetime Republican presidential candidate, as did Springfield's *Staats-Anzeiger*.[41] When moderate Germans exhibited more caution, once again revealing the fragile threads that united German Republicans on the Middle Border, Friedrich Münch wrote a scathing editorial chastising his countrymen: "What I find deplorable in the present political movement is the split that has occurred in the progressive element." He reasoned, "This naturally gives the enemies of progress an advantage," and asked, "Is it not highly lamentable that the Germans of this country, who could in their unity be so significant, have instead gathered in two different, hostile groups?"[42]

Hoping to prevent Frémont from siphoning precious votes, the Republican political machine scrambled to secure radical German Republicans, suddenly a legitimate threat to Lincoln's nomination. While in New York in late March 1864, Lincoln's personal secretary, John G. Nicolay, spoke with Wisconsin's German Republican leader Carl Schurz. Nicolay reported that Schurz was "under impression that the German movement for Fremont is earnest and will be pretty strong, and that they seriously intend to run him as a third candidate"[43]Attorney General Edward Bates reported that in June 1864, during a Republican convention in Missouri, German representatives "did desert the M[issouri] Convention: and every[one] knows that the Germans constitute the heart and nucl[e]us—the body and strength of the Radicals of Mo."[44]

To counter Frémont's popularity, Lincoln's ally in St. Louis, Frank Blair, lured the former editor of the *Anzeiger des Westens,* Heinrich Börnstein, back from a diplomatic appointment in Bremen to swing the newspaper back to Lincoln. Börnstein's subsequent return forced George Hillgaertner, Börnstein's more radical replacement, to break off and form his own newspaper, the *Neue Zeit,* and immediately support Frémont. Meanwhile, Börnstein's brief stint proved largely ineffective; his sensationalized brand of journalistic magic seemed to have worn off.[45]

Gustav Körner also received entreaties to leave a diplomatic post and rally southern Illinois Germans to Lincoln's aid. Though he did return, Körner, ever the consummate politician, realized the risk in openly supporting an unpopular president. "I have the most serious doubts as to the propriety of my taking the stump in the presidential canvass," Körner explained. Assessing the situation, he believed that Frémont's many supporters were "peculiarly sensitive" and therefore concluded, "I am for the present of the opinion that by public speaking I would do more harm than good."[46] In fact, most German Republican leaders in the region who advocated tirelessly for Lincoln in 1860 were absent from the campaign trail in 1864, filling diplomatic posts, serving in the Union army, or distancing themselves from Lincoln's administration.[47]

Peace Democrat George B. McClellan's nomination garnered little excitement from Germans, but it did provide a stark reminder of what would happen should they fail to elect a candidate willing to prosecute the war to its successful conclusion. Assessing the options, Emil Preetorius, the *Westliche Post*'s radical new editor, initially concluded, "Against McClellan and Against Lincoln—Both are equally incapable and worthless."[48] But Frémont's campaign never truly stood on solid ground. Union military victories, particularly the fall of Atlanta, restored confidence in Lincoln, and soon after, Frémont bowed out.[49] Given the alternative, the *Neue Zeit* supported Lincoln, but only "under protest." The *Westliche* surrendered its hopes for Frémont but refused to openly stump for Lincoln. In southern Illinois, Rudolph Mueller wrote, "It is difficult to find one's way in this political chaos and find the man who is capable of bringing back to the nation its sinking credit." Ultimately, he determined to vote "for Lincoln, this sleepy head, in any case only with reluctance."[50]

In the end, the majority of German Republican voters on the Middle Border, whether moderate or radical, went for Lincoln rather than turn the war over to a Peace Democrat.[51] At the beginning of the war, Joseph Hotz was a farmer and, like most people in Jackson County, Indiana, a Democrat—never truly believing the Republicans had eradicated nativism. But after serving in the Union army for two years, he informed his wife in May 1863, "I was once a democrat but not anymore." A year later, he complained, "There [are] a lot of lazy bums [in Jackson County], they shout off their mouths and do all their fighting at home behind a whiskey glass." Before the election, he assured his wife, "I know Lincoln will be reelected, and that is the biggest victory we can have in this war." Yet he felt the need to clarify his position once again. "You may think I am an Abolitionist . . . but I would never vote for McClellan, he is a traitor." Ultimately, for Hotz, Lincoln represented the best chance to save the Union. Ending his letter, he swore, "We will not make peace until the devil has every rebel and when they lay down their weapons."[52]

With a victory for the Republican Party, the election further revealed the growing fissures between radical, moderate, and conservative Germans. Though some remained tethered to the Democratic Party, Germans on the Middle Border almost unilaterally supported the Union war. But as radical Germans asserted themselves politically, the big-tent coalition of free soil and free labor Unionism began to break down over particulars. This proved especially true in Missouri, the epicenter of radical German activity. After radicals demanded universal emancipation, conservative German newspapers, including *Der Lutheraner*, the *Neue Anzeiger des Westens*, and the Catholic *Tages-Chronik* went to great effort to dissociate themselves from their radical brethren. Though they claimed far fewer readers, their editorials provide "evidence of a significant conservative base within the German population."[53]

Despite conservatives' efforts, voting eligibility in Missouri during the 1864 election required white men to swear allegiance to the Union, known as a test oath, and this, coupled with the lack of a viable Democratic Party, undermined any and all conservative aspirations. Indeed, Radical Republicans carried the day, winning St. Louis's mayoral election with strong majorities in German wards, with similar results in the heavily German Gasconade and St. Charles Counties. Radical voters proved strong enough to elect Thomas C. Fletcher as governor, control the state legislature, and call for a new convention to debate the state's constitution, including slavery and emancipation.[54]

As far as Leonhard Tafel was concerned, the radicals' ascendance served as proof that all had gone according to plan. In St. Louis in January 1864, Leonhard wrote to his son, Gustav, a prominent Republican in Cincinnati, to explain that Germans in his city and Missouri in general had grown weary of conditional Unionists and half-hearted Republicans. Tafel was particularly upset about the ineffective and, in his eyes, traitorous activities of Union general John Schofield, commander of the Department of Missouri. "Our state is still not satisfied that Lincoln has not yet arrested Schofel [Schofield]," Tafel fumed. "He himself was responsible for the business [of continued guerrilla activity] in Missouri and it seems the imbecile behaved as though he was Lincoln's highest, wisest advisor." That Schofield, and by extension Lincoln, had not crushed the guerrillas incensed Tafel and other radical Germans, who believed lingering sympathy for slave owners was to blame.

Approaching the election in August 1864, Leonhard Tafel continued to express disdain for "the scamps," those, he explained, who had "shown themselves to be against our Radicals." Emancipation inspired hostility among the many conditional Unionists in the state, where support for the war dissipated once abolition seemed likely. Tafel and many other radical Germans saw the retreat as treacherous and disloyal. "They have armed themselves and given their guns to the so-called Conservatives, who couldn't wait to go, with sack and pack, over to the enemy," Tafel wrote. But Schofield's removal signaled Radical Republicans' tightening grip in the state, and Tafel optimistically predicted, "Now the department is finally Radical, and will twist the necks of the guerrillas." Outlining a plan for Germans in the West, he predicted, "What the future will be for the Germans in the Union naturally hangs on whether we are clever in constituting the German Party and avoid the appearance of wanting to have a party of our own." Germans, then, would subtly take command and lead the way in implementing reform in a region where native-born leadership continued to reveal itself to be wholly lacking. If successful, it would follow that "then the Republican can be master of the world, and our position the most elevated since the world was created." The elections confirmed Tafel's expectation that radicals would assume control and dictate the state's future; the elevated role he and many others expected Germans to play, however, remained less clear.[55]

German liberalism's radical turn on the Middle Border accelerated alongside battlefield success, emancipation, and Radical Republican victories in 1864. But by interlacing unconditional support for the Union with universal emancipation, Germans adopted a radical position incongruous with the region's dominant conservatism. Although radical Germans enjoyed profound success in 1864, they also further alienated themselves from not only native-born conservatives but also conservative Germans, who disapproved of extreme positions concerning race and nascent reconstruction policies. Feeling the ground split beneath them, moderate Germans began to seek out alternatives to Radical Republican rule, steering German liberalism away from its radical path.

CHAPTER 8

"A TERRIBLE MISTAKE WAS MADE"

THE RETREAT OF GERMAN LIBERALISM

The alliance between Germans and Radical Republicans along the Middle Border was born out of sectional crisis and disunion, but those debates dissipated in April 1865. So, too, did the alliance. Germans' support for radical antislavery and a punishing, hard war was predicated on liberal nationalism, individual freedom, and self-improvement—the philosophical underpinnings of *Bildung*. With the Southern aristocracy's putative death, a clear road to abolition opened and a free West was secured. Thus radical policies lost their urgency in a region where racial equality and black civil rights were tremendously unpopular and even feared. Consequently, as resistance to Radical Reconstruction grew, the region's Germans distanced themselves from divisive Republican policies that favored African Americans, renewed nativism, and promoted temperance. As the Germans concluded, a radical agenda that first and foremost addressed political and economic discrimination against African Americans prevented national progress; they therefore shifted their focus to national reunion and local economic development, including growing class inequities.

Reacting to the Middle Border's racial conservatism, the Germans rationalized their retreat from radicalism by insisting that they were following liberal principles grounded in Jeffersonian democracy that were inconsistent with Radical Republicanism. They continued to uphold black freedom's necessity but crucially argued that elevating African Americans to social equality with white people was not the role of government. Instead, government in a liberal nation should protect individual rights and property without affording privileges to any one group. Therefore, they reiterated the need for national reunion, contending that a federally occupied South was both a despotic obstruction to national unity and a drain of resources to ensure special protections for Southerners, white and black.[1]

Building on the larger context of ethnic consciousness, liberal Germans along the border were reacting to more provincial, regional demands. As black migrants began to crowd into river cities like St. Louis and at several points across the Ohio River, many white workers accused Radical Republicans of upending society. Perhaps coincidentally, Germans recognized nativist and temperance strains resurfacing in the Republican Party, no longer obscured by national exigencies. Alarmed, Germans in the West feared they might become political pawns and increasingly doubted their place in Northern Republicans' postwar plans.[2]

By the war's end, Radical Republicans' political opponents in Missouri had either fled the state or were disenfranchised, which left the newly elected governor, Thomas C. Fletcher, nearly unchallenged when he signed an order of emancipation on January 14, 1865.[3] Though they had long called for an act of liberation following slavery's demise in Missouri, German Radical Republicans were suddenly in an uncomfortable and possibly untenable situation. Though nearly unilateral in their support of emancipation, many Germans opposed the Radical Republicans' widely unpopular agenda and their fiery spokesman Charles Drake's "Draconian" proposals for the new state constitution.[4] Before the war, Drake, a St. Louis attorney, had been a Whig with ties to the Know-Nothings and had briefly denounced antislavery in Missouri. Despite the abrupt about-face and his association with nativism, some radical Germans, including Emil Pretorius, editor of the *Westliche Post*, endorsed Drake's efforts, maintaining that outright secessionists had "forfeited their rights to be instrumental in government." But after Drake's actual proposals started to emerge, even radical Germans began to suspect they had been seduced.[5]

Both radical and moderate Germans opposed Drake on several points. Though they believed former rebels should be punished, what Drake proposed went to extremes, beginning with an "ironclad oath" that severely proscribed individuals holding the thinnest of ties to rebellious activity. After mustering out of service in 1865, Louis Benecke returned to Brunswick, Missouri, and was elected mayor, running as a Republican. But Benecke opposed Drake, later explaining that "the Republican Party made a very great mistake at that time by not inviting the ex-Confederates to join them." Though careful to exclude guerrillas, Benecke contended that most ex-Confederates "were mistaken when they risked their lives to break up this grand Republic, but they had been misled and now were in the right."[6] Benecke and other Germans complained that the oath stripped political participation away from any and all who were deemed, potentially arbitrarily, disloyal. Such harsh restrictions suggested to many Germans a dangerous precedent, one that sparked memories of European repression and censorship. Crucially, many Germans also opposed the religious language in the constitution's prose and believed nativism and temperance could be read between the lines.[7]

As proceedings became heated, German delegates Isidor Bush and George Husmann threatened to resign. Soon after, a German mass meeting held at Turner Hall denounced Radical Republican leadership. Germans en masse spoke out against strict suffrage restrictions that would effectively disenfranchise a great number of Missourians potentially for political gain. That a former nativist who had not long ago made his anti-German feelings well known led these efforts caused much consternation over what group might be targeted next. Finally, even the radical *Westliche Post* denounced Drake.[8] In what was both an ideological and personal battle, Germans opposed disenfranchisement because, as John McKerley explains, they regarded it "as encouraging despotism and corruption, both of which they associated with the suffrage provisions' prime architect, Charles D. Drake." Crucially, these tactics were all too familiar, seemingly ripped from the pages of a European despot's manual.[9]

All the while, radical Germans insisted on black political rights, including suffrage. At one point in the convention, Husmann even protested use of the word *white* in the constitution's final draft. This stance, however, left radical Germans in no-man's-land, stuck between the autocratic Drake and conservative Democrats attempting to regain lost ground by opposing black suffrage.[10] Ultimately, though Drake and other non-German Radical Republicans tacitly upheld black suffrage, it was left out of the 1865 constitution in hopes of preventing dissension during the march to ratification. William Parrish argues that most Missourians "held reservations about [African American] suffrage. Indeed, probably very few outside the ranks of the German Radicals were willing to accept 'universal freedom, equality, humanity.'" Already at odds with Drake's Radical Republicans, by supporting black suffrage, radical Germans found even fewer allies among white conservatives on the other side of the aisle, leaving them standing almost entirely alone.[11]

The Missouri Democratic Party's rapid reorganization resigned radical Germans to a swiftly shrinking island. Capitalizing on the situation, German Democrats, though still much in the minority in Missouri, clamored for Germans to return to what was once a nearly unbreakable coalition. As Forty-Eighter Ernest Bruncken explained in his 1904 study of German political refugees in America, "The fact that the German Republicans of that generation had Democratic rather than Whig antecedents must not be forgotten when it is sought to explain why so many of them drifted back into the Democratic ranks after the slavery question had been disposed of."[12] Having traveled full circle from Democratic mouthpiece to Republican organ and back again, the *Anzeiger des Westens* proclaimed, "There does not exist any further community between the present tendency of the radical party and the Germans; . . . their connection therefore is unnatural and pernicious, and the only correct policy after the solution of the slavery question lies in the return of the Germans to the Democratic party." Though such a reunion did not immediately materialize, the notion that Germans and the "radical party" were increasingly antagonistic marked the beginning of their separation.[13]

The conflict surrounding Missouri's constitutional ratification widened the space between Germans and Radical Republicans. Ratification was expected to benefit from a largely disfranchised opposition—former Confederates and those accused of disloyalty—who would have overwhelming voted against the new constitution. Yet in St. Louis and St. Charles County, both heavily German, the constitution was easily defeated; in southeastern Missouri, several counties also rebuked Drake's proposals, a development that William Parrish attributes to "the German influence in combination with the Conservative strength."[14] Still, rural voters, including some Germans, saw the constitution as a just punishment for guerrillas and their sympathizers and overwhelmingly supported ratification. In Lafayette County, 98 percent of voters approved the constitution in the heavily German Freedom Township.[15]

At the final tally, the constitution fell roughly one thousand votes shy of ratification. But then the soldiers' ballots arrived, giving Drake and the Radical Republicans a two-thousand-vote victory. Before the vote, Radical Republicans published a letter to German veterans in the German press, warning, "The copperheads and rattlesnakes hidden under Union flowers . . . are endeavoring to swindle us out of our victories . . . and to destroy the Republic." Harboring resentment and anger, German soldiers likely contributed significantly to the radicals' victory.[16]

Still, ratification revealed that even among those Missourians, including many Germans, who were deemed loyal and eligible to vote, Radical Republicans found less and less support. Radical Germans, too, swam in dangerous waters. In September 1866, the *Anzeiger des Westens* reported that as a "radical candidate for legislature," Colonel Conrad Weinrich made clear that "he regards the Negro as quite his equal in political and social terms. He also remarked that if four of his five daughters were to marry white men, and one married a Negro, he would treat his black son-in-law just like the white husbands." The *Anzeiger*'s disbelief and outrage indicated the internal rifts between radicals and the rest of the German community.[17]

At home among neither conservative Democrats nor Radical Republicans, many Germans on the Middle Border who once pursued a radical war now instead forged a path toward a new political movement—Liberal Republicanism. The combination of regional conservatism toward race and the Democratic Party's rebirth in the region led prominent German Republicans to carve a path back to the moderate middle ground. In doing so, they contributed to the creation of the Liberal Republican movement. Liberal Republicans, much like their counterparts in Bismarck's Germany, championed hard-line nationalism as the ultimate goal. Just as national preservation had led Germans to support the war and even abolition, it now subverted radical policies to secure reunification.[18] Alison Efford argues that for German Americans, "defending citizenship rights of African Americans . . . had become an obstacle to national unity."[19]

Across the Middle Border, Liberal Republicans gained traction among Germans seeking a moderate plank to stand on. In Jefferson City, Missouri, a Liberal Republican meeting in 1870 outlined a party platform, asked for a national meeting, and nominated a presidential candidate. Points of emphasis included a demand for free trade without government interference, civil service reform, and reconciliation with the South. In southern Illinois, Gustav Körner, along with his ally Lyman Trumbull, joined the Liberal Republicans in Belleville. And in 1872, a national meeting in Cincinnati attracted leading German Republicans.[20] Mischa Honeck outlines that in addition to defeating Radical Republicans and President Grant, Germans in Cincinnati condemned "state interventionism" in accordance with their "emerging middle-class consciousness that celebrated individual excellence and dreaded class conflict."[21]

Applauding Liberal Republicans' focus on national reunion, the reenfranchisement of former rebels, and the struggling economy, Germans uniquely grounded their support in liberal nationalism and the individualism inherent in *Buildung*, much as they had in the 1850s when they first embraced free soil and free labor ideology. At the same time, the need to respond to local expectations and pressures on the Middle Border caused liberal Germans to abandon their wartime radicalism and adopt more moderate, popularly acceptable positions.[22]

Illustrating the transition that many Germans underwent, the curious career of George Thilenius began in July 1863 at a "Union Emancipation Meeting" in Cape Girardeau, Missouri. Thilenius, a Forty-Eighter fighting for the Union, had jumped to the Republican Party in the late 1850s and successfully ushered the German vote in the city away from what was once a firm alliance with local Democrats. In the 1864 election, heavily German Cape Girardeau went overwhelmingly for Abraham Lincoln, and every city office went to the Republicans.[23] On the state level, Thilenius also supported legislation that would abolish slavery. But when the question of civil rights for freedmen arose at the state convention in early 1865, leading non-German Radical Republicans hesitated, fearing the divisive issue might split their supporters.[24] Outraged by the sudden timidity, Thilenius, along with fellow Germans Isidor Busch and George Husmann, endorsed black male suffrage, boldly announcing, "We hold, that we were not sent here to pander to a prejudice which may unfortunately exist, but to deal equal justice to all, without regard to color."[25]

Despite such activism, by 1871, the year Liberal Republicanism appeared on the national stage, Thilenius, then serving as mayor of Cape Girardeau, had pulled away from his radical position on race and citizenship. With city elections approaching, the *Cape Girardeau Argus*, the city's conservative Democratic paper, inexplicably came out as one of Thilenius's strongest supporters. The *Argus* barnstormed on the mayor's behalf, finding it regrettable that his radical opponents were "expecting to be elected to rule over the destinies of this city, by the votes of forty or fifty ignorant colored men. It behooves our people to watch this dark-lantern movement."[26] Only a few years removed from advocating for black male suffrage, Thilenius now saw his name atop a ticket supported by a powerful Democratic newspaper that made it a point to disparage black voters and the program of Radical Reconstruction. The strange career of George Thilenius, from European revolutionary to leading antislavery Republican and ultimately to the moderate middle, mirrors the changing regional and local mentalities that pushed leading Germans to the Liberal Republican movement.

George Thilenius's retreat to the moderate middle began with declining enthusiasm for Radical Republicans combined with tension within the German community in Missouri. In 1867, Thilenius won Cape Girardeau's mayoral election as a Republican, effectively capitalizing on wartime momentum and disenfranchised local Democrats. But as mayor, Thilenius soon proved too extreme for the Democratic *Argus*. The paper claimed no party loyalty, but with time and a growing sympathetic readership, its conservative Democratic leanings became far more pronounced. Not long after Thilenius took office, one editorial pointed to his involvement in the Grand Army of the Republic (GAR) and his unabashed support of black equality as damning evidence of radicalism. One bold headline proclaimed, "White men can and shall rule in this a White Man's Government!" and warned that "the 'Nigger' [is] to be set over white men!" The article went on to describe Thilenius's alliance with

"'Billy,' the Buck Cannon," a black military recruiter who, with Thilenius's help, raised three hundred black volunteers for military service. "Think of it, White Men!" the *Argus* pleaded. "Three hundred semi barbarian Africans to be placed over you, in order to intimidate voters, sufficient to perpetuate in power the vagabonds and rapscallions who now misrepresent the people."[27]

Arguing that radicals intended to place black over white, a rejuvenated Democratic Party in Missouri stepped back into the fray by protesting black suffrage and political rights. In November 1868, the State Democratic Association of Missouri sent out calls for the reorganization of county associations; in southeast Missouri, a special election saw Democrats successfully elect their candidate, Dr. James R. McCormick. The unifying platform quickly became the repudiation of black suffrage. Democrats, William Parrish outlines, skillfully denounced black voting rights "at a time when thousands of whites were still unable to vote and participate in political affairs." And while radicals won state elections in 1868—again in large part because of disenfranchised former Confederates—black enfranchisement was defeated by twenty thousand votes, sending a clear message.[28]

Much like the rest of the state, in Cape Girardeau County, Democrats sought to rally support for white labor and white interests. "At the risk of not being considered 'loil,'" the *Argus* advised, "whenever these blacks shall be found assembling . . . [white men] should get together with their shotguns." Demonstrating a keen grasp of local temperaments, the *Argus* wanted to reach out to the many residents of southeast Missouri who had fought to preserve the Union but understood emancipation purely as a wartime necessity. They most definitely had not fought to secure black equality, nor did they agree with Missouri's Radical Republicans, who, they believed, aspired to place former slaves on equal terms with free white men. Those radicals, like Mayor George Thilenius, were playing with fire. "Now, if these worse than rebels desire to inaugurate Civil War by quartering negroes upon us," the *Argus* announced, damning the radicals with alacrity, "let them take the consequences."[29]

Sitting in his mayoral office, George Thilenius surely received the message loud and clear. True, he enjoyed the support of local German Republicans, but the solid ground he stood on was shifting underneath his feet. So in an effort to stay true to the liberal principles that had led him to join the fight for the Union, while also preserving his political clout, Thilenius occupied a moderate middle ground. By focusing on the local economy, political reform, and white reunion, Thilenius, along with other prominent Germans, could still claim the liberal progressive mantle while eschewing racial equality and Radical Reconstruction—sweeping the dust under the rug.

After Carl Schurz, the most well-known German American politician in the nation, arrived in 1867 to work as the *Westliche Post*'s coeditor, St. Louis Germans began outlining their exit from Radical Republicanism—a road map Germans throughout the region would follow. As a liberal nationalist, Schurz engaged in healing wounds. He was joined by prominent Germans on the Middle Border who proposed that black suffrage would coincide with the reenfranchisement of former rebels and the end of federal occupation of the South.[30] By doing so, Germans believed they could reunite and secure an inclusive democracy. More tactically, by promoting liberal suffrage for black and white people, Germans would clearly dissociate themselves from Radical Republicans while simultaneously appeasing moderates who were willing to exchange the black vote for what would likely amount to the return of the Democratic Party in some form.

Industrialization and growing class antagonisms posed another challenge to the German-Republican alliance. Republican free labor ideology, emphasizing white workers' ability to rise up in society and join a robust middle class, had attracted liberal Germans before the war and continued to do so after. But growing class consciousness among industrialized German workers undermined free labor ideology. Many workers and laborers no longer believed their rise up the socioeconomic ladder was a possibility. They attributed their stagnation to greedy capitalists who profited from the war but were also frustrated by the government's continued concerns over Southern black people, which seemed to come at the expense of their own struggles.[31] Not coincidentally, liberal Germans, seeking to move away from Radical Republicanism, began to reclaim economic policies they had once fought for under the Democratic Party's banner. Agitating over protective tariffs, which they argued unfairly placed a tax burden on the individual while aiding manufacturers, liberal Germans claimed to represent white middle- and working-class interests. In that vein, just as they condemned government interference to benefit an economic industrial elite, liberal Germans also denounced Radical Reconstruction and its misguided attention solely on the South.

Still, some radical Germans never wavered, and by remaining rooted, they drifted farther out to sea. Within liberal German America, socialist labor radicals had always existed on the periphery, espousing ideas that only under the threat of secession and the promise of abolition coalesced, begrudgingly, with mainstream liberal German thought. Overthrowing slave masters was an important first step, but the war's conclusion did not signal the end of the struggle.[32] Joseph Weydemeyer, the *Westliche Post*'s radical contributor, in 1865 expressed his fear that race would undercut growing working-class consciousness. He argued that black and white workers would need to unite in "the great struggle between labor and monopolistic capital," asking, "Where, then, to find these comrades in the South when not among the workers themselves, regardless of what ancestry determines their skin color?" But Weydemeyer's appeals largely failed to overcome German workers' mounting fears that Radical Republicans and black laborers threatened their position in cities and towns along the Middle Border, where black migrants began to settle in staggering numbers.[33]

Though much of southern Indiana supported the Union, the region remained fiercely averse to African American settlement. This was true even in Evansville, where Republicans, with their German allies' backing, controlled the growing city's politics. Republicans in Evansville had largely endorsed emancipation, following the *Evansville Journal*'s reasoning that the measure was first and foremost a punishment for the South. But by 1865, black migrants began crossing the Ohio River in droves and often settled in the surrounding area.[34] They soon discovered that racial antipathies remained firmly in place after white workers in the industrializing city, already struggling with falling wages, turned their wrath on black job competitors. Local Democrats enthusiastically argued that Radical Republicans promoted black equality at the expense of white workers and began reaching out to Germans, who constituted a significant segment of the working class.[35]

By making entreaties to German workers, Democrats hoped to regain what was once a solid Democratic voting bloc in Evansville, before Kansas-Nebraska and free soil and free labor ideology snatched them away. By the late 1850s, German Republicans in Evansville successfully convinced a majority of their countrymen that the slave South had hijacked the Democratic Party. When Germans gathered in 1857 to discuss the dangers slavery posed, they concluded that "to open the door to slavery in the territories . . . is to close it upon the free labor and free laborers of the Northern States and of the old world."[36] That same year, Republicans publicly denounced the Democratic *Enquirer* after the newspaper argued that local Republicans were "so intensely American [Know-Nothing], or anti-Democratic, that they would rather have a free negro for a neighbor or a laborer than a German . . ." and wanted to "make equals with [black people]—eat at the same table and sleep in the same bed with them, as though they were whites." Ultimately, the *Enquirer*'s attempts to play on nativism and racial equality could not overshadow many Germans' fear that a "slavocracy" would destroy the nation, and thus they marched off in Union blue.[37]

When German soldiers returned to Evansville, they found a city transformed by industrial growth, as well as a burgeoning black population. Though black men were excluded from most sectors of the economy, they did find employment in the less-desired and lower-paying mines and tobacco factories. Tensions soon developed between African Americans and German laborers, and these tensions spilled out into the community. In August 1865, a German Catholic woman reported being attacked and "outraged" by two black men. The Republican *Journal*'s headline the next day read, "A Diabolical Outrage." Later that day, a white mob forced its way into the jail, shot the two accused men, and hanged both from a lamppost. Soon after, a number of black families fled the city. In the fallout, local Republican leaders quietly condemned German Catholic Butternuts for targeting black families and threatening to burn local tobacco factories where many black men were employed. Over the next few years, Evansville Germans and African Americans lived in increasingly segregated neighborhoods.[38]

German working-class consciousness in Evansville began to push back against German Republican leadership in the city for what was perceived as a preference for black votes over German workers. Such thinking was symptomatic of growing class division within Evansville's German community. Industrialization sharpened previously subdued discord between German professionals and managers and the rapidly expanding German working class. The *Evansville Demokrat* charged local wealthy Germans with corruption and accused the city's Republican council of turning its back on German workers, pointing to the construction of a new school in the wealthier, largely non-German section of the city.[39] Black laborers' arrival in Evansville exacerbated class anxieties, causing the considerable number of German workers in the mines and cotton mills to abandon German Republican leaders in the next election, returning local Democrats to city offices for the first time in eight years.[40]

African American migration into southern Illinois, where antiblack sentiment had existed for decades, began during the war's last years and immediately ignited debate over free black migrants' place in the community. Initially, Germans scoffed at white resistance to black residents. After receiving his medical discharge from the Eighty-Second Illinois in late 1863, Friedrich Braütigam, a Republican and strong supporter of emancipation, returned to St. Clair County, Illinois. In his absence, Southern black migrants moved into the area, settling down on the outskirts of Lebanon. But what most disturbed Braütigam was not the growing black population, but native-born white people's reaction to changing demographics. "The unrest against the numerous Negroes who are here and whose numbers have increased in recent times is growing daily and becoming seriously apparent," he reported. "The reason the working class is running them off is frightening." He explained,

"[White workers] believe to be working for their own self-interest." When he met with other local Germans, they also engaged in "a lively conversation which mostly was in regard to the all-absorbing Negro issue," but with only deepened encouragement for the radical war and emancipation.

Just one month later, Germans in Lebanon, Illinois, turned their attention to new challenges—the plight of newly arrived African Americans overshadowed by local interests and concerns. After a meeting in the German schoolhouse to discuss the upcoming city election, Braütigam believed, "The support is primarily toward the Germans," as "the other party consisted primarily of temperance people who want nothing less than to close all drinking establishments on Sundays which would have a very unpleasant effect on the predominant German population here." Though local Germans in Lebanon buttressed local Republicans and were strongly committed to the war, temperance's reemergence suddenly attracted all attention. "Despite the fact that all the German citizens of Lebanon stood together," they lost the city election. Determining the failure's source, Braütigam explained, "The anticipation of getting the 20 votes of the liberal section of the Americans (the Union club) was not fulfilled." The Germans' "liberal" Republican allies having forsaken them for temperance not only was disappointing but also served as a warning. Despite the war and debates concerning black migrants raging in the background, Braütigam and other Germans in southern Illinois concentrated their attention on "the German population whose civil rights have been seriously violated."[41]

In the postwar years, temperance, Sabbatarianism, and nativist sympathies, which in the 1850s had been submerged beneath free soil and free labor's coalition, reappeared. In Illinois, temperance was positioned as a moral imperative taken up by state Republicans. In 1867, the *Belleviller Zeitung* warned Republicans that "the German element in the country are a unit upon this question [temperance], and will abandon the Radical party in a body, if that organization persists in favoring the enforcement of prohibitory measures and Sunday observance by law."[42] When a state temperance law passed in 1872 under the Republicans' watch, widespread outrage poured out of the German community and hastened their exit from the coalition.[43]

In southern Indiana, Germans interpreted this fascination with temperance and black political rights as an attack on their culture and further indication that the Republicans had discarded them. William Hofmann, a brewer in Posey County, explained, "One knows this: Temperance and nativism brood from the New England states." Linking nativism and temperance to faraway Radical Republicans, Hofmann predicted, "The Negroes will be given the right to vote in order to use them as voting cattle in order to accomplish their devil's plan, while they will deprive white people the right to vote." In 1874, a contentious debate broke out over the pro-temperance, Republican-proposed Baxter Law. Hofmann reported, "The entire German press in the State of Indiana held a convention in Terre Haute and decided not to support any candidate for any official position who is not positively against the Baxter Law." Despite German threats, "the Republican Party in their state platform declared themselves for, the Democratic Party against this Baxter Law, so the latter won." The threads of Union that once bound Germans to the Republican coalition appeared to be quickly unraveling.[44]

While Liberal Republicanism focused nationally on reunion, civic reform, and the economy, on the local level, German political leaders like George Thilenius embraced the movement in order to break away from Radical Republicans and any sign of nativism or temperance. In late 1868, Thilenius's major critic, the Democratic *Argus*, took up the call to connect Cape Girardeau by rail to St. Louis. As a major network of railroad lines spread across the West, the Mississippi River's importance began to wane. For a city that owed its existence to river commerce, this was a frightening development. City leaders thus made a major rail spur's completion the singular political issue. The *Argus* announced its demands in clear terms: "We want, and must have a Railroad outlet; and whoever may be the pioneer to supply this much needed desideratum, will deserve and receive the thanks and blessings of the whole community—irrespective of past or present political affiliations." To back up its claims, the newspaper mentioned the recent work of Mayor Thilenius to push the rail line forward, which it supported fully. "Thilenius certainly carries with him our ardent wish that he may meet full fruition . . . and when the *Argus* can aid the good work, it will be found ever ready to do so."[45]

In addition to improving the local economy, Thilenius was driven by personal interests. Around the time he began to advocate for the railroad, the new State Line Company, formed by local businessmen (over half of whom were German), publicly endorsed the Cape Girardeau, Pilot Knob, and Belmont line spur to the city of Cape Girardeau. They named Thilenius president, paying him a yearly salary of $3,000, and soon after, as a source of additional financing, the city sold a $150,000 bond, which was matched by Cape Girardeau County. Thilenius also owned a large mill outside the city and stood to benefit from direct access to the railroad. His political and financial investment marked the beginning of a new political alliance with the *Argus*, the paper having suddenly shifted its views on the mayor, becoming one of his biggest supporters.[46]

Thilenius's emphasis on local economic developments marched in step with the Missouri Democrat Party's resurgence and advocacy for the white working class. The *Argus* asked voters to recall "that the whole country prospered and grew powerful under the Democratic administration," and then further tailored its message to reach out to the city's German population reminding that "it was the Democrats who encouraged foreign emigration of white people." The subtext was that radicals preferred to import Southern black people, whereas the *Argus* declared that it was "against negro equality. . . . [and] are for a white man's government." This depiction of radicals was further reinforced when the paper cited an episode where "the leader of the Radical party declared in a speech that he would prefer to have a white woman marry 'buck negroes' to Germans."[47] Such evidence suggests that conservatives willfully went to great lengths to imply that with the radicals, Germans played second fiddle to the interests of black Americans.

In an editorial titled "Warning to Germans," Democrats continued to hammer home the accusation that Radical Republicans had forsaken Germans for the black vote. The *Argus* pointed to "the persistent and often repeated expressions of the editor of the [*Cape Girardeau*] *News* [the city's Republican paper] of 'd—n the Dutch'" and "his unceasing war on Sheriff Bader, Mayor Thilenius, and other adopted citizens." As the paper went on to report, during a recent procession of black veterans along Second Street in front of the German Turner Hall, the editor of the *Cape Girardeau News* pointed his finger at the hall and told the men in the procession, "Never vote for a man who belongs to it.'" Dismayed, the *Argus* asked a series of pointed questions for the Turners and the German community to ponder: "Have the colored men forgot who filled the first regiment in Missouri to strike the shackles from their limbs? Have they forgot where the loyal people of Cape Girardeau met for the first time to form themselves into organized bodies of soldiers, to set them free? Was it not in the Turner Hall? Was it not the Turners? Was it not the Germans?" The story told by the *Argus*, echoed by Democrats across the Middle Border, was one of betrayal and incompetence. Germans had fought to save the Union and led the charge of emancipation, yet now, just a few years removed from the battlefield, freedmen and radicals had cast them off. The *Argus* questioned whether those Germans, "who profess to be, and are, sensible and respectable men, [were] going to submit to such a course."[48]

In 1871, as the next city election approached, the struggling radical ticket in Cape Girardeau nominated a black candidate for councilman in opposition to George Thilenius. The *Argus* concluded that radicals offered a "Black man's ticket." Following the election a few months later, the *Argus* reported on the outcome: "this city—hitherto always Radical—gave a majority for our [Democratic] ticket. Our labors for years have been directed to convincing the

Germans, who compose a majority of our voting population, that the Democratic Party is not hostile to them." In that same election, George Thilenius was reelected, but this time as a Liberal Republican—the arc of his career an ominous foreshadowing of Radical Reconstruction's fate.

As Germans on the Middle Border retreated from Radical Reconstruction policies, they likewise slowly abandoned any notions of racial equality within a lily-white society. Like most of white America, Germans generally accepted race as a necessary point of division in American society. Though asserting the existence of racial differences, German liberals felt that freedom by its very nature conferred equal opportunity in a republic, which they had long argued was the bedrock of a free nation. This position, however, also allowed Germans to tacitly agree with assessments that blamed Reconstruction's shortcomings on black inferiority.[49]

From the Civil War's opening salvo, Emil Mallinckrodt was convinced that "a permanent restoration of the Union is no longer possible other than through the total and final abolition of slavery." Abolition, then, was historical progress in that it secured the nation, a goal that liberal Germans like Mallinckrodt had spent decades pursuing. In 1868, Mallinckrodt wrote an editorial for the radical *Westliche Post* titled "The Dark Continent and Its Residents." In it, he traced the slave trade's history back to Africa and concluded that African Americans possessed a biological deficiency that threatened America should "race mixing" take place. "Viewed entirely without prejudice, an amalgamation would be a misfortune for the white, or Caucasian, element," he explained. Emancipation was not the problem, for "legal freedom and equality is forever guaranteed to the colored in the United States, as was just." Instead, Mallinckrodt warned that "social equalization" could "lead to physical mixing and a creation of a mixed race, would be a national misfortune." By 1874, he expressed outright regret over the Emancipation Proclamation, writing that "a terrible mistake was made" and concluding that African Americans "would have been better off in slavery."[50]

CONCLUSION

German America's story on the Middle Border ended remarkably close to where it began. In 1850, the *St. Charles Demokrat*, a German-language newspaper in Missouri, fiercely supported the Democratic Party. In agreement with the majority of Germans on the Middle Border, the *Demokrat* touted the party's liberal ideologies based on Jeffersonian individualism and Jacksonian mass democracy. Yet only a decade later, the newspaper endorsed Abraham Lincoln and the Republicans, eschewing the aristocratic slave masters who they claimed had led the Democrats to their doom. The election season editorials seemed to be echoing the heavily German St. Charles County, which went Republican. As the *Demokrat* explained, "There was a time in the political history of this country when the expression 'Democratic Party' meant something. . . . Nothing has remained of the expression other than an empty shell." Voters in St. Charles County and throughout the region would likewise declare for the Republicans and Union in the 1864 election. Illustrative of the lengths to which Germans were willing to go to move the nation forward was Augusta, "the most radical little German town on the Missouri River." There, it was reported in April 1866, "Colored children now also take part in instruction at the public school. The other children get along very well with them, and the stouthearted teacher, Mr. Gütlich, says the Colored children pay close attention and behave orderly."[1] Such racial harmony in a former slave state was the ultimate expression of the inclusive liberalism Germans in the region had argued was necessary to preserve the nation-state's high ideals. But none of this was to last atop the shifting sands of Reconstruction.

German American ideological evolution on the Middle Border from the sectional debates of the 1850s to the end of the Civil War was profound but far from complete. Only a few years removed from celebrating black and white schoolchildren's coexistence, in 1870 the *St. Charles Demokrat* announced that the newly formed Liberal Republican Party represented "the new part of progress which has the courage to break with reactionaries and German-devourers.

Its victory means the victory of progress." Denunciation of the Grant administration's declaration of martial law in South Carolina and its attempt to "disseminate in the North a false view of the situation in the South . . . and to keep carpetbaggers in office in the South" followed accordingly. An 1872 editorial disagreed with Massachusetts senator Charles Sumner's call to end segregation, explaining that "as long as enough schools for Negroes are available with teachers equally as good as for whites, we do not see why Negroes should be forced into white schools." Emphasizing individual liberties, the *Demokrat* reasoned, "Whoever wants to have a theater exclusively for whites, cannot be forced to admit Negroes." By 1880, the newspaper had returned to the Democratic Party, where it had resided thirty years before. Rather than a contradiction, this progression represented, to the prominent German paper's editorial board, a logical outcome.[2]

German Americans on the Middle Border had always maintained that free, independent citizens were necessary for a nation to prosper. Within this paradigm, slavery worked in diametric opposition, undermining individualism and *Bildung*. Recognizing a Hegelian conflict between slave and free labor, Germans believed reconciliation or synthesis was predictable, leaving a unified nation of free men to move inexorably westward.[3] As historians Elizabeth Flower and Murray G. Murphey argue, having read "Hegel's analysis of slavery in the *Phenomenology*—the master is more enslaved than the slave—with enthusiasm," philosophical German thinkers could see the "collapse of slavery as a system of labor was inevitable."[4] Those who had not read Hegel nonetheless saw clearly the coming conflict. Fearing national dissolution, few Germans immediately advocated extreme means to achieve this end, condemning abolitionists and Southern Fire-Eaters alike. Their antislavery position was instead rooted in a combination of *Bildung* and free soil and free labor ideology, arguing that preventing slavery's western expansion would protect and elevate white workers and farmers above a withering Southern aristocracy. It was only when disunion became a reality, representing the very death knell of liberal nationalism, that they justified a radical war to protect their vision.

Ironically, the very arguments Germans made to support wartime emancipation were used in the postwar period to justify their retreat from Radical Reconstruction. Insisting that a liberal nation required free individuals, leading German voices claimed that Southern occupation and white Southerners' disenfranchisement represented government oppression, too closely resembling the absolutism that once thwarted nationalism in central Europe. On the Middle Border, where black equality and civil liberties were unpopular, German leaders argued that if suffrage were extended to black men, former

Confederates should also receive voting rights. Rather than spend resources to protect African Americans in the South, Germans found it easier to shift the debate to regional economic improvement, including the condition of white workers and the growing middle class. As historian Alison Efford outlines, through the newfound Liberal Republican Party, Germans sought to "subordinate questions of African-American rights to free trade, civil service reform, and reconciliation between Northern and Southern whites."[5]

Though the Liberal Republican movement quickly and unsuccessfully exited national politics, it opened the gates for some Germans to return to the Democrats. Before becoming one of the most influential German Republicans in the West, Gustav Körner once received consideration for the Democrats' gubernatorial candidacy in Illinois. Even after his conversion to the Republican side of the aisle, he remarked that beyond slavery, "On all other questions which had divided the two great parties, I was as sincere a Democrat as ever." Following the war and slavery's defeat, the one major wall separating Körner from the party responsible for his early political career crumbled, opening the path to reunion and reconciliation.[6]

Running as a Liberal Republican in Illinois's 1872 gubernatorial race, Körner was defeated by the Republican candidate, which left him further disillusioned. In 1876, he came full circle by publicly endorsing Democrat Samuel J. Tilden for president. As Körner explained, "The questions that compelled my severance from the Democratic Party had been settled by the war, and the principles which brought the Republican Party into power and sustained the organization . . . had also been settled by the arbitration of the sword."[7] More cynically, the *Missouri Cashbook* in Jackson, Missouri, claimed that because Germans "were needed to save the Union they were petted and caressed with a fondness unspeakable. After the war, Radicalism sought to still further use this element . . . but the practical German mind realizes the fact that the war is over."[8] Körner's journey back to the Democratic Party seems to ring out in affirmation.

Though Democrats on the Middle Border were only too happy to welcome Germans back into the fold, not all followed Gustav Körner's withdrawal. In Körner's St. Clair County, Edward Treutlein believed Republicans remained "the party of progress, of equal rights for all and everyone without distinction of station or color," while Democrats, "if no longer exactly reactionary [were] still very conservative . . . they would like to leave everything the old way like it was before the war."[9] Immediately following peace at Appomattox, Johann Bauer reported, "In the state of Missouri we are looking forward to a better future; *Sclavery* [*sic*] (or trade in human beings) has ceased forever." As Democrats began their resurgence, he insisted that Southerners should lose their citizenship, "otherwise all the blood was shed for naught and the fruits of victory lost and it would not be long before people were again sold like animals."[10] To his dismay, former Confederates, Butternuts, Peace Democrats, and politicians along the border simply campaigning on an antiblack platform slowly returned to positions of power. Bauer's worldview quickly slipped into the minority position and then almost totally disappeared.[11]

In many ways, committing to a radical war on the Middle Border cost Germans deeply. Though victorious in preserving the nation, to do so they had adopted a position that would prove impossible to maintain during Reconstruction, losing in local and regional politics during the "war after the war." German Liberal Republicans like Carl Schurz and Gustav Körner understood this and began to map out their retreat. Those radical Germans who stayed the course ultimately fought a losing battle. After the war, Germans gained enormous power in Freedom Township in Lafayette County, Missouri, where so much of their political opposition found themselves disenfranchised or banished. In this vacuum, Germans overwhelmingly supported the radical 1865 state constitution and in 1869 elected a German to a county position, a feat unheard of before the war. But by the 1870s, former Confederates retook their old seats of power. In 1875, Francis Cockrell replaced U.S. senator Carl Schurz. In 1884, John Marmaduke, a Confederate general under Sterling Price, was elected governor of Missouri. In short order, "the Lafayette County Germans found themselves, despite being on the winning side of a devastating war, governed by former Confederates who were not just Missourians but their near neighbors."[12]

In addition to the changing political winds, many Germans believed that given the war's successful conclusion and the Union's restoration, the pursuit of radical policies on the border represented a bridge too far. Black migrants' arrival and Radical Reconstruction policies combined with resuscitated nativist and temperance strains convinced many Germans that their interests no longer received consideration in the Republican Party. William Hofmann declared his opposition to the Civil Rights Act then being debated in 1874, writing, "This is the most fanatic senselessness and will also it is to be hoped not become a law." Hofmann, a brewer in southern Indiana, was wary of black voting rights and became convinced that radicals were bent on handing over society to African Americans. He reasoned:

> Let us suppose a ragged Negro comes into an inn; the innkeeper will not keep him on account of his ragged appearance, so he faces the uppermost penalty; but at the same time comes also a white person who also does not appear at the best and the inn keeper says: You may not stay with me;

> here nobody cares two hoots about it. Is that not preferring the Negro to the White? The same also with the school. The Negroes have separate schools in our state and generally the whole country; they are taught from the public funds to which everyone must pay just as the whites.

Besides, he concluded, "because of their skin, particularly in the summer, the perspiration circulates a not so very acceptable odor."[13]

That so many German Americans who once passionately fought for emancipation quietly walked away from Radical Reconstruction says much about Reconstruction's shortcomings. Historians point to a number of factors. Some argue that Germans feared black migration would bring economic competition or that they simply came to see the benefits of white privilege.[14] Cincinnati's August Willich articulated a larger class struggle that transcended race, insisting that "black and white slavery derive from the same principle," and he argued that until the white worker became conscious of this fact, he would "not even have set foot on the battlefield for the advancement of human rights."[15] But he found few willing to listen. Instead, German socialists turned their attention to the conflict brewing between labor and capital in the North's industrial cities. Economic turmoil in the early 1870s not only turned German laborers against German ownership but also undermined any cooperation between black and white workers. During the general strike of 1877, German workers and industrialists in St. Louis both identified the city's black residents as the source of the problem.[16] Martin W. Öfele adds another layer, pointing out that "for the sake of assimilation, ethnic public memory had to conform with generally accepted interpretations of the war." Adopting white nationalist memory meant Germans gradually deemphasized black equality or the importance of black soldiers.[17]

On the Middle Border, all these explanations contributed to German liberalism's retreat from its wartime position, along with more provincial pressures that appeared more immediate. Nativism loomed around every corner, and temperance remained a constant refrain in Republican circles, whereas neither resided among Democrats. Furthermore, between 1866 and 1870, one hundred thousand new German immigrants arrived each year in America. Rather than confront slavery, they focused on organized labor in an industrializing society, citizenship rights, and their own status as white Americans in a racially conscious society.[18] For German Americans, challenging the Middle Border's racial hierarchy in the postwar years would not preserve the Union or open western lands to independent workers; both had been secured in 1865. Having helped save the nation, German leadership believed they could claim victory, but in accepting uneven and unequal progress, they largely faded into obscurity.

Triumphant in their war to save the Union, German Americans' story on the Middle Border ultimately became one of loss by politics. Germans were unable to remain politically and culturally salient while simultaneously supporting rights for African Americans and the reintegration of white Southerners. Still, many tried, and this strategy proved disastrous. The 1871 nomination of Horace Greeley and Democrats' successful machinations led Friedrich Hecker to conclude that Liberal Republican Carl Schurz "was completely duped. The whole thing was calculated to get rid of him and to strike the Germans a blow (and how!)."[19] As Hecker soon discovered, the moderate ground had already disappeared. White residents along the border denounced the federal government and retreated to a conservative, unreconstructed political economy despite—or perhaps to spite—Germans' conciliatory efforts, which did not go far enough to effect lasting social change.

Perhaps all was foretold in Louisville, long before secession and war. In that border city in 1854, a small group of Germans wrote a radical antislavery tract in response to fiery sectional debates that consumed the Ohio Valley. It was not well received—in fact, it was violently rejected, and many associated with the publication fled the city. Those who remained took the lesson to heart, and rather than aid the free soil and free labor movement as their fellow Germans did in Cincinnati, St. Louis, Evansville, Belleville, and other small towns and cities on the border, Germans in Louisville remained tied to pro-Union Democrats rather than side with the Know-Nothings and nativists who dominated the city's fledgling Republican Party.[20] At the beginning of the war, German city council member Philip Tompert called on Louisville's Germans to crush secession, warning that shame would be heaped on them if they remained observers while Germans in other loyal states rushed to enlist. But then in 1865, running as a Peace Democrat, Tompert was elected mayor. Politically, Tompert's actions proved expedient; those German who toed the radical line found far less success.[21]

Standing in stark contrast, for the Louisville Germans who fought a radical war to save the nation, little tribute would be offered. Pauline Tafel, whose husband and brothers formed the first German Turner Society in America upriver in Cincinnati, recalled that in Louisville immediately after the war, "animated by the Turners who wished to erect a monument to the fallen soldiers," a committee was established to build the memorial. But "we never got any farther than to put up the foundation." The unfinished memorial serves as a perfect metaphor for the Germans' subverted legacy and unfulfilled promise on the Middle Border.[22]

NOTES

BIBLIOGRAPHY

INDEX

NOTES

Introduction: *Im Abendlande*

1. *Mississippi Blätter*, April 21, 1861, quoted in Rowan, *Germans for a Free Missouri*, 182–84.

2. Forster, *Zion on the Mississippi*, 84.

3. Levine, *Spirit of 1848*, 60; Debow, *Statistical View*, 399 and appendix; Kennedy, *Population of the United States in 1860*, xxvii, 599, 603–5; Lipin, *Producers, Proletarians, and Politicians*; Kamphoefner, *Westfalians*, 70–105; Keil, "Continuity and Change," 21–24.

4. Phillips, *Rivers Ran Backward*, 5–9; Aron, *American Confluence*, xii, xvii–xxi; Astor, *Rebels on the Border*, 3; Cayton, "Artery and Border," 19–23; Smith, *Borderland in the Civil War*, 2; Stanley, "'Between Two Fires,'" 2.

5. Astor, *Rebels on the Border*, 3; Morrison, *Slavery and the American West.*

6. Blackbourn, *Long Nineteenth Century*, 138–43; Sperber, *Rhineland Radicals.* On the connections between America and European liberalism, see Fleche, *Revolution of 1861*; Levine, *Spirit of 1848*; Brancaforte, *German Forty-Eighters in the United States.*

7. Freehling, *Road to Disunion*, 2:97; Arenson, *Great Heart of the Republic*, 2–3; Stanley, "'Between Two Fires,'" 2–6; Thornbrough, *Indiana in the Civil War Era*, 13. See also Etcheson, *Emerging Midwest*; Smith, *Borderland in the Civil War.*

8. Merkel, "Anti-Slavery Movement in Missouri," 59.

9. Stampp, *Indiana Politics during the Civil War*, 13; Nation, *At Home in the Hoosier Hills*, 3–4; Marshall, *Creating a Confederate Kentucky*, 10; Astor, *Rebels on the Border*, 29; Foner, *Free Soil, Free Labor, Free Men*, 49. See also Hubbart, "'Pro-Southern' Influences," 45–47; Stanley, "'Between Two Fires,'" 20, 92; *Charleston Courier*, December 21, 1860. On the presence of slavery in the early history of southern Illinois, see Simeone, *Democracy and Slavery in Frontier Illinois.*

10. Nagel, "German Forty-Eighters' Critique," 55; Öfele, *German-Speaking Officers*, 231; Freitag, *Friedrich Hecker*, 25–26.

11. Forty-Eighter is the designation given to German immigrants who arrived following the failed nationalist revolutions in 1848 and 1849. It has been

broadly applied to both those immigrants who were fleeing political persecution and those who were displaced by economic turmoil.

12. Anderson, "German Americans, African Americans," 1–3.

13. Efford describes the creation of this myth during and after the Civil War "as a form of ethnic self-definition" that continued as German American understandings of the era. Efford, *German Immigrants, Race, and Citizenship*, 53–85

14. Sheehan, *German Liberalism in the Nineteenth Century*, 5, 14; Beiser, *Romantic Imperative*, 88. For a broader history, see Bruford, *German Tradition of Self-Cultivation.* In *Experience of the Foreign* (43), Berman explains that "through *Bildung* an individual, a people, a nation, but also a language, a literature, a work of art in general are formed and thus acquire a form, a *Bild*."

15. De Ruggiero, *History of European Liberalism*, 211–51.

16. Vick, *Defining Germany*, 16, 43.

17. Printed in the *Missouri Republican*, August 26, 1848.

18. Koerner, *Memoirs*, 1:341.

19. Bowman, "Antebellum Planters and *Vormärz* Junkers," 779–808.

20. Efford, *German Immigrants, Race, and Citizenship*, 53–54; Fleche, *Revolution of 1861*, 16.

21. Flower and Murphey, *History of Philosophy in America*, 2:470, 494. In *Defining Germany* (39), Brian Vick contends that if one characteristic of German liberals "stands out above all others, it is their continued faith in the course of history as the advance of culture."

22. Foner, *Free Soil, Free Labor, Free Men*, 59.

23. *Deutsche Tribüne*, February 15, 1850.

24. Levine, *Spirit of 1848*, 151, 154–55, 149.

25. *Anzeiger des Westens*, July 21, 1854.

26. *Evansville (IN) Daily Journal*, February 25, 1854.

27. Bender, *Nation among Nations*, 126.

28. Magnus Brucker, Letter to Wife, September 18, 1864, M0324, Indiana Historical Society (hereafter cited as IHS).

29. Albert O. Allen to Jap Pinnell, December 3, 1863, in Siddali, *Missouri's War*, 119.

1. Building a *Neuen Deutschland*: The Dreissiger Immigration and the Origins of German Liberalism on the Middle Border

1. Theodor Engelmann, Letter to Parents, February 28, 1829, Engelmann-Kircher Papers, Box 2, Abraham Lincoln Presidential Library (hereafter cited as ALPL); Blackbourn, *The Long Nineteenth Century*, 21–22; Sheehan, *German Liberalism in the Nineteenth Century*, 8–9.

2. Theodor Engelmann, Letter to Sister, May 22, 1829, and Letters to Parents, November 28, 1831, January 18, 1832, Engelmann-Kircher Papers, Box 2, ALPL; Koerner, *Memoirs*, 2:13–15; Vierhaus, "Wir nennen's Gemeinsinn," 21–32.

3. Theodor Engelmann, Letter to Classmate, March 24, 1833, Letter to Fiancée, Hannchen (Hannah) Kribben, April 3, 1845, Engelmann-Kircher Papers, Box 2, ALPL.

4. Kamphoefner, *Westfalians*, 15–25; Levine, *Spirit of 1848*, 22–25. In tracing the socioeconomic conditions in Germany before 1848, Levine emphasizes the rise of industrial capitalism following the defeat of the French and formation of the German states as a product of a "revolution from above," meaning industrial and agrarian elites.

5. Theodor Engelmann, Letter to Classmate, March 24, 1833, Engelmann-Kircher Papers, Box 2, ALPL; Keil, "Continuity and Change," 21.

6. Phillips, *Missouri's Confederate*, 45; Tucker, "Political Leadership," 83. On the beginnings of radical liberalism in Germany, see Blackbourn, *Long Nineteenth Century*, 132–33;

7. Vick, *Defining Germany*, 16–17; De Ruggiero, *History of European Liberalism*, 211–51. Vick points to the establishment of a "culture of nationhood" in the decades before 1848 that fostered a desire for public and political awareness and consciousness of the German state.

8. Blackbourn, *Long Nineteenth Century*, 12–17.

9. Ibid., 82–89. Patriotism, Blackbourn argues, was "conditioned by the disappearance of the Holy Roman Empire, sharpened by French occupation, and fed by the growing interest in German language, history and folkways" (88). On patriotism as a product of the Napoleonic war of liberation, see Heideking, "Festive Culture and National Identity," 218.

10. Vick, *Defining Germany*, 39–41; Blackbourn, *Long Nineteenth Century*, 130; Rowan, *Germans for a Free Missouri*, 23. Rowan draws a line from the emerging German nationalism of the early nineteenth century to later waves of immigration to the United States, saying that "the revolutionary movement of the 1830s promoted a romantic nationalism with few concrete social or political goals beyond justice and brotherhood in a united German nation."

11. Blackbourn, *Long Nineteenth Century*, 120–25; Sheehan, *German Liberalism in the Nineteenth Century*, 10–11.

12. Albert Lange, Autobiographical Letter, March 25, 1858, IHS.

13. Paul Weber, *America in Imaginative German Literature*, 169; Stevens, "Making of a Superior Immigrant," 122–24.

14. Ferdinand Ernst, "Observations Made upon a Journey through the Interior of the United States of North America, in the Year 1819," translated by E. P. Baker (1823), ALPL; Kamphoefner, "Immigrant Epistolary and Epistemology," 34–54; Kamphoefner, "Uprooted or Transplanted?" 71–89. In "Uprooted or Transplanted?" Kamphoefner challenges Oscar Handlin's seminal work on American immigration, *The Uprooted*, demonstrating that German immigration was marked by great continuity through "chain migration."

15. Gottfried Duden, "Report on a Journey to the Western States of North America and a Stay of Several Years along the Missouri (during the Years 1824, '25, '26, and 1827)," translated by Elsa Nagel, 2600, State Historical Society of Missouri (hereafter cited as SHSM).

16. On Duden's influence on emigration to America, see Weber, *America in Imaginative German Literature*, 115.

17. Mauer, "Earlier German Nationalism in America," 521; Siegmar Muehl Collection, "Friedrich Muench: Man of Letters on the Missouri Frontier," C0952, SHSM.

18. On the Giessen Society and similar colonization efforts, see Kamphoefner, Helbich, and Sommer, *News from the Land of Freedom*, 8; Gustav Koerner Papers, "The Germans in Missouri," 1880, SHSM.

19. Wyman, *Immigrants in the Valley*, 4, 17, 63.

20. Koerner's own treatise on the German-American experience, titled *An Illumination of Duden's Report on the Western States of North America: From the American Side*, was meant to curb the enthusiasm of his fellow countrymen. Koerner downplayed the natural beauty of the Ohio and Mississippi Valleys, pointing instead to "rapidly varying temperatures" and disease-ridden swamps and lowlands. Koerner, *Illumination of Duden's Report*, 6–31.

21. Gert Goebel Typescript, *Laenger Als Ein Menschleben in Missouri*, 1879, SHSM; Krause, "German Americans in the St. Louis Region," 295–310.

22. Theodor Engelmann, Letter to Sister, February 1, 1836, Engelmann-Kircher Papers, Box 2, ALPL.

23. William H. Law and John Law Papers, SC 0963, IHS; Gilbert, *History of Evansville and Vanderburg County*, vol. 1; Lipin, *Producers, Proletarians, and Politicians*; Fritsch, *German Settlers and German Settlements*, 21–22.

24. Bartel, "Institutional Influence of the German Element," 9.

25. Gustav Hiller, Letter to Carl Mayer, February 2, 1840, Charles (Carl) Mayer, SC 1055, IHS.

26. Kamphoefner, Helbich, and Sommer, *News from the Land of Freedom*, 103.

27. Letter containing journal prospectus to Joseph Engelmann and possible contributors, February 1, 1836, Engelmann-Kircher Papers, ALPL.

28. *Letters of a German from North-America to his Friends and Relatives in Germany: Reading for Instructive Entertainment*, IHS, Schramm Family Papers, 1842–1930 (bulk 1851–1911).

29. Ibid. See also *Letters of Jacob Schramm and Family from Indiana to Germany in 1836* and "The Schramm Letters, Written by Jacob Schramm and Members of his Family from Indiana to Germany in the year 1838," Schramm Family Papers, 1842–1930, IHS. Schramm sold land to railroad companies, which, contrary to his initially dire predictions, opened up across central and southern Indiana.

30. Guelzo, *Lincoln*, 6.

31. Lammers, "Shaping a True German Identity," 33.

32. Zimmermann, "Travels into Missouri," 40–41 (italics mine).

33. Weber, *America in Imaginative German Literature*, 79–83, 188.

34. Cayton, "'Going over the River,'" 3–8; Phillips, "'The Chrysalis State,'" 145–50. Rockenbach, "'War upon Our Border,'" 10.

35. Edward Mühl Papers, C3744, WHMC; Gerstäcker, *Streifund Jagdzüge durch die Vereignigten Staaten* (1844) in Weber, *America in Imaginative German Literature*, 153; Di Maio, "Unity and Diversity."

36. Klauprecht, *German Chronicle*, 172–78.

37. Levine, *Spirit of 1848*, 182–84; Wade, *Urban Frontier*.

38. Reemelin, *Life of Charles Reemelin*, 38–40, 50; Levine, *Spirit of 1848*, 185–86.

39. Theodor Engelmann, Letter to Sister, Gretchen Hilgard, January 21, 1837, Engelmann-Kircher Papers, ALPL.

40. Kamphoefner, "Missouri Germans," 118.

41. Koerner, *Illumination of Duden's Report*, 18, 44; Eversmann Family Papers, 1810–1982, C3743, SHSM.

42. Göbel, *Länger Als Ein Menschen Leben in Missouri*, Gert Goebel Typescript, SHSM.

43. Muench, "The State of Missouri: An Account with Special References to Immigration," Friedrich Münch Papers, SHSM.

44. Kamphoefner, *Westfalians*, 69.

45. Robert Tonnies, "A Brief Biography of Mary Gertrude Kroger, Nee Schlebbe," Pamphlets, fB K93t (1991), Cincinnati History Library and Archives (hereafter cited as CHLA); Lamott, *History of the Archdiocese of Cincinnati*. Francis Joseph Stallo, a wealthy Dreissiger, originally purchased several large tracts eighty miles outside of Cincinnati in 1832 in hopes of attracting immigrants. Stallostown would later be known as Minster in honor of Münster, Germany, where many of the immigrants originated.

46. Frizzell, *Independent Immigrants*, 2–21.

47. Letters of Frederick Steines in Bek, "Followers of Duden," Fifth Article, *Missouri Historical Review* 15 (July 1921): 661.

48. Efford, *German Immigrants, Race, and Citizenship*, 56–57.

49. Bek, *German Settlement Society*, 250; Muehl, "Hermann's 'Free Men,'" 363.

50. Göbel, *Länger Als Ein Menschen Leben in Missouri.*

51. Dunson, "Notes on the Missouri Germans on Slavery," 359.

52. Koerner, *Memoirs*, 1:36–38; *Anzeiger des Westens*, October 11, 1836.

53. Koerner, *Memoirs*, 1:57–58.

2. The Politicization of German Liberals: The Revolution of 1848 and the Second Wave of German Immigration

1. Tucker, "Political Leadership," 114. On the history of German American editors and newspapers, including the *Anzeiger*, see Arndt and Olson, *German-American Newspapers and Periodicals.*

2. Koerner, *Memoirs*, vols. 1 and 2. For a summary of Jacksonian contribution to early antislavery politics, see Earle, *Jacksonian Antislavery*, 5.

3. On the details of Wilmot's proviso and the beginnings of the Northern Democratic rebellion against slavery's western expansion, see Earle, *Jacksonian Antislavery*, chapter 5.

4. *Anzeiger des Westens*, July 22, 1848, quoted in Tucker, "Political Leadership," 133–34; Anderson, "German Americans, African Americans," 66.

5. Sheehan, *German Liberalism in the Nineteenth Century*, 52–54.

6. On the German revolutions in 1848, see Siemann, *German Revolution of 1848–49*; Blackbourn, *Long Nineteenth Century*; Hamerow, *Restoration, Revolution, and Reaction.*

7. Boernstein, *Memoirs of a Nobody*, 139.

8. Earle, *Jacksonian Antislavery*, 3–5.

9. *Anzeiger des Westens*, July 10, 1850, reprinted in the *Missouri Republican*, July 30, 1850. On Börnstein's joining the *Anzeiger* and reshaping its politics, see Rowan, *Germans for a Free Missouri*, 40.

10. Blackbourn, *Long Nineteenth Century*, 138–43; Honeck, *We Are the Revolutionists*, 6. The concept of an "imagined people" is in line with Anderson's *Imagined Communities.*

11. Vick, *Defining Germany*, 43.

12. Ibid., 37.

13. Efford, *German Immigrants, Race, and Citizenship*, 18.

14. Levine, *Spirit of 1848*, 35–37; Wittke, *Against the Current*, 61.

15. Levine, *Spirit of 1848*, 19–23, 54; Hörst, "'More Than Ordinary . . . ,'" 76. Hörst follows immigrants from Mussloch, Baden, a small agricultural community, to Cincinnati. One hundred emigrated between 1848 and 1849, all belonging to the *arbeitenden Bevölkerung* (working people).

16. Hansen, "Revolutions of 1848 and the German Emigration," 630–32.

17. Hamerow, "Two Worlds of the Forty-Eighters," 20.

18. Blackbourn, *Long Nineteenth Century*, 145.

19. Levine, *Spirit of 1848*, 38; Wittke, *Refugees of Revolution*, 341.

20. Behlendorff, "Recollections of a Forty-Eighter," 312, 315–16.

21. Harris, "The Arrival of the Europamude," 2.

22. Kamphoefner, *Westfalians*, 67.

23. Ibid.

24. Levine, *Spirit of 1848*, 7.

25. Bek, "Followers of Duden," Twelfth Article, *Missouri Historical Review* 17 (July 1923): 479–504.

26. Reemelin, *Life of Charles Reemelin*, 88; Earle, *Jacksonian Antislavery*.

27. "Was ist der Staat" and "Zur Frage der Menschenrechte," in *Gesammelte Schriften von Friedrich Münch*, quoted in Tucker, "Political Leadership," 113–14.

28. Bazil B. Edmonston Papers, S 406, Indiana State Library.

29. Solomon Eby, Letter, 1847, Missouri Collection 3982, SHSM.

30. Forster, *Zion on the Mississippi*, 69, 274.

31. Anbinder, *Nativism and Slavery*.

32. Reemelin, *Life of Charles Reemelin*, 81.

33. Koerner, *Memoirs*, 2:516, 284.

34. Ibid., 535–37.

35. Tucker, *Political Leadership*, 92; "Friedrich Hecker: The Beloved of the People," Friedrich Hecker Papers, SHSM; Freitag, *Friedrich Hecker*, 131–32.

36. Foner, *Free Soil, Free Labor, Free Men*, 13.

37. Freitag, *Friedrich Hecker*, 23, 47.

38. Levine, *Spirit of 1848*, 85–86, 91.

39. Heinrich Bornstein, "Seventy-Five Years in the Old and New World," translated by William Bek, 1884, 90, 101, C1054, SHSM.

40. Tucker, *Political Leadership*, 118, 130; Koerner, *Memoirs*, 2:548; Klauprecht, *German Chronicle*, 170.

41. Siegmar Muehl Collection, "Friedrich Muench: Man of Letters on the Missouri Frontier," 27–30, C0952, SHSM.

42. Edward Muehl, "Friedrich Muench," 31, C0952, Edward Mühl Papers, SHSM.

43. Muehl, "Eduard Muhl," 33–34, ibid.

44. Baron, *Abraham Lincoln and the German Immigrants*, 4; Heideking, "Festive Culture and National Identity," 228.

45. Newspaper clipping, H. A. Rattermann, "Dr. Johan Friedrick Leonhard Tafel," *Der Deutsche Pionier* 9 (December 1880), Gustav Tafel Papers, 1847–1994, 1070, CHLA.

46. Rattermann, "Die Pionier-Turngemeinde Amerika's," 178–82; Metzner, *Brief History of the American Turnerbund*, 6–18; "Biographical Sketch," 1940, 1847–1994, 1070, Gustav Tafel Papers, CHLA; Woellert, *Cincinnati Turner Societies*.

47. Honeck, *We Are the Revolutionists*, 13. For background on the American Turners, see Hofmann, "Turners' Loyalty for Their New Home Country."

48. Levine, *Spirit of 1848*, 92–93.

49. Stierlin, *Der Staat Kentucky und die Stadt Louisville*, 81–85. See also Baldwin, "Public Image of Germans."

50. Honeck, *We Are the Revolutionists*, 34.

51. Wittke, *Against the Current*; Schinnerer, "Karl Heinzen," 84–144.

52. Stierlin, *Der Staat Kentucky und die Stadt Louisville*, 84; Baldwin, "Public Image of Germans," 83–85.

53. Lipin, *Producers, Proletarians, and Politicians*, 78.

54. Bornstein, "Seventy-Five Years in the Old and New World," 90–94; Grimstead, *American Mobbing*, viii; *St. Louis Intelligencer*, April 5, 1852; Schneider, "Riot and Reaction in St. Louis," 172–73.

55. *Missouri Courier*, February 14, 1850.

56. Anderson, "German Americans, African Americans," 1–3.

57. Muehl, "Eduard Mühl," 33.

3. "I Was an Enthusiastic Democrat in Those Days": Free Soil, Free Labor, and the Realignment of German Liberals, 1852–1856

1. While outlining the eventual fallout between nativism and the Republican Party, Eric Foner demonstrates the belief among Republicans, especially western Republicans, that free soil and antislavery Germans were essential to the party's success. Eric Foner, *Free Soil, Free Labor, Free Men*, 233.

2. Ibid., ix, 18–19; Earle, *Jacksonian Antislavery*, 4–5.

3. Levine, *Spirit of 1848*, 218.

4. *Evansville (IN) Daily Journal*, July 24, 30, 1850.

5. Lang, "Germans in Vanderburgh County," 7–9.

6. Lang, "Germans of Dubois County," 238.

7. Lang, "Germans in Vanderburgh County," 8–11.

8. Lee Rodman "History of the Indiana Cotton Mills," 1, Indiana Cotton Mills Mss., Lilly Library.

9. Joseph Kundek, Letter to Hamilton Smith, May 28, 1851, Joseph Kundek Mss., Hamilton Smith Papers, ibid.

10. Stanton, "Brought, Borrowed, or Bought," 60–61.

11. Kuppers, Gabriel, and Bidnar, "Beginning Anew," 342.

12. Lang, "Some Characteristics of German Immigrants,"39.

13. Bergquist, "Political Attitudes of the German Immigrant," 11–12. Bergquist argues that while northern Illinois filled with new transportation routes and migrants from the northeastern and Middle Atlantic states, with Chicago as its epicenter, in southern Illinois dependency on the river waned, and upland southerners continued to lose political and economic power.

14. *Evansville (IN) Daily Journal*, July 22, 23, August 2, 1852.

15. Ibid., August 2, November 19, 1852.

16. Bergquist, "Political Attitudes of the German Immigrant," 25, 13.

17. *Belleviller Zeitung*, May 12, 1853.

18. Bergquist, "Political Attitudes of the German Immigrant," 117–18.

19. Morton, "'This Magnificent New World,'" 284–308. See also Forbes, *Missouri Compromise and Its Aftermath.*

20. Mergenthal, "Border Lines," 86.

21. Arenson, *Great Heart of the Republic*, 29.

22. Earle, *Jacksonian Antislavery*, 13; Chambers, *Old Bullion Benton*, 337; Merkel, "Slavery Issue," 389–90. See also McCandless, "Rise of Thomas H. Benton," 145–58.

23. Phillips, *Missouri's Confederate*, 170; Chambers, *Old Bullion Benton*, 340–41.

24. Chambers, *Old Bullion Benton*, 345.

25. Ibid., 357. See also Morton, "'High Wall and a Deep Ditch,'" 1–24.

26. Merkel, "Slavery Issue," 397–98; Chambers, *Old Bullion Benton*, 377; Arenson, *Great Heart of the Republic*, 41; Boernstein, *Memoirs of a Nobody*, 183–93.

27. Kellner, "German Element on the Urban Frontier," 235–36.

28. Ibid., 228–29; Schneider, "Riot and Reaction in St. Louis," 172–73.

29. *Anzeiger des Westens*, July 27, 1850; Chambers, *Old Bullion Benton*, 382; Kamphoefner, "St. Louis Germans and the Republican Party," 72.

30. *St. Charles Demokrat*, January 1, 1852, quoted in Mallinckrodt, *History of Augusta*, 1:5.

31. Howe, *Political Culture of the American Whigs*; Potter and Fehrenbacher, *Impending Crisis*, 151–76. On the origins of the slave power, see Foner, *Free Soil, Free Labor, Free Men*, 73–102.

32. *Evansville (IN) Daily Journal*, February 13, 15, 25, 1854.

33. Foner, *Free Soil, Free Labor, Free Men*, 59. See also Gienapp, *Origins of the Republican Party.*

34. Foner, *Free Soil, Free Labor, Free Men*, 27–28. See also Sexton, *Rise and Fall of the White Republic*; Wilentz, *Chants Democratic.*

35. *St. Charles Demokrat*, January 1, 1852; Bergquist, "Political Attitudes of the German Immigrant," 161; Arenson, *Great Heart of the* Republic, 58; *Anzeiger des Westens*, July 16, 1854, quoted in Anderson, "German Americans, African Americans," 91.

36. Wittke, *German-Language Press*, 139; Levine, *Spirit of 1848*, 151–54, 158; Lipin, *Producers, Proletarians, and Politicians*, 113.

37. Reemelin, *Life of Charles Reemelin*, 87–88, 97–100.

38. Koerner, *Memoirs*, 2:34; Tucker, *Political Leadership*, 154, 200–202.

39. Wittke, *German-Language Press*, 180; Peterson, *Popular Narratives and Ethnic Identity*, 107–8.

40. Levine, *Spirit of 1848*, 192; Schinnerer, "Karl Heinzen," 130; Wittke, *Against the Current*, 92–98.

41. Levine, *Spirit of 1848*, 102–4; Wilentz, *Chants Democratic*, 335–43; *Louisville Democrat*, March 4, 1854; Honeck, *We Are the Revolutionists*, 29.

42. *Evansville (IN) Daily Journal*, February, 15, 25, March 18, 1854.

43. Bergquist, "Political Attitudes of the German Immigrant," 82.

44. *Evansville (IN) Daily Journal*, February 25, 1854.

45. *Anzeiger des Westens*, July 21, 24, 1854, as quoted in Mauer, "Earlier German Nationalism in America," 521.

46. Freitag, *Friedrich Hecker*, 157, 172–73.

47. Anbinder, *Nativism and Slavery*, ix–xiii. On nativism in America, see Billington, *Protestant Crusade*, and Stephenson, "Nativism in the Forties and Fifties."

48. Eric Foner argues that nativism in the West "was much less dramatic," largely as a result of the foreign-born population. Foner, *Free Soil, Free Labor, Free Men*, 244–45.

49. Bergquist, "Political Attitudes of the German Immigrant," 70; Foner, *Free Soil, Free Labor, Free Men*, 246–47.

50. *Evansville (IN) Daily Journal*, June 23, 1854.

51. Tucker, *Political Leadership*, 166–67, 169; Hawgood, *Tragedy of German-America*, 240–41.

52. Münch, "The State of Missouri: An Account with Special References to Immigration," translated by Elsa Nagel, 1859, SUN2462, WHMC.

53. For a discussion on the downfall of the Whig Party and the response of Southern Whigs to sectionalism, see Howe, *Political Culture of the American Whigs*, Chapter 10.

54. Anbinder, *Nativism and Slavery*, 93.

55. Rattermann and Körner, *Kentucky's German Pioneers*, 97–99.

56. Stierlin, *Der Staat Kentucky und die Stadt Louisville*, 161–62.

57. "An Address to the Native Americans of Fayette Congressional District," 1848, CA ovsz, Filson Historical Society (hereafter cited as FHS).

58. Overdyke, *Know-Nothing Party in the South*, 36–37.

59. Kleber, *Encyclopedia of Louisville*, 97; Bruncken, *German Political Refugees*, 4.

60. *Louisville Daily Courier*, October 8, 1853; Baldwin, "Public Image of Germans," 83–90; Stierlin, *Der Staat Kentucky und die Stadt Louisville*, 161–62.

61. Joshua Speed, "Bloody Monday" Letter, September 8, 1855, A S742, Speed Family Papers, FHS; *Louisville Anzeiger*, August 11, 1855; Mittlebeeler, "Aftermath of Louisville's Bloody Monday," 197–219; O'Toole and Aebersold, "Louisville's Bloody Monday Riots," 425.

62. Excerpt from Humphrey Marshall speech, "Reasons for the Formation of a Native American Party"; Letter from Henry Middleton to Humphrey Marshall, December 31, 1855, A M368, Humphrey Marshall Papers, FHS.

63. *Louisville Daily Journal*, July 1855, cited in Charles Cusick, "Gentleman of the Press: The Life and Times of Walter Newmann Haldeman," 27, FB C985, FHS; Overdyke, *Know-Nothing Party in the South*, 45.

64. Overdyke, *Know-Nothing Party in the South*, 198, 201; *Louisville Journal*, quoted in Anbinder, *Nativism and Slavery*, 170–73.

65. Cusick, "Gentleman of the Press." For background on Haldeman, see Price, "Storm of Disunion over a Border State"; Brand, "History of the Know-Nothing Party in Indiana."

66. Towers, *Urban South and the Coming of the Civil War*, 210. Louisville, and Kentucky as a whole, voted for John Bell and the Constitutional Union Party in 1860, and as Towers explains, Louisville remained the "South's most pro-Union city."

67. Trexler, "Slavery in Missouri," 165; Fellman, *Inside War*, 39; *Anzeiger des* Westens, July 7, 1854.

68. Kamphoefner, "St. Louis Germans and the Republican Party," 74–76, 77–88; Kamphoefner, "German-Americans and Civil War Politics," 238–241; Anderson, "German Americans, African Americans," 158.

69. Arenson, *Great Heart of the Republic*, 60.

70. Kamphoefner, "St. Louis Germans and the Republican Party, 74; Parrish, *Frank Blair*, 50–52; Arenson, *Great Heart of the Republic*, 95–96. Demonstrating the German distaste for proslavery Democrats, Kamphoefner explains that with Republican candidate John C. Fremont off the Missouri ballot in the 1856 presidential election, Frank Blair's *Missouri Democrat* begrudgingly

supported Buchanan. Outraged, Heinrich Börnstein rebuked the National Democratic ticket and published an "Under Protest" ticket in the *Anzeiger*, which included American Party candidates and Whig candidate Millard Fillmore. Kamphoefner argues that in this one instance, the German vote did shift to nativist Whigs, evidence of the determination of Germans to steer their own ship against proslavery Democrats. Kamphoefner, "St. Louis Germans and the Republican Party, 81.

71. Tucker, "Political Leadership," 68, 171.

72. Freitag, *Friedrich Hecker*, 167–68.

73. *Evansville (IN) Daily Journal*, August 6, 1856; *Indianapolis Freie Presse*, October 16, 1856.

74. Foulke, *Life and Works of Oliver P. Morton*, 90; Blackbourn, *Long Nineteenth Century*, 12–14, 17; Arenson, *Great Heart of the Republic*, 108; Brose, *German History*, 4; Levine, *Spirit of 1848*, 218. Blackbourn cites Goethe's *Faust* and the oft-quoted drinking song "Das liebe heil'ge röm'sche Reich, Wie hält's nur noch zusammen?" (The dear old Holy Roman Empire, How does it hold together?). Blackbourn, *Long Nineteenth Century*, 17. Arenson makes a strong point: with "the final collapse of interregional compromise in the election of 1860, they were astounded by the call for secession: memories of *Kleinstaaterei*, or small-statism, that had doomed German unity for hundreds of years led to immediate suspicions." Arenson, *Great Heart of the Republic*, 108.

75. Gustav Tafel to Hugo Tafel, April 20, 1857, Gustav Tafel Papers, 1847–1994, 1070, CHLA.

76. William Hofmann, Letters to Brother, October 5, 1856, February 7, 1857, SC 1995, William Hofmann Papers, IHS.

77. William Henry Schrader, "Reminiscences," n.d., C1519, SHSM.

78. Levine, *Spirit of 1848*, 233.

79. *Evansville Daily Journal*, August 14, 1856.

4. "Continuous Vigilance Is the Price of Freedom": Antislavery Germans and the Election of 1860

1. Levine, *Spirit of 1848*, 242. Levine argues that approaching the 1860 election, "German Republicans sought to turn the attention of other German voters away from issues such as nativism, temperance, and sabbatarianism and back toward those of slavery and the West" (242).

2. Jewett, "Gustave Koerner and the Republican Party," 27; Koerner, *Memoirs*, 1:617–18, 2:23–25; *Belleviller Zeitung*, July 22, 1860.

3. *Anzeiger des Westens*, December 17, 1860, quoted in Rowan, *Germans for a Free Missouri*, 147.

4. Ibid.

5. Phillips, *Missouri's Confederate*, 49; Stanley, "'Between Two Fires,'" 35, 20; Simeone, *Democracy and Slavery in Frontier Illinois*, 3–15. See also Litwack, *North of Slavery.*

6. Merkel, "Anti-Slavery Movement in Missouri," 59. See also Dillon, *Elijah P. Lovejoy.*

7. Bergquist, "Political Attitudes of the German Immigrant," 122; Koerner, *Memoirs*, 2:82, 97.

8. Levine, *Spirit of 1848*, 217, 242.

9. *Anzeiger des Westens*, December 3, 1860. On the radical turn in St. Louis, see Anderson, *German Americans, African Americans*, 188.

10. Saalberg, "*Westliche Post* of St. Louis," 33–35; Rowan, *Germans for a Free Missouri*, 45–47.

11. *Westliche Post,* September 27, 1857, quoted in Rowan, *Germans for a Free Missouri*, 50–51.

12. Saalberg, "*Westliche Post* of St. Louis," 72.

13. Arenson, *Great Heart of the Republic*, 20; Kellner, "German Element on the Urban Frontier," 228–29, 240.

14. Anderson, *German Americans, African Americans*, 117.

15. *Anzeiger des Westens*, June 6, 1858, quoted in Kamphoefner, "St. Louis Germans and the Republican Party," 83.

16. Mallinckrodt, *History of Augusta*, 1:26–31; *Westliche Post*, January 13, 1858.

17. W. B. Napton, Letter to Claiborne Fox Jackson, 1857, C1879, SHSM.

18. Friedrich Muench, "The State of Missouri: An Account with Special References to Immigration," 1859, translated by Elsa Nagel, SUN2462, Friedrich Münch Papers, SHSM.

19. Koerner, *Memoirs*, 1:316.

20. Roske, *His Own Counsel*, 54.

21. *Belleviller Zeitung*, May 20, 1858. See also Tucker, "Political Leadership," 202–4; Levine, *Spirit of 1848*, 225; Bergquist, "People and Politics in Transition," 196–226.

22. Holtmann, *Lost American Dream*, 33; Nation, *At Home in the Hoosier Hills*, 474–76.

23. Nation, *At Home in the Hoosier Hills*, 474–76. In Evansville, Indiana, the Democratic *Enquirer* expressed outright shock after learning that local German organizations had announced their support for 1856 Republican presidential candidate John C. Fremont. Hoping to redirect the city's many Germans back to the righteous path, the *Enquirer* instructed them that "vot[ing] for the Abolition State ticket . . . will be to re-elect the temperance law . . . and

the most dangerous sectional party this country ever beheld, and merely out of misguided sympathy for the negro race." *Evansville (IN) Daily Enquirer*, August 15, 1856.

24. Arenson, "Dred Scott versus the Dred Scott Case," 35–36.

25. Monaghan, *Civil War on the Western Border*, 102; Ponce, "'Noise of Democracy,'" 81–96; Tucker, "Political Leadership," 199–201.

26. Bergquist, "People and Politics in Transition," 196. Koerner, *Memoirs*, 2:75. For background on the amendment, see Anbinder, *Nativism and Slavery*, 250–53.

27. German representatives from both East and West had assembled at the Deutsches Haus Meeting before the convention. Of the gathering, Karl Bernays claimed, "All hell broke loose." Western attendees believed they would be best served by joining the Republicans, while the eastern delegation voiced general caution. Bergquist, "Forty-Eighters and the Republican Convention," 141–56; Baron, *Abraham Lincoln and the German Immigrants*, 124–25.

28. Bergquist, "People and Politics in Transition," 196–226; *Anzeiger des Westens*, May 24, 1860.

29. *Anzeiger des Westens*, June 7, 1860; Baron, "Abraham Lincoln and the German Immigrants," 217–18; Levine, *Spirit of 1848*, 248; Herriott, "Conference in the Deutsches Haus," 101–91.

30. *Cincinnati Volksfreund*, September 4, 27, 1860, quoted in Schick, "'For God, Mac, and Country," 47, 52.

31. Easton, *Hegel's First American Followers*, 181, 190. Willich claimed the *Republikaner* was free of outside influence because it was sponsored by the Social Workingman's Club and the Germania Institute and therefore was "truly by and for workers." The paper's masthead under Willich: "Value in Return for Value."

32. Levine, *Spirit of 1848*, 223; Honeck, *We Are the Revolutionists*, 72–73; *Cincinnati Daily Enquirer*, December 6, 1859, quoted in Honeck, *We Are the Revolutionists*, 73–74; Easton, *Hegel's First American Followers*, 190.

33. *Anzeiger des Westens*, October 29, 1860, quoted in Rowan, *Germans for a Free Missouri*, 137.

34. George Julian, Letter to Theodore Hielscher, November 30, 1860, L 81, George Julian Papers, IHS.

35. *St. Charles Demokrat*, April 26, 1860, quoted in Mallinckrodt, *History of Augusta*, 49.

36. Koerner, *Memoirs*, 2:61; *Belleviller Zeitung*, July 22, 1860.

37. Sabine Freitag writes, "Whether and how money came cannot be proven. It must be assumed that Hecker received some support from the Republican Party." Freitag, *Freidrich Hecker*, 177.

38. Kamphoefner, Helbich, and Sommer, *News from the Land of Freedom*, 158–59.

39. Gustav Tafel, "Speech to Cincinnati Turners," 1070, Gustav Tafel Papers, CHLA.

40. *Daily Missouri Democrat*, quoted in Fleche, *Revolution of 1861*, 41.

41. Baron, "Abraham Lincoln and the German Immigrants," 88–89.

42. Tucker, "Political Leadership," 219–21; Baron, "Abraham Lincoln and the German Immigrants," 91, 200–205.

43. Tafel, *Cincinnati Germans in the Civil War*, 16.

44. Cassius Marcellus Clay, Letter to Cephas Brainerd, January 8, 1859, FHS. Frederick C. Luebke's collection of essays does much to trace the evolution of the debate, beginning with a discussion of the contributions of William Dodd and Donnal Smith, who unequivocally claimed the singular importance of the German vote in the West to Lincoln's victory. However, as Luebke outlines, these early studies' evidentiary reliance on German American sources were likely biased. Instead, using the tools of social history, Luebke points to studies using more quantifiable approaches. In Wisconsin, where the Republican Party embraced nativist elements, Joseph Schafer demonstrates that Germans largely remained in the Democratic fold, despite the claims of Carl Schurz. Similarly, citing nativism and temperance, George H. Daniels finds strong Democratic ties among the majority of Germans in Iowa. Ronald P. Formisano underlines a number of variables, including religion and class, that largely split the German vote in Michigan. See Luebke, *Ethnic Voters and the Election of Lincoln*, xi–xxii, 3, 7–8. See also Dodd, "Fight for the Northwest," 774–88; Smith, "Influence of the Foreign-Born," 1–15; Schafer, "Who Elected Lincoln?" 46–61; Daniels, "Immigrant Vote in the 1860 Election," 110–28; Formisano, "Ethnicity and Party in Michigan," 175–95. On a national level, despite continued support for Democratic candidates, Walter Kamphoefner and Wolfgang Helbich conclude that Germans "were still probably the social group that made the largest net shift away from the Democratic Party during the decade of the 1850s." Kamphoefner and Helbich, *Germans in the Civil War*, 4–5.

45. Monaghan, "Did Abraham Lincoln Receive the Illinois German Vote?" 65–66.

46. Bergquist, "People and Politics in Transition," 198, 210–16. On the German Catholic vote in Illinois, see Fehrenbacher, "Illinois Political Attitudes," 130–35.

47. Levine, *Spirit of 1848*, 250; Lipin, *Producers, Proletarians, and Politicians*, 114–20; Snepp, "Evansville's Channels of Trade," 325–91; Smith, *Borderland*

in the Civil War, 69; Gienapp, "Who Voted for Lincoln?" 67. On Indiana, see Kelso, "German-American Vote," and Elbert, "Southern Indiana Politics."

48. Levine, *Spirit of 1848*, 252; Efford, *German Immigrants, Race, and Citizenship*, 83–84; Kelso, "German-American Vote."

49. Smith, *Borderland in the Civil War*, 73, 65; Gienapp, "Who Voted for Lincoln?" 67.

50. Kamphoefner, "St. Louis Germans and the Republican Party," 75–76. Mallinckrodt, *History of Augusta*, 49.

51. *Missouri Republican*, October 20, 1860, quoted in Taylor, "Neither North nor South," 338.

52. *St. Charles Demokrat*, February 14, 1861.

53. Saalberg, "*Westliche Post* of St. Louis," 71. See also Taylor, "Neither North nor South," 359.

54. *Belleviller Zeitung*, quoted in Öfele, *German-Speaking Officers*, 1.

55. *Cincinnati Volksblatt*, April, 24, 1856; *Cairo City Gazette*, December 6, 1860, quoted in Stanley, "'Between Two Fires,'" 92, 94; *Charleston (MO) Courier*, December 21, 1860; Fleche, *Revolution of 1861*, 145. Matt Stanley explains, "Conservatives in southern Illinois, geographically, culturally, and politically the southernmost part of any free state, were even more openly southern" (94).

56. Meyer Friede speech, January 30, 1860, Friede Family Papers, 1849–1977, SHSM; Gustav Tafel, "Speech to Cincinnati Turners," 1070, Gustav Tafel Papers, CHLA.

57. *Belleviller Zeitung*, April 11, 1861.

5. The West's Most Loyal Unionists: Union, Emancipation, and German Soldiers' Motivations

1. In his memoirs, Heinrich Börnstein reasoned that German Americans "did not want the glorious and powerful union of the United States to turn from a great and strong nation into an array of independent and small states." Quoted in Öfele, *True Sons of the Republic*, 45.

2. August Horstmann, Letter to Family, June 16, 1862, quoted in Kamphoefner and Helbich, *Germans in the Civil War*, 122; Henry Voelkner, Letter to Family, April 13, 1862, Henry Voelkner Papers, SHSM.

3. *St. Charles Demokrat*, October 10, 1861, quoted in Mallinckrodt, *What They Thought*, 64.

4. Aaron Astor argues that conservative Unionists in the Border West held both the ideological and geographical middle ground and therefore denounced both Northern and Southern extremism. Astor, *Rebels on the Border*, 8–10.

5. Öfele, *True Sons of the Republic*, 69.

6. Josephine Kircher, Letter to Henry Kircher, June 4, 1861, Engelmann-Kircher Papers, ALPL.

7. Reinhart, *August Willich's Gallant Dutchmen*, 22–23.

8. Fleche, *Revolution of 1861*, 43.

9. Freitag, *Friedrich Hecker*, 220.

10. Bek, "Followers of Duden," Seventeenth Article, *Missouri Historical Review* 19 (October 1924): 124.

11. Kamphoefner and Helbich, *Germans in the Civil War,* xi; Engle, *Yankee Dutchmen*, 19.

12. Ural, *Civil War Citizens*, 1–2; Keller, *Chancellorsville and the Germans*, 24–25. Surveying the field of Civil War scholarship, Kamphoefner and Helbich cite the lack of German inclusion in standard histories such as Wiley's *The Life of Billy Yank*, Robertson's *Soldiers Blue and Gray*, and McPherson's *Battle Cry of Freedom*. Kamphoefner and Helbich, *Germans in the Civil War,* xxx–xxxiii.

13. Kamphoefner and Helbich, *Germans in the Civil War*, xiii, 26. Although 24 percent of the Union army consisted of foreign-born soldiers, they made up only 8 percent of James McPherson's letter writers in *What They Fought For*, a paucity McPherson acknowledges. From McPherson's sample, "67 percent voiced simple but strong patriotic convictions and 40 percent went further, expressing ideological purposes such as liberty and democracy." McPherson, *What They Fought For*, 35. In a separate essay, Helbich concludes, "On the grounds of simple plausibility I claim that people who have no alternative to manual labor and who cannot find any work at all, and who also have a very different cultural background and know little about America, would be rather unlikely to write declarations of American patriotism." Helbich's conclusions are based on a sample of 36 German soldiers. He finds that German officers (sample of 9) matched their American counterparts in terms of patriotic expression, but German enlisted men registered at a far lower number—3 of 27. Questions arise, however, when comparing Helbich's sample size of 36 soldiers with McPherson's 562. Helbich, "German-Born Union Soldiers," 308–11. Martin W. Öfele concludes that "the degree to which German and other immigrant soldiers were motivated by patriotism as opposed to the mere desire for adventure monetary rewards is not clear." Öfele, *German-Speaking Officers*, 15.

14. *St. Charles Demokrat*, April 10, 1862, quoted in Mallinckrodt, *What They Thought*, 4.

15. Kamphoefner and Helbich, *Germans in the Civil War,* xi; Tafel, *Cincinnati Germans in the Civil War*, 3, 25–27; McMurtry, "Lincoln Visited by a German Delegation," 2; Öfele, *True Sons of the Republic,* 34. See also Miller, "Contribution of the German Immigrants," 466–69.

16. Hofmann, "Turners' Loyalty for Their New Home Country," 156.

17. Barnett, "August Willich," 60.

18. Keller, *Chancellorsville and the Germans*, 28.

19. Engle, *Yankee Dutchmen*, 29.

20. Kamphoefner and Helbich, *Germans in the Civil War*, 8–9; Reinhart, *Two Germans in the Civil War*, xxix.

21. Nation, *At Home in the Hoosier Hills*, 199–204; Henry Reed, "Southern Slavery and Its Relations to Northern Industry," Catholic Institute of Cincinnati, January 24, 1862, PAM 326 R324, CHLA.

22. Stanley, "'Between Two Fires,'" 3; Astor, *Rebels on the Border*, 43–50. See also Etcheson, *Emerging Midwest.*

23. Kautz, "Fodder for Cannon," 48.

24. On the problems of assuming feelings toward the war based on religion, see Kamphoefner, "German-Americans and Civil War Politics," 232–46.

25. Stanley, "'Between Two Fires,'" 96; Kautz, "Fodder for Cannon," 40.

26. Lang, "Germans of Dubois County," 229–48; Christina Katterhenry, Letter to Relatives, November 25, 1861, SC 0896, IHS.

27. Lause, *Price's Lost Campaign*, 133.

28. Albright Koehler Diary, May 18, 1862, SC 875, ALPL.

29. Frederick Heuring Journal, November 2, 1861, M 590, IHS; Adolf Engelmann, clipping, December 16, 1861, Engelmann-Kircher Papers, ALPL; Friedrich August Braeutigam (Braütigam) Diary, August 13, October 5, 1862, ALPL. Adolf Engelmann served at the time as the lieutenant colonel of the 43rd Illinois Infantry.

30. McPherson, *For Cause and Comrades*, 24; Balzer Grebe, "Autobiography and Civil War Diary of Balzer Grebe, 2nd Lieutenant, 14th Illinois Regiment, United States Infantry," SC 2681 ALPL; Amalie Rückels, Letter to Regina Kessel, January 27, 1862, quoted in Kamphoefner and Helbich, *Germans in the Civil War*, 389–90.

31. Holtmann, *Lost American Dream*, 40–44, 62.

32. Schramm Family Papers, August Schramm Diary, May 29, 1861, M 0248, BV 1736–38, BV 2107–8, F 0286–92, IHS; Eduard Ochsner, Letter to Brother, January 1862, Eduard Ochsner Letters, Lilly Library; Stephen Werly Diary, 1862–64, Missouri History Museum Library (hereafter cited as MHML); Engle, *Yankee Dutchman*, 56–57.

33. Reinhart, *August Willich's Gallant Dutchmen*, 52. See also Barnett, "Willich's Thirty-Second Indiana Volunteers," 48–70; Peake, *Indiana's German Sons.*

34. Reinhart, *August Willich's Gallant Dutchmen*, 28–29, 93, 96.

35. Mallinckrodt, *What They Thought*, 331, 334.

36. Astor explains that conditional Unionists "felt that the perpetuation of the Union was the only way to preserve the slave-based social order." Astor, *Rebels on the Border*, 4.

37. Guelzo, *Lincoln's Emancipation Proclamation*, 33; Astor, *Rebels on the Border*, 94–120; Stanley, "'Between Two Fires,'" 124.

38. Anton Herman Bullenhaar, Letter to Family in Germany, quoted in Kamphoefner and Helbich, *Germans in the Civil War*, 373; Nagel, "German Forty-Eighters' Critique," 61; Karl Adolph Frick, Letters to Parents, 1861 (n.d.), May 11, 1862, quoted in Kamphoefner and Helbich, *Germans in the Civil War*, 350; *Anzeiger des Westens*, November 6, 1861, quoted in Anderson, "German Americans, African Americans," 289.

39. *Anzeiger des Westens*, September 4, 1861, quoted in Rowan, *Germans for a Free Missouri*, 284. See also Gerteis, *Civil War St. Louis*, 136–41. On Frémont, see also Nevins, *Frémont*; Arenson, *Great Heart of the Republic*, 120–21.

40. On Frémont's conflict with the city's Unionist leaders and his dependency on German support, see Gerteis, *Civil War St. Louis*, 142–44, 147; Öfele, *German-Speaking Officers*, 13. On the outbreak of guerrilla warfare in Missouri, see Fellman, *Inside War*.

41. *Anzeiger des Westens*, August 28, 1861, quoted in Rowan, *Germans for a Free Missouri*, 278–79.

42. Guelzo, *Lincoln's Emancipation Proclamation*, 49–50; Gerteis, *Civil War St. Louis*, 156–58.

43. *Anzeiger des Westens*, September 18, November 13, 1861, quoted in Rowan, *Germans for a Free Missouri*, 289.

44. Honeck, *We Are the Revolutionists*, 100–101. See also Bowman, *Lincoln and Citizens' Rights*, 67–68.

45. Henry Voelkner, Letter to Family, November 27, 1861, Henry Voelkner Papers, SHSM; Tucker, *Political Leadership*, 286. See also Anderson, "German Americans, African Americans," 205–14.

46. Anderson, "German Americans, African Americans," 192–96; Arenson, *Great Heart of the Republic*, 122; Tucker, *Political Leadership*, 286; LeChien, "Lyman Trumbull and Gustave Koerner," 29–30; Cole, "President Lincoln and the Illinois Radical Republicans," 422.

47. *Anzeiger des Westens*, March 2, 1862; Saalberg, "*Westliche Post* of St. Louis," 82; Tucker, *Political Leadership*, 260, 298; Öfele, *German-Speaking Officers*, 23.

48. Anderson, "German Americans, African Americans," 210.

49. *St. Charles Demokrat*, May 1, 1862, quoted in Mallinckrodt, *What They Thought*, 49.

50. For a detailed analysis of the 1862 state convention, see Parrish, *Missouri under Radical Rule*, 2–4; Gerteis, *Civil War St. Louis*, 264–65; Anderson, "German Americans, African Americans," 210.

51. One of the most prominent examples of this interpretation is Manning, *What This Cruel War Was Over*.

52. On conservative Unionism and opposition to abolition in the Lower North, see Stanley, "'Between Two Fires,'" 112–49. Astor describes those conservative Unionists in Missouri and Kentucky who opposed emancipation as "belated Confederates." Astor, *Rebels on the Border*, 90–120.

53. Henry Kircher Diary, September 2, 1862, entry, Engelmann-Kircher Papers, ALPL.

54. Magnus Brucker, Letter to Wife, September 10, 1862, M0324, Magnus Brucker Letters, IHS.

55. Guelzo, *Lincoln's Emancipation Proclamation*, 123–25; Smith, *Borderland in the Civil War*, 338. See also Bigham, *On Jordan's Banks*.

56. *Anzeiger des Westens,* October 1, 1862, quoted in Anderson, "German Americans, African Americans," 208.

57. *St. Charles Demokrat*, October 30, 1862, quoted in Mallinckrodt, *History of Augusta*, 81.

58. Adolf Engelmann, Letter to Father, December 16, 1862, Engelmann-Kircher Papers, ALPL.

59. Friedrich August Braeutigam (Braütigam), Letters to Family, January 3, 4, 1863, ALPL.

60. Kamphoefner and Helbich, *Germans in the Civil War*, 350.

61. Frederick A. Heuring Journal, December 21, 1862, M 590, IHS.

62. *St. Charles Demokrat*, December 14, 1862, quoted in Mallinckrodt, *History of Augusta*, 92, 85.

63. Lause, *Race and Radicalism*, 4.

64. Stampp, *Indiana Politics during the Civil War*, 151–52; Nation, *At Home in the Hoosier Hills*, 206, 210–16; William Hofmann, Letter to Family in Germany, September 3, 1862, William Hofmann Papers, SC 1995, IHS.

65. *Cincinnati Volksfreund,* July 4, 1862, quoted in Holtmann, *Lost American Dream*, 45–47.

66. *Belleviller Volksblatt*, quoted in Schick, "'For God, Mac, and Country,'" 123.

67. Louis Houck, "Some Reminiscences of Louis Houck," 4–8, 121, Special Collections and Archives, Southeast Missouri State University; Rhodes, *Missouri Railroad Pioneer*, 7–10, 15.

68. *Cincinnati Volksfreund*, May 20, 1863, quoted in Reinhart, *August Willich's Gallant Dutchmen*, 142–43.

69. Kamphoefner and Helbich, *Germans in the Civil War*, 362.

70. Adolf Engelmann, Letter to Father, February 2, 1863, Engelmann-Kircher Papers, ALPL.

6. Rebel Bushwhackers and the "Damned Dutch": Radical Germans and the Deeper Roots of Missouri's Guerrilla War

1. Hildebrand's status was discussed in the *St. Louis Republican*, August 29, 1863; *Perryville (MO) Union*, July 17, 1863. Ironically, according to Hildebrand, his ancestors included German-speaking Bavarians who, after a brief stay in the Netherlands, came to Pennsylvania in the seventeenth century. Quickly, though, he emphasizes the family's transition to "literally a race of backwoodsmen" and rugged Missouri pioneers and never mentions his ancestry again. Ross, *Autobiography of Samuel S. Hildebrand*, 3.

2. Ross, *Autobiography of Samuel S. Hildebrand*, 78–79, 103, 108. As Hildebrand was illiterate, his autobiography was ghostwritten and edited by James W. Evans and A. Wendell Keith, M.D., in 1870 with the subtitle *The Renowned Missouri "Bushwhacker" and Unconquerable Rob Roy of America.*

3. Fellman, *Inside War*, xv, 252. Examining the psychological component of combat, Fellman's groundbreaking study argues that chaotic violence reflected the "battering and reshaping of moral structure." In *A Savage Conflict*, Daniel E. Sutherland largely adopts Fellman's model by avoiding ideological, political, and economic motivations.

4. Kamphoefner and Helbich, *Germans in the Civil War*, 9–10. Of the 10,730 Union volunteers in 1861, four-fifths were German. Total German enlistment in Missouri neared 31,000 in Union regiments, or roughly 36 percent. Faust, *German Element in the United States*, 1:523. See also Niven, "Role of German Volunteers in St. Louis," 29–30.

5. Hurt, *Agriculture and Slavery in Missouri's Little Dixie*, 127–30.

6. Ross, *Autobiography of Samuel S. Hildebrand*, 5. Henry C. Thompson, a journalist and amateur historian of southeast Missouri, wrote that Hildebrand's family originated in Hanover and arrived in northern Pennsylvania in 1680 but provides no source for his claim. Thompson, *Sam Hildebrand Rides Again*, 1.

7. Ross, *Autobiography of Samuel S. Hildebrand*, 6.

8. Thompson, *Sam Hildebrand Rides Again*, 2.

9. The role of the Southern yeoman is discussed in Ford, Origins of Southern Radicalism, and McCurry, Masters of Small Worlds.

10. Initially, studies that did exist were highly personal and carried considerable agendas, either hoping to romanticize and even celebrate the legend of

the "noble guerrilla" or seeking to demonize their exploits as those of immoral, evil men. On the construction of the "noble guerrilla," see Fellman, *Inside War*, 247; Hulbert, "Constructing Guerrilla Memory," 58–81. In "Sideshow No Longer," Daniel Sutherland traces the treatment of guerrilla warfare as a separate piece of Civil War historiography and the trend's recent reversal with the evolution of scholarship on guerrilla warfare. See also Beilein, "Household War."

11. Stiles, *Jesse James*, 80–86.

12. Beilein, "Guerrilla Shirt," 151, 154. On the role of women in guerrilla warfare, see Whites, "Tale of Three Kates," 73–94.

13. Bowen, "Guerrilla War in Western Missouri," 30–51; Geiger, "Indebtedness and the Origins of Guerrilla Violence," 49–52.

14. Michael Fellman argues that native-born, rural Missouri white people regarded Germans generally as "'nigger lovers' . . . foreign elements to be purged from the properly American community." Fellman, *Inside War*, 39, 70.

15. Ross, *Autobiography of Samuel S. Hildebrand*, 134.

16. Stephen Engle notes that Abraham Lincoln "recognized from the very beginning of the war that as a border state, Missouri's ethnic makeup made it much more complicated to deal with than Maryland or Western Virginia and just how important it was to capitalize on the Germans' loyalty to keep Missouri in the Union." Engle, *Yankee Dutchmen*, 34.

17. *Liberty Tribune*, June 29, 1860, quoted in Frizzell, *Independent Immigrants*, 92.

18. St. Charles County Historical Society Archives, Missouri State Cases, quoted in Mallinckrodt, *Freed Slaves*, 48, 21.

19. Friedrich Münch, "The State of Missouri: An Account with Special References to Immigration," translated by Elsa Nagel, 1859, SUN2462, SHSM.

20. Ibid.

21. On the early immigration to Missouri, see Hurt, "Seeking Fortune in the Promised Land," 4–19; Astor, *Rebels on the Border*, 15.

22. *Missouri Gazette and Advertiser*, October 26, 1816.

23. Levine, *Half Slave and Half Free*, 136–37; Mergenthal, "Border Lines," 107–14. See also Chambers, *Old Bullion Benton*. The free state of Maine was admitted to the Union simultaneously with Missouri's admittance to keep sectional balance in the U.S. Senate.

24. Reprinted in "Missouri History Not Found in Textbooks," 100–101; Kamphoefner, *Westfalians*, 108.

25. Göbel, *Länger Als Ein Menschen Leben in Missouri*, C1854, Gert Goebel Typescript, SHSM.

26. Bek, "Followers of Duden," Eighth Article, *Missouri Historical Review* 16 (April 1922): 343.

27. McMaster, *History of the People of the United States*, 372.

28. *Cape Girardeau (MO) Eagle*, September 14, 1855.

29. *Charleston (MO) Courier*, February 11, 1859.

30. Originally printed in the *Democrat* sometime in late May and reprinted in the *Charleston (MO) Courier*, June 7, 1861.

31. Joseph Cowgill Maple, "Incidents of the Campaign of 1861 in Southeast Missouri," 3–4, Cape Girardeau County Archive Center, Jackson, Missouri.

32. Ibid., 20–24. These Germans most likely belonged to Hecker's Regiment, the all-German 24th Illinois comprising Germans from both southern Illinois and southern Missouri.

33. Ibid., 28–31.

34. Lindsay W. Murdoch, "Narrative of the Service of Lindsay W. Murdoch in the War of the Rebellion, 1861–1865," Kent Library, Southeast Missouri State University.

35. Diary entry, ca. 1862, Charles F. Hinrichs Papers, 1862–1902, C0335, SHSM.

36. "The Swamp Fox," *St. Joseph Gazette*, April 13, 1919, M. Jeff Thompson Papers, WHMC. On M. Jeff Thompson, see McGhee, *Voices of the Swamp Fox Brigade.*

37. Frizzell, "Southern Identity in Nineteenth Century Missouri," 238–60. See also Hurt, *Agriculture and Slavery in Missouri's Little Dixie.*

38. Frizzell, *Independent Immigrants*, 54–56.

39. Walkenhorst, *Walkenhorst Homestead*, 13–15. This memoir, or "pen picture," consists of articles written by Walkenhorst in the *Concordian* describing his youth in Lafayette County. See also Burke, *On Slavery's Border.*

40. Walkenhorst, *Walkenhorst Homestead*, 15–21.

41. *Lexington Weekly Express*, January 7, 1860, quoted in Padberg, "German Ethnic Theatre in Missouri," 175n81.

42. *Westliche Post*, May 8, 1861, quoted in Rowan, *Germans for a Free Missouri*, 191–92.

43. Frizzell, *Independent Immigrants*, 97.

44. Louis A. Meyer, "Memoirs," Louis A. Meyer Papers, private collection; Frizzell, *Independent Immigrants*, 99–100; Frizzell, "Killed by Rebels," 369–95.

45. Meyer, "Memoirs."

46. Frizzell, *Independent Immigrants*, 99–105.

47. On mid-nineteenth-century St. Louis, see Arenson, *Great Heart of the Republic.*

48. Behlendorff, "Recollections of a Forty-Eighter," 327–31; John Buegel, Civil War Diary, 1861–1864, translated by William. G. Bek, C1844, WHMC.

49. Boernstein, *Memoirs of a Nobody*, 268–272; Arenson, *Great Heart of the Republic*, 113–16.

50. Phillips, *Missouri's Confederate*, 231–42.

51. Gerteis, *Civil War St. Louis*, 82; Freehling, *South vs. the South*, 55.

52. Rowan, *Germans for a Free Missouri*, 4. By 1860, the German population in the city had grown to 50,520, constituting 31 percent of the overall population. U.S. Bureau of the Census, *Population of the United States in 1860*, 29, 32, 299–300. See also Gerteis, *Civil War St. Louis*, 82.

53. Kaufmann, *Germans in the American Civil War*, 111.

54. Bull Family Papers, A123, Civil War Manuscript Collection, SHSM; Phillips, "Radical Crusade," 22–43; Winter, *Civil War in St. Louis*; Rowan, *Germans for a Free Missouri*, 143.

55. Buegel, Civil War Diary. For Lyon's role, see Phillips, *Damned Yankee.*

56. George Daniel Schuster, Civil War Memoir, Mss. A353, MHML; Kargau Collection, "St. Louis in Former Years," SHSM; Memoir, Loesch Family Papers, 3931, MHML; Buegel, Civil War Diary.

57. For a more detailed account of the events leading up to Camp Jackson, see Gerteis, *Civil War St. Louis*; for details on key military and political figures involved in Camp Jackson, see Phillips, "Radical Crusade," 22–43; for more details on the military aspect of Camp Jackson, scc Winter, *Civil War in St. Louis.*

58. Daniel M. Grissom Papers, C995, Vol. XXIX, 767, WHMC.

59. Hill, *Mrs. Hill's Journal*, 13; Winter, *Civil War in St. Louis*, 52–53.

60. Rombauer, *Union Cause in St. Louis in 1861*, 241; Buegel, Civil War Diary.

61. Heinrich Bornstein Memoir, "Seventy-Five Years in the Old and New World," 1884, 1054, SHSM, 166.

62. Arenson, *Great Heart of the Republic*, 112–15; *Evansville (IN) Daily Journal*, May 13, 1863.

63. Kaufmann, *Germans in the American Civil*, 108–9; Rowan, *Germans for a Free Missouri*, vii.

64. *Fayetteville (TN) Observer*, June 6, 1861.

65. Edward Conrad Smith resolves, "One is forced to the conclusion that [Camp Jackson] was a political blunder of the first magnitude, which occasioned inestimably more damage to the cause of the Union." While Smith is correct in regard to turning conditional Unionists in Missouri against the federal government, given the strategic importance of St. Louis, it was far more crucial to secure the city. Smith, *Borderland in the Civil War*, 221, 238.

66. *Missouri Republican*, quoted in Arenson, *Great Heart of the Republic*, 117.

67. Taylor, "Neither North nor South," 374; Siddali, *Missouri's War*, 68

68. Kaufmann, *Germans in the American Civil War*, 145; Öfele, *German-Speaking Officers*, 11. On Lincoln's approach to the Border West, see Phillips, "Lincoln's Grasp of War," 184–210.

69. Fellman, *Inside War*, 158.

70. Kamphoefner and Helbich, *Germans in the Civil War*, 345.

71. *Plaindealer*, February 28, 1862, quoted in Stepenoff, *From French Community to Missouri Town*, 66.

72. Münch's essay was originally published in the *St. Charles (MO) Demokrat*, quoted in Mallinckrodt, "Freed Slaves," 5. For more on Münch, see Muench, *Autobiography*; Tolzmann, "Far West," 5–10.

73. Bowman, "All Politics Are Local," 207–17; *Westliche Post*, January 29, 1863.

74. Mallinckrodt, "Freed Slaves," 5.

75. Mallinckrodt, *History of Augusta*, 102.

76. Ibid., 81.

77. *Westliche Post*, November 20, 1862.

78. *St. Charles (MO) Demokrat*, November 27, 1862, quoted in Mallinckrodt, *History of Augusta*, 83.

79. Phillips, "Hard-Line War," 1–2, 14–15.

80. Guelzo, *Lincoln's Emancipation Proclamation*, 45–46.

81. Phillips, "Hard-Line War," 21–22.

82. Astor, *Rebels on the Border*, 103.

83. *St. Louis Democrat*, quoted in Lause, *Price's Lost Campaign*, 124. For other examples, see ibid., 38, 61, 116, 140.

84. Lause, *Race and Radicalism*, 1; Lause, *Price's Lost Campaign*, 185.

85. Meyer, "Memoirs"; *Anzeiger des Westens*, October 21, 1864. In regard to the treatment of the German women, Frizzell concludes that rape and sexual abuse likely did occur. Frizzell, *Independent Immigrants*, 114–17.

86. Lause, *Race and Radicalism*, 6; Wood, *Two Civil War Battles of Newtonia*, 116–18.

87. Neely, "Quantrill Men Reunions," 243–57.

88. Fellman, *Inside War*, 70.

89. Mallinckrodt, "Freed Slaves," 43.

7. The Radical Turn: Abolition and the Crisis of German Liberalism

1. Christopher Phillips argues that the federal government's "hard war" truly began in these western states. See Phillips, "Lincoln's Grasp of War,"

184–210. Though Mark Grimsley contends that it did not begin until early 1864, he defines "hard war" as "deliberately or concomitantly subjecting the civilian population to the pressures of war." Grimsley, *Hard Hand of War*, 3–6.

2. Calhoun, *Roots of Radicalism*, 4.

3. On the Thirteenth Amendment, see Vorenberg, *Final Freedom*; Anderson, "German Americans, African Americans," 34–36; Parrish, *Missouri under Radical Rule*, 6–7; Honeck, *We Are the Revolutionists*, 71–103; Tucker, "Political Leadership." On the attraction of the Republican Party's free soil and free labor ideology, see Levine, *Spirit of 1848*; Efford, *German Immigrants, Race, and Citizenship*.

4. Augusta Kircher, Letter to Henry Kircher, September 8, 1862, Engelmann-Kircher Papers, ALPL.

5. *Westliche Post*, November 20, 1862, quoted in Mallinckrodt, *What They Thought*, 82.

6. Fellman, "Emancipation in Missouri," 42.

7. *St. Charles Demokrat*, November 27, 1862, quoted in Mallinckrodt, *History of Augusta*, 83–85.

8. Leonhard Tafel, Letter to Gustav Tafel, August 7, 1864, Gustav Tafel Papers, 1847–1994, 1070, CHLA.

9. Newspaper clipping, H. A. Rattermann, "Dr. Johan Friedrick Leonhard Tafel," *Der Deutsche Pionier* 9 (December 1880), ibid.

10. Benjaminson, "Regiment of Immigrants," 175.

11. Gallagher, *Union War*, 2, 40–44. Gallagher has recently argued that most Northern soldiers enlisted to save the Union, and therefore "the loyal citizenry initially gave little thought to emancipation." He notes that this was particularly true along the Middle Border. Gallagher, *Union War*, 2. For a detailed analysis of the lower North, see Stanley, "'Between Two Fires.'"

12. Marshall, *Creating a Confederate Kentucky*, 5–6, 10; Astor, *Rebels on the Border*, 120–50.

13. Guelzo, *Lincoln's Emancipation Proclamation*, 189. On the limits of the Emancipation Proclamation, see Voegeli, *Free but Not Equal*; Hess, *German in the Yankee Fatherland*, 119n25.

14. Adolf Engelmann, Letters to Wife, May 6, June 10, 1864, Engelmann-Kircher Papers, ALPL. Antiwar or Peace Democrats received the label of Copperheads after attaching the liberty heads from copper pennies onto their uniforms or clothing.

15. Stampp, *Indiana Politics during the Civil War*, 151–52.

16. *Evansville (IN) Enquirer*, February 14, 1862; Jaspin, *Buried in the Bitter Waters*, 15–30; Stanley, "'Between Two Fires,'" 117–20.

17. Klement, *Dark Lantern*; Weber, *Copperheads*.

18. Levine, *Spirit of 1848*, 260; Daniel Kreiling, Letter to Brother, August 8, 1863, S 453, Isaac Farver Letters, IHS.

19. Hess, "Obscurity of August Mersy," 127–38.

20. Magnus Brucker, Letter to Wife, September 18, 1864, M0324, Magnus Brucker Papers, IHS.

21. Friedrich August Braeutigam (Braütigam), Letter to Wife, February 15, 1863, Friedrich August Braeutigam (Braütigam) Papers, ALPL.

22. Adolf Engelmann, Letters to Wife, December 15, 1862, February 2, 1863, Engelmann-Kircher Papers, ALPL.

23. Frederick A. Heuring, Newspaper Clipping, *Evansville (IN) Daily Journal*, ca. 1862, and Journal Entry, January 20, 1863, M 590, Frederick Heuring Journal, IHS. "Butternuts" was a slang term for Confederates derived from the uniforms worn by poor soldiers who could not properly dye their clothing, but in this context it referred to Northerners who desired peace with the South.

24. Magnus Brucker, Letter to Wife, Sept. 18, 1864, M0324, Magnus Brucker Papers, IHS.

25. Karl Fülle, Letters to Julius Buechel, January 17, February 15, 1863, translated by Amy Scaffer, Julius Buechel Papers, MHML.

26. Kamphoefner and Helbich, *Germans in the Civil War*, 250–54.

27. Friedrich August Braeutigam (Braütigam), Letters to Wife, April 24, 26, 1863, ALPL.

28. After serving the first three months of the war in the Ninth Illinois, Henry Kircher crossed the Mississippi River in 1861 to join the Twelfth Missouri, a German regiment led by former Prussian Army officer Peter Osterhaus. For more background information on Kircher, see Hess, *German in the Yankee Fatherland*.

29. Henry Kircher, Letters to Father, March 2, April 19, 1863, Engelmann-Kircher Papers, ALPL.

30. Kronenberg, *Lives and Letters of an Immigrant Family*, 173–75.

31. Ibid., 179–80.

32. *Belleviller Volksblatt*, July 28, 1863, quoted in Schick, "'For God, Mac, and Country,'" 240.

33. Ibid., February 21, May 10, 1864. For background on Houck, see Rhodes, *Missouri Railroad Pioneer*. Alison Clark Efford notes that the *Neue Anzeiger*, Carl Dänzer's attempt to resurrect the *Anzeiger des Westens* as a conservative paper, did not enjoy much success and attracted only a small percentage of St. Louis's German readership. Efford, *German Immigrants, Race, and Citizenship*, 95.

34. Taylor, *Frontiers of Freedom*, 196–97.

35. Schick, "'For God, Mac, and Country,'" 123.

36. William Hofmann Papers, 1840–1888, SC 1995, IHS.

37. Levine, *Spirit of 1848*, 261.

38. Anderson, "German Americans, African Americans," 213, 225–26; Parrish, *Missouri under Radical Rule*, 4.

39. Mallinckrodt, *What They Thought*, 346.

40. Koerner, *Memoirs*, 2:410, 432.

41. Tucker, "Political Leadership," 310–11, 325; Nagler, "Lincoln-Fremont Debate," 157–78; *Mississippi Blätter* (weekly edition of the *Westliche Post*), April 10, 1864.

42. *Neue Zeit*, April 14, 1864, quoted in Mallinckrodt, *History of Augusta*, 112.

43. John G. Nicolay, Letter to President Lincoln, March 30, 1864, quoted in Burlingame, *With Lincoln in the White House*, 133.

44. Edward Bates, Diary Entry, June 10, 1864, in Beale, *Diary of Edward Bates*, 374–75.

45. Gerteis, *Civil War St. Louis*, 265; Tucker, "Political Leadership," 316–18; Nagler, "Lincoln-Fremont Debate," 170–75.

46. Gustave Koerner, Letter to William C. Flagg, September 1864, SC 876, Gustave Koerner Papers, ALPL.

47. Tucker, "Political Leadership," 329. Tucker notes that "not a single member of the *Dreissiger* or Forty-Eighter refugees of Illinois and Missouri made a useful contribution to Lincoln's 1864 campaign." Ibid.

48. Saalberg, "*Westliche Post* of St. Louis," 119.

49. McPherson, *Battle Cry of Freedom*, 775–56.

50. Benjaminson, "Regiment of Immigrants," 169.

51. Lipin, *Producers, Proletarians, and Politicians*, 124–29; Anderson, "German Americans, African Americans," 268. Lincoln won overwhelmingly in St. Charles County in Missouri, while Evansville's Germans gave a comfortable majority to both Lincoln and Indiana's Republican governor, Oliver Morton. In St. Louis, the heavily German first and second wards went over 70 percent for Lincoln.

52. Joseph Hotz, Letters to Family, May 13, 1863, September 5, November 8, 1864, M 0710, F 0079, IHS.

53. Anderson, "German Americans, African Americans," 215–17, 260; Gerteis, *Civil War St. Louis*, 281.

54. Parrish, *Missouri under Radical Rule*, 9; McKerley, "Citizens and Strangers," 77–78; Gerteis, *Civil War St. Louis*, 307–9.

55. Leonhard Tafel, Letters to Gustav Tafel, January 9, August 7, 1864, Gustav Tafel Papers, 1847–1994, 1070, CHLA.

8. "A Terrible Mistake Was Made": The Retreat of German Liberalism

1. Blight, *Race and Reunion.*

2. Efford, *German Immigrants, Race, and Citizenship*; Roediger, *Wages of Whiteness*; Ignatiev, *How the Irish Became White*; Jacobson, *Whiteness of a Different Color.*

3. Gerteis, *Civil War St. Louis*, 308–11.

4. Parrish, *Missouri under Radical Rule*; Arenson, *Great Heart of the Republic*, 155–56. On Missouri's road to emancipation, see Gerteis, "Legacy of the *Dred Scott* Case, 77–78.

5. Parrish, *Missouri under Radical Rule*, 6; Saalberg, "*Westliche Post* of St. Louis," 127–31. Charles Drake condemned alcohol on Sundays, citing "infidel Germans" and the "open lewdness of the beer garden and beer house." He went on to describe "the vulgar and obscene theatricals," where, he argued, "it is a matter of public notoriety that they are to large extent of the most obscene character, outraging decency and offending all our ideas of propriety and morality." *Lexington Weekly Express*, 1860, quoted in Padberg, "German Ethnic Theatre in Missouri, 175n82.

6. Benecke, *Historical Sketch*, 28.

7. Efford, *German Immigrants, Race, and Citizenship*, 96, 104–7; Arenson, *Great Heart of the Republic*, 157. Parrish notes that Drake's article regarding voter qualifications "went to extreme lengths in providing for 'rebel' disenfranchisement," including an oath requiring one to swear never to have engaged in any of the eighty-six acts of disloyalty. Parrish, *Missouri under Radical Rule*, 20, 27–28.

8. Parrish, *Missouri under Radical Rule*, 21, 27–29.

9. McKerley, "'We Promise to Use the Ballot as We Did the Bayonet,'" 217.

10. Efford, *German Immigrants, Race, and Citizenship*, 102. On Husmann, see Hooker, "George Husmann," 353–60; Gerteis, *Civil War St. Louis*, 312.

11. Parrish, *Missouri under Radical Rule*, 117.

12. Bruncken, *German Political Refugees*, 59.

13. *Anzeiger des Westens*, December 13, 1867, quoted in Tucker, "Political Leadership," 344, 346.

14. Parrish, *Missouri under Radical Rule*, 38, 45–46.

15. Frizzell, *Independent Immigrants*, 142; Efford, *German Immigrants, Race and Citizenship*, 113–14.

16. Parrish, *Missouri under Radical Rule*, 48, 103; Gerteis, *Civil War St. Louis*, 315.

17. Kamphoefner and Helbich, *Germans in the Civil War*, 346.

18. Bender, *Nation among Nations*, 178; Anderson, "German Americans, African Americans," 34–51. See also Barclay, *Liberal Republican Movement in Missouri.*

19. Efford, *German Immigrants, Race and Citizenship*, 9. See also Anderson, "German Americans, African Americans," 34–51; Barclay, *Liberal Republican Movement in Missouri.*

20. Freitag, *Friedrich Hecker*, 283, 286–87, 297.

21. Honeck, *We Are the Revolutionists*, 181.

22. Efford, *German Immigrants, Race, and Citizenship*, 171; Freitag, *Friedrich Hecker*, 263. On the Liberal Republicans and Reconstruction, see Slap, *Doom of Reconstruction.*

23. *Cape Girardeau (MO) Argus*, July 9, 1863, November 10, 1864.

24. Parrish, *Missouri under Radical Rule*, 17.

25. Efford, *German Immigrants, Race, and Citizenship*, 102; *Cape Girardeau (MO) Argus*, April 27, 1865.

26. *Cape Girardeau (MO) Argus*, March 30, 1871.

27. Ibid., October 1, 1868.

28. Parrish, *Missouri under Radical Rule*, 235–39, 258.

29. *Cape Girardeau (MO) Argus*, October 1, 1868.

30. Efford, *German Immigrants, Race and Citizenship*, 116; Freitag, *Friedrich Hecker*, 263. On Schurz, see Trefousse, *Carl Schurz.*

31. Foner, *Reconstruction*; Efford, *German Immigrants, Race, and Citizenship*, 4; Freitag, *Friedrich Hecker*, 27.

32. Honeck, *We Are the Revolutionists*, 175–77.

33. *Westliche Post*, September 14, 1865, quoted in Efford, *German Immigrants, Race, and Citizenship*, 127.

34. Lipin, *Producers, Proletarians, and Politicians*, 14–16, 105; Bigham, *We Ask Only a Fair Trial*, 16.

35. Lipin, *Producers, Proletarians, and Politicians*, 126–35.

36. Ibid., 113; Snepp, "Evansville's Channels of Trade," 325–91.

37. Bigham, *We Ask Only a Fair Trial*, 15–18.

38. Ibid., 27, 39.

39. Lipin, *Producers, Proletarians, and Politicians*, 112, 135–36.

40. Elliot, *History of Evansville and Vanderburgh County*, 297.

41. Friedrich August Braeutigam (Braütigam), Letters to Wife, April 24, 26, May 2, 4, 1863, ALPL.

42. Tucker, "Political Leadership," 345–46.

43. Freitag, *Friedrich Hecker*, 275.

44. William Hofmann, Letters to Family in Germany, June 22, 1866; November 14, 1874, SC 1995, William Hofmann Papers, IHS.

45. *Cape Girardeau (MO) Argus*, November 26, 1868.

46. Story reprinted in the *Cape Girardeau (MO) Bulletin*, June 27, 1968.

47. *Cape Girardeau (MO) Argus*, November 15, 1868.

48. Ibid., August 8, 18, 1870.

49. Öfele, *German-Speaking Officers*, 229; Jacobson, *Whiteness of a Different Color*, 68–90; Anderson, "German Americans, African Americans," 270.

50. Mallinckrodt, *What They Thought*, 381, 400.

Conclusion

1. *St. Charles (MO) Demokrat*, February 2, 1860, April 26, 1866, quoted in Mallinckrodt, *History of Augusta*, 38, 148.

2. *St. Charles (MO) Demokrat*, September 8, 1870, November 9, 1871, February 15, 1872, quoted in Mallinckrodt, *History of Augusta*, 214–15, 232, 238–39.

3. Pochmann, *New England Transcendentalism and St. Louis Hegelianism*, 13, 32–33.

4. Flower and Murphey, *History of Philosophy in America*, 1:494.

5. Efford, *German Immigrants, Race, and Citizenship*, 171.

6. Jewett, "Gustave Koerner and the Republican Party," 27.

7. *History of St. Clair County, Illinois*, 203; Freitag, *Friedrich Hecker*, 286.

8. *Missouri Cashbook*, July 10, 1872.

9. Kamphoefner, "'Auch unser Deutschland muss einmal frei warden,'" 96.

10. Kamphoefner, Helbich, and Sommer, *News from the Land of Freedom*, 160–62.

11. See Blight, *Race and Reunion*; Phillips, *Missouri's Confederate*; Astor, *Rebels on the Border*, 135–45; Marshall, *Creating a Confederate Kentucky*.

12. Parrish, *History of Missouri*, 324; Frizzell, *Independent Immigrants*, 143.

13. William Hofmann, Letter to Wife, November 14, 1874, William Hofmann Papers, SC 1995, IHS.

14. See Roediger, *Wages of Whiteness*; Anderson, "German Americans, African Americans," 42–43.

15. Honeck, *We Are the Revolutionists*, 94.

16. Efford, *German Immigrants, Race, and Citizenship*, 228. On the conflict between race and class in the labor movement in Cincinnati, see Ross, *Workers on the Edge*; Roediger, "'Not Only the Ruling Classes,'" 213–39.

17. Öfele, *German-Speaking Officers*, 231–34.

18. Tucker, "Political Leadership," 347.

19. Freitag, *Friedrich Hecker*, 286.

20. Astor, *Rebels on the Border*, 175.

21. Yater, *Two Hundred Years at the Fall of the Ohio*, 92–93.

22. Pauline Tafel (Mrs. Karl Tafel), "Out of My Life," New Port Kentucky, 1907, translated by Mary Konersam Tafel, 1939, A T124p, FHS.

BIBLIOGRAPHY

Primary Sources

UNPUBLISHED SOURCES

Abraham Lincoln Presidential Library (ALPL), Springfield, Illinois
- Albright Koehler Diary
- Balzer Grebe Autobiography
- Engelmann-Kircher Papers
- Ferdinand Ernst Papers
- Friedrich August Braeutigam (Braütigam) Diary

Cape Girardeau County Archive Center, Jackson, Missouri
- Joseph Cowgill Maple Typescript

Cincinnati History Library and Archives (CHLA), Cincinnati Museum Center, Cincinnati, Ohio
- Gustav Tafel Papers
- Mary Gertrude Kroger Papers
- Robert Tonnies, "A Brief Biography of Mary Gertrude Kroger, Nee Schlebbe"

Filson Historical Society (FHS), Louisville, Kentucky
- Cassius Marcellus Clay
- Humphrey Marshall Papers
- Speed Family Papers
- Pauline Tafel, "Out of My Life"

Indiana Historical Society (IHS), Indianapolis
- Albert Lange Papers
- Charles (Carl) Mayer Papers
- Frederick Heuring Journal
- Isaac Farver Letters
- Joseph Hotz Papers
- Magnus Brucker Papers
- Schramm Family Papers
- William H. Law and John Law Papers
- William Hofmann Papers

Indiana State Library, Indianapolis
- Bazil B. Edmonston Papers
- George Julian Papers

Kent Library, Special Collections and Archives, Southeast Missouri State University, Cape Girardeau
- Lindsay W. Murdoch Typescript
- Louis Houck, "Some Reminiscences of Louis Houck"

Lilly Library, Bloomington, Indiana
- Eduard Ochsner Letters
- Hamilton Smith Papers
- Indiana Cotton Mills Mss.

Missouri History Museum Library (MHML), St. Louis
- George Daniel Schuster Memoir
- Julius Buechel Papers
- Loesch Family Papers
- Stephen Werly Diary

Private Collection
- Louis A. Meyer Papers

State Historical Society of Missouri (SHSM), Columbia
- Bull Family Papers
- Charles F. Hinrichs Papers
- Eversmann Family Papers
- Friede Family Papers
- Friedrich Hecker Papers
- Friedrich Münch Papers
- Gert Goebel Typescript
- Gottfried Duden Typescript
- Gustav Koerner Papers
- Heinrich Bornstein Memoir
- Henry Voelkner Papers
- Kargau Collection
- William Henry Schrader Papers
- Siegmar Muehl Collection
- Solomon Eby Letters
- W. B. Napton Letters

Western Historical Manuscript Collection (WHMC), Columbia, Missouri
- Daniel M. Grissom Papers
- Edward Mühl Papers

John Buegel Diary
M. Jeff Thompson Papers

PRINTED SOURCES

Beale, Howard K., ed. *The Diary of Edward Bates, 1859–1866.* Washington: U.S. Government Printing Office, 1933.

Behlendorff, Frederick. "Recollections of a Forty-Eighter." In Goebel, *Jahrbuch*, 310–51.

Benecke, Louis. *Historical Sketch of the "Sixties" in Chariton County, Missouri.* Brunswick, MO, 1909.

Boernstein, Henry [Heinrich Börnstein]. *Memoirs of a Nobody: The Missouri Years of an Austrian Radical, 1849–1866.* Translated and edited by Steven Rowan. St. Louis: Missouri Historical Society Press, 1997.

Burlingame, Michael, ed. *With Lincoln in the White House: White House: Letters, Memoranda, and Other Writings of John G. Nicolay, 1860–1865.* Carbondale: Southern Illinois University Press, 2000.

Fritsch, William A. *German Settlers and Settlements in Indiana.* Evansville, IN: printed by the author, 1915.

Gilbert, Frank M. *History of the City of Evansville and Vanderburg County, Indiana.* Vol. 1. Chicago: Pioneer, 1910.

Goebel, Julius. *Jahrbuch der Deutsche-Amerikanischen Historischen Gesellschaft von Illinois*, vol. 15. Chicago: University of Chicago Press, 1916

Hess, Earl J., ed. *A German in the Yankee Fatherland: The Civil War Letters of Henry A. Kircher.* Kent, OH: Kent State University Press, 1983.

Hill, Sarah Jane Full. *Mrs. Hill's Journal: Civil War Reminiscences.* Edited by Mark M. Krug. Chicago: R. R. Donnelley, 1980.

History of St. Clair County, Illinois. Philadelphia: Brink, McDonough, 1881.

Holtmann, Antonius. *A Lost American Dream: Civil War Letters (1862/63) of Immigrant Theodor Heinrich Brandes in Historical Contexts.* Translated by Eberhard Reichmann. Indianapolis: Max Kade German-American Center, Indiana University–Purdue University Indianapolis and Indiana German Heritage Society, 2005.

Koerner, Gustave [Gustav Körner]. *An Illumination of Duden's Report on the Western States of North America: From the American Side.* Translated by Steven W. Rowan. St. Louis: University of Missouri, 2009.

———. *Memoirs of Gustave Koerner, 1809–1896: Life Sketches Written at the Suggestion of His Children.* 2 vols. Edited by Thomas J. McCormack. Cedar Rapids: Torch Press, 1909.

Krapf, Norbert, ed. *Finding the Grain: Pioneer German Journals and Letters from Dubois County, Indiana*. Indianapolis: Max Kade German-American Center, 1996.

Kronenberg, Kenneth, trans. and ed. *Lives and Letters of an Immigrant Family: The van Dreveldts' Experiences along the Missouri, 1844–1866*. Lincoln: University of Nebraska Press, 1998.

Mallinckrodt, Anita M., trans. and ed. *Freed Slaves: Ex-Slaves and Augusta, Missouri's Germans During and After the Civil War*. Augusta: Mallinckrodt Communications and Research, 1999.

———. *A History of Augusta, MO, and Its Area as Reported in the* St. Charles Demokrat. Vol. 1, *1850s–1860s*. Augusta, MO: Mallinckrodt Communications and Research, 1998.

———. *What They Thought: Missouri's German Immigrants Assess Their World, 1860s*. Vol. 2. St. Louis: Mallinckrodt Communications and Research, 1995.

McGhee, James E. *Voices of the Swamp Fox Brigade: Supplemental Letters, Orders and Documents of General M. Jeff Thompson's Command, 1861–1862*. Independence, MO: Two Trails, 1999.

Muench, Friedrich [Friedrich Münch]. *Autobiography of Friedrich Muench*. Translated by Ralph Godfrey. 1964. Reprint, Marthasville, MO: Three Pines, 2001.

Reemelin, Karl. *Life of Charles Reemelin, In German: Carl Gustav Rümelin, from 1814–1892*. Cincinnati: Weier and Daiker, 1892.

Reinhart, Joseph R., trans. and ed. *August Willich's Gallant Dutchmen: Civil War Letters from the 32nd Indiana Infantry*. Kent, OH: Kent State University Press, 2006.

———, trans. and ed. *Two Germans in the Civil War: The Diary of John Daeuble and the Letters of Gottfried Rentschler, 6th Kentucky Volunteer Infantry*. Knoxville: University of Tennessee Press, 2004.

Ross, Kirby, ed. *Autobiography of Samuel S. Hildebrand: The Renowned Missouri Bushwhacker*. Fayetteville: University of Arkansas Press, 2005.

Siddali, Silvana R., ed. *Missouri's War: The Civil War in Documents*. Athens: Ohio University Press, 2009.

U.S. Bureau of the Census. *Population of the United States in 1860*. Washington, DC: Government Printing Office, 1864.

Walkenhorst, William F. *The Walkenhorst Homestead*. Concordia, MO: *Concordian*, 1976.

NEWSPAPER AND PERIODICALS

Alton Freie Presse
Anzeiger des Westens
Belleviller Zeitung
Cape Girardeau (MO) Argus
Cape Girardeau (MO) Bulletin
Cape Girardeau (MO) Eagle
Charleston (MO) Courier
Cincinnati Volksfreund
Deutsche Tribüne
Evansville (IN) Daily Enquirer
Evansville (IN) Daily Journal
Evansville (IN) Gazette
Fayetteville (TN) Observer
Indianapolis Freie Presse
Louisville Daily Courier
Mississippi Blätter
Missouri Cashbook
Missouri Courier
Missouri Democrat
Missouri Gazette and Advertiser
Missouri Republican
Perryville (MO) Union
St. Charles (MO) Demokrat
St. Louis Commercial Bulletin
St. Louis Republican

Secondary Sources

BOOKS

Anbinder, Tyler. *Nativism and Slavery: The Northern Know-Nothings and the Politics of the 1850s.* New York: Oxford University Press, 1995.

Anderson, Benedict. *Imagined Communities: Reflections on the Origins and Spread of Nationalism.* New York: Verso, 1983.

Arenson, Adam. "Dred Scott versus the Dred Scott Case: The History and Memory of a Signal Moment in American Slavery, 1857–2007." In Finkelman, Konig, and Bracey, *The* Dred Scott *Case*, 25–48.

———. *The Great Heart of the Republic: St. Louis and the Cultural Civil War.* Cambridge, MA: Harvard University Press, 2011.

Arndt, Karl J. R., and May E. Olson. *German-American Newspapers and Periodicals, 1732–1955*. Heidelberg: Quelle and Meyer, 1961.

Aron, Stephen. *American Confluence: The Missouri Frontier from Borderland to Border State*. Bloomington: Indiana University Press, 2006.

Astor, Aaron. *Rebels on the Border: Civil War, Emancipation, and the Reconstruction of Kentucky and Missouri*. Baton Rouge: Louisiana State University Press, 2012.

Barclay, Thomas S. *The Liberal Republican Movement in Missouri*. Columbia: University of Missouri Press, 1926.

Barney, William. *The Road to Secession*. New York: Praeger, 1972.

Baron, Frank. *Abraham Lincoln and the German Immigrants: Turners and Forty-Eighters*. Lawrence: Society for German American Studied, 2012.

Beilein, Joseph M., Jr., and Matthew C. Hulbert, eds. *The Civil War Guerrilla: Unfolding the Black Flag in History, Memory, and Myth*. Lexington: University Press of Kentucky, 2015.

Beiser, Frederick C. *The Romantic Imperative: The Concept of Early German Romanticism*. Cambridge, MA: Harvard University Press, 2003.

Bek, William G. *The German Settlement Society of Philadelphia and Its Colony, Hermann, Missouri*. 1907. Reprint, Boston: American Press, 1984.

Bender, Thomas. *A Nation among Nations: America's Place in World History*. New York: Hill and Wang, 2006.

Bergquist, James M. "The Forty-Eighters and the Republican Convention of 1860." In Brancaforte, *German Forty-Eighters in the United States*, 141–56.

———. "People and Politics in Transition: The Illinois Germans, 1850–1860." In Luebke, *Ethnic Voters and the Election of Lincoln*, 196–226.

Berman, Antoine. *The Experience of the Foreign: Culture and Translation in Romantic Germany*. Albany: State University of New York Press, 1992.

Berry, Stephen. *Weirding the War: Stories from the Civil War's Ragged Edges*. Athens: University of Georgia Press, 2011.

Bigham, Darrel E. *On Jordan's Banks: Emancipation and Its Aftermath in the Ohio River Valley*. Lexington: University Press of Kentucky, 2005.

———. *We Ask Only a Fair Trial: A History of the Black Community of Evansville, Indiana*. Bloomington: Indiana University Press, 1987.

Billington, Ray A. *The Protestant Crusade, 1800–1860: A Study of the Origins of American Nativism*. Chicago: Quadrangle Books, 1938.

Blackbourn, David. *The Long Nineteenth Century: A History of Germany, 1780–1918*. New York: Oxford University Press, 1998.

Blight, David. *Race and Reunion: The Civil War in American Memory*. Cambridge, MA: Belknap Press of Harvard University Press, 2001.

Bowman, Dennis K. "All Politics Are Local: Emancipation in Missouri." In *Lincoln Emancipated*, edited by Brian R. Dirck, 207–17. Dekalb: Northern Illinois University Press, 2007.

———. *Lincoln and Citizens' Rights in Civil War Missouri.* Baton Rouge: Louisiana State University, 2011.

Brancaforte, Charlotte L., ed. *The German Forty-Eighters in the United States.* New York: Peter Lang, 1989.

Brose, E. D. *German History, 1789–1871: From the Holy Roman Empire to the Bismarckian Reich.* Oxford: Berghahn Books, 1997.

Bruncken, Ernest. *German Political Refugees in the United States during the Period from 1815–1860.* Milwaukee: Deutsch-Amerikanische Geschichtsblätter, 1904.

Bruford, W. H. *The German Tradition of Self-Cultivation: "Bildung" from Humboldt to Thomas Mann.* London: Cambridge University Press, 1975.

Burke, Diane Mutti. *On Slavery's Border: Missouri's Small Slaveholding Households, 1815–1865.* Athens: University of Georgia, 2010.

Calhoun, Craig. *The Roots of Radicalism: Tradition, the Public Sphere, and Early Nineteenth-Century Social Movements.* Chicago: University of Chicago Press, 2012.

Chambers, William Nisbet. *Old Bullion Benton: Senator from the New West.* Boston: Little, Brown, 1956.

Daniels, George H. "Immigrant Vote in the 1860 Election: The Case of Iowa." In Luebke, *Ethnic Voters and the Election of Lincoln*, 110–28.

Debow, J. D. B. *Statistical View of the United States* [. . .] *Compendium of the Seventh Census.* Washington, DC: A. O. P. Nicholson, 1854.

De Ruggiero, Guido. *The History of European Liberalism.* Translated by R. G. Collingwood. Boston: Beacon Press, 1959.

Dillon, Merton L. *Elijah P. Lovejoy, Abolitionist Editor.* Champaign-Urbana: University of Illinois Press, 1980.

Di Maio, Irene S. "Unity and Diversity in Friedrich Gerstäcker's Novels of North American Immigration." In *German? American? Literature? New Directions in German-American Studies*, edited by Winfried Fluck and Werner Sollors, 113–34. New York: Peter Lang, 2002.

Earle, Jonathan H. *Jacksonian Antislavery and the Politics of Free Soil, 1824–1854.* Chapel Hill: University of North Carolina Press, 2004.

Earle, Jonathan H., and Diane Mutti Burke, eds. *Bleeding Kansas, Bleeding Missouri: The Long Civil War on the Border.* Lawrence: University of Kansas Press, 2013.

Easton, Loyd D. *Hegel's First American Followers: The Ohio Hegelians: John B. Stallo, Peter Kaufmann, Moncure Conway, and August Willich, with Key Writings*. Athens: Ohio University Press, 1966.

Efford, Alison Clark. *German Immigrants, Race, and Citizenship in the Civil War Era*. New York: Cambridge University Press, 2013.

Elliot, Joseph P. *A History of Evansville and Vanderburgh County, Indiana*. Evansville, IN: Keller Print Company, 1897.

Engle, Stephen D. *Yankee Dutchman: The Life of Franz Sigel*. Fayetteville: University of Arkansas Press, 1993.

Etcheson, Nicole. *The Emerging Midwest: Upland Southerners and the Political Culture of the Old Northwest, 1787–1861*. Bloomington: Indiana University Press, 1996.

Faust, Albert Bernhardt. *The German Element in the United States: With Special Reference to Its Political, Moral, Social, and Educational Influence*. 2 vols. Boston: Houghton and Mifflin, 1909.

Fellman, Michael. *Inside War: The Guerrilla Conflict in Missouri during the American Civil War*. New York: Oxford University Press, 1989.

Finkelman, Paul, David Konig, and Christopher Bracey, eds. *The* Dred Scott *Case: Historical and Contemporary Perspectives on Race and Law*. Athens: Ohio University Press, 2010.

Fleche, Andre M. *The Revolution of 1861: The American Civil War in the Age of Nationalist Conflict*. Chapel Hill: University of North Carolina Press, 2012.

Flower, Elizabeth, and Murray G. Murphey. *A History of Philosophy in America*. 2 vols. New York: Capricorn Books, 1977.

Foner, Eric. *Free Soil, Free Labor, Free Men: The Ideology of the Republican Party before the Civil War*. New York: Oxford University Press, 1995.

Forbes, Robert Pierce. *The Missouri Compromise and Its Aftermath: Slavery and the Meaning of America*. Chapel Hill: University of North Carolina Press, 2007.

Ford, Lacy K. *Origins of Southern Radicalism: The South Carolina Upcountry, 1800–1860*. New York: Oxford University Press, 1988.

Formisano, Ronald P. "Ethnicity and Party in Michigan, 1854–1860." In Luebke, *Ethnic Voters and the Election of Lincoln*, 175–95.

Forster, Walter O. *Zion on the Mississippi: The Settlement of the Saxon Lutherans in Missouri, 1839–1841*. St. Louis: Concordia Publishing House, 1953.

Foulke, William Dudley. *Life and Works of Oliver P. Morton*. Indianapolis: Bowen-Merrill, 1899.

Freehling, William A. *The Road to Disunion*. Vol. 2, *Secessionists Triumphant, 1854–1861*. New York: Oxford University Press, 2007.

———. *The South vs. the South: How Anti-Confederate Southerners Shaped the Course of the Civil War*. New York: Oxford University Press, 2001.

Freitag, Sabine. *Friedrich Hecker: Two Lives for Liberty*. Translated by Steven Rowan. St. Louis: St. Louis Mercantile Library, University of Missouri, 2006.

Frizzell, Robert W. *Independent Immigrants: A Settlement of Hanoverian Germans in Western Missouri*. Columbia: University of Missouri, 2007.

Gallagher, Gary W. *The Union War*. Cambridge, MA: Harvard University Press, 2011.

Gerteis, Louis S. *Civil War St. Louis*. Lawrence: University Press of Kansas, 2001.

———. "The Legacy of the *Dred Scott* Case: The Uncertain Course of Emancipation in Missouri." In Finkelman, Konig, and Bracey, *The* Dred Scott *Case*, 68–82. Athens: Ohio University Press, 2010.

Gienapp, William E. *Origins of the Republican Party, 1852–1856*. New York: Oxford University Press, 1987.

———. "Who Voted for Lincoln?" In *Abraham Lincoln and the American Political Tradition*, edited by John L. Thomas, 50–97. Amherst: University of Massachusetts, 1986.

Gordon, Lesley J., and John Inscoe, eds. *Inside the Confederate Nation: Essays in Honor of Emory M. Thomas*. Baton Rouge: Louisiana State University Press, 2005.

Grimsley, Mark. *The Hard Hand of War: Union Military Policy toward Southern Civilians, 1861–1865*. Cambridge: Cambridge University Press, 1995.

Grimstead, David. *American Mobbing, 1828–1861: Toward Civil War*. New York: Oxford University Press, 1998.

Guelzo, Allen C. *Lincoln: A Very Short Introduction*. New York: Oxford, 2009.

———. *Lincoln's Emancipation Proclamation: The End of Slavery in America*. New York: Simon and Schuster, 2004.

Hamerow, Theodore S. *Restoration, Revolution, Reaction: Economics and Politics in Germany, 1815–1871*. Princeton, NJ: Princeton University Press, 1958.

———. "The Two Worlds of the Forty-Eighters." In Brancaforte, *German Forty-Eighters in the United States*, 19–36.

Harris, James F. "The Arrival of the Europamude: Germans in America after 1848." In Brancaforte, *German Forty-Eighters in the United States*, 1–17.

Hawgood, John A. *The Tragedy of German-America: The Germans in the United States of America during the Nineteenth Century and After*. New York: G. P. Putnam, 1940.

Heideking, Jürgen. "Festive Culture and National Identity in America and Germany, 1760–1860." In Heideking and Henretta, *Republicanism and Liberalism*, 209–34.

Heideking, Jürgen, and James A. Henretta, eds. *Republicanism and Liberalism in America and the German States, 1750–1850*. Publications of the German Historical Institute. Cambridge: Cambridge University Press, 2002.

Helbich, Wolfgang. "German-Born Union Soldiers: Motivation, Ethnicity, and 'Americanization.'" In *German-American Immigration and Ethnicity in Comparative Perspective*, edited by Wolfgang Helbich and Walter D. Kamphoefner, 308–11. Madison, WI: Max Kade Institute for German-American Studies, 2004.

Honeck, Mischa. *We Are the Revolutionists: German Speaking Immigrants and American Abolitionists after 1848*. Athens: University of Georgia Press, 2011.

Howe, David Walker. *The Political Culture of the American Whigs*. Chicago: University of Chicago Press, 1984.

Hurt, R. Douglas. *Agriculture and Slavery in Missouri's Little Dixie*. Columbia: University of Missouri Press, 1992.

Ignatiev, Noel. *How the Irish Became White*. New York: Routledge, 2009.

Jacobson, Matthew Frye. *Whiteness of a Different Color: European Immigrants and the Alchemy of Race*. Cambridge, MA: Harvard University Press, 1999.

Jaspin, Elliot. *Buried in the Bitter Waters: The Hidden History of Racial Cleansing in America*. New York: Basic Books, 2007.

Kamphoefner, Walter. "'Auch unser Deutschland muss einmal frei warden': The Immigrant Civil War Experience as a Mirror on Political Conditions in Germany." In *Transatlantic Images and Perceptions: Germany and America Since 1776*, edited by David E. Barclay and Elisabeth Glaser-Schmidt, 87–108. New York: Cambridge Press, 1997.

———. *The Westfalians: From Germany to Missouri*. Princeton, NJ: Princeton University Press, 1987.

Kamphoefner, Walter D., and Wolfgang Helbich, eds. *Germans in the Civil War: The Letters They Wrote Home*. Translated by Susan Carter Vogel. Chapel Hill: University of North Carolina Press, 2006.

Kamphoefner, Walter D., Wolfgang Helbich, and Ulrike Sommer. *News from the Land of Freedom: German Immigrants Write Home*. Ithaca, NY: Cornell University Press, 1991.

Kaufmann, Wilhelm. *The Germans in the American Civil War, with a Biographical Directory*. Translated by Steven Rowan. Edited by Don Heinrich Tolzmann with Werner D. Mueller and Robert E. Ward. Carlisle: John Kallmann Publishers, 1999.

Keller, Christian B. *Chancellorsville and the Germans: Nativism, Ethnicity and Civil War Memory.* New York: Fordham University Press, 2007.

Kennedy, Joseph C. G. *Population of the United States in 1860; Compiled from the Original Returns of the Eighth Census* [. . .]. Washington, DC: Government Printing Office, 1864.

Klauprecht, Emil. *German Chronicle in the History of the Ohio Valley and Its Capital City, Cincinnati, in Particular.* Translated by Dale V. Lally Jr. Edited by Don Heinrich Tolzmann. Bowie, MD: Heritage Books, 1992.

Kleber, John E. ed. *The Encyclopedia of Louisville.* Lexington: University Press of Kentucky, 2001.

Klement, Frank L. *Dark Lanterns: Secret Political Societies, Conspiracies, and Treason Trials during the Civil War.* Baton Rouge: Louisiana State University Press, 1984.

Lamott, John Henry. *History of the Archdiocese of Cincinnati, 1821–1921.* New York: Frederick Pustet Company, 1921.

Lause, Mark A. *Price's Lost Campaign: The 1864 Invasion of Missouri.* Columbia: University of Missouri Press, 2011.

———. *Race and Radicalism in the Union Army.* Champaign: University of Illinois Press, 2009.

Levine, Bruce. *Half Slave and Half Free: The Roots of Civil War.* New York: Hill and Wang, 2005.

———. *The Spirit of 1848: German Immigrants, Labor Conflict, and the Coming of the Civil War.* Urbana: University of Illinois Press, 1992.

Lipin, Lawrence M. *Producers, Proletarians, and Politicians: Workers and Party Politics in Evansville and New Albany, Indiana, 1850–1887.* Chicago: University of Illinois, 1994.

Litwack, Leon. *North of Slavery: The Negro in the Free States, 1790–1860.* University of Chicago, 1961.

Luebke, Frederick C., ed. *Ethnic Voters and the Election of Lincoln.* Lincoln: University of Nebraska, 1971.

Manning, Chandra. *What This Cruel War Was Over: Soldiers, Slavery, and the Civil War.* New York: Alfred A. Knopf, 2007.

Marshall, Anne. *Creating a Confederate Kentucky: The Lost Cause and Civil War Memory in a Border State.* Chapel Hill: University of North Carolina Press, 2010.

McCurry, Stephanie. *Masters of Small Worlds: Yeoman Households, Gender Relations and the Political Culture of the Antebellum South Carolina Low Country.* New York: Oxford University Press, 1995.

McKerley, John W. "'We Promise to Use the Ballot as We Did the Bayonet': Black Suffrage Activism and the Limits of Loyalty in Reconstruction Missouri." In Earle and Burke, *Bleeding Kansas, Bleeding Missouri*, 205–24.

McMaster, John Bach. *A History of the People of the United States, from the Revolution to the Civil War.* Vol. 7, *1841–1850*. New York: D. Appleton and Company, 1914.

McPherson, James M. *Battle Cry of Freedom: The Civil War Era.* New York: Oxford University Press, 1988.

———. *For Cause and Comrades: Why Men Fought in the Civil War.* New York: Oxford University Press, 1997.

———. *What They Fought For, 1861–1865.* New York: Anchor Books, 1995.

Metzner, Henry. *A Brief History of the American Turnerbund.* Pittsburgh: National Executive Committee of the American Turnerbund, 1924.

Monaghan, Jay. *Civil War on the Western Border, 1854–1865.* Lincoln: University of Nebraska Press, 1955.

———. "Did Abraham Lincoln Receive the Illinois German Vote?" In Luebke, *Ethnic Voters and the Election of Lincoln*, 62–67.

Morrison, Michael A. *Slavery and the American West: The Eclipse of Manifest Destiny and the Coming of the Civil War.* Chapel Hill: North Carolina University Press, 1997.

Nagel, Daniel. "The German Forty-Eighters' Critique of the U.S. South, 1851–1860." In *The U.S. South and Europe: Transatlantic Relations in the Nineteenth and Twentieth Centuries*, edited by Cornelis A. van Minnen and Manfred Berg, 51–72. Lexington: University of Kentucky Press, 2013.

Nagler, Jörg. "The Lincoln-Fremont Debate and the Forty-Eighters." In Brancaforte, *German Forty-Eighters in the United States*, 157–78.

Nation, Richard F. *At Home in the Hoosier Hills: Agriculture, Politics, and Religion in Southern Indiana, 1810–1870.* Bloomington: Indiana University Press, 2005.

Neely, Jeremy. "The Quantrill Men Reunions." In Earle and Burke, *Bleeding Kansas, Bleeding Missouri*, 243–58.

Nevins, Allan. *Frémont: Pathmarker of the West.* 1939. Reprint, Lincoln: University of Nebraska Press, 1992.

Öfele, Martin W. *German-Speaking Officers in the U.S. Colored Troops, 1863–1867.* Gainesville: University of Florida Press, 2004.

———. *True Sons of the Republic: European Immigrants in the Union Army.* Westport, CT: Praeger.

Overdyke, W. Darrell. *The Know-Nothing Party in the South.* Baton Rouge: Louisiana State University Press, 1950.

Parrish, William E. *Frank Blair: Lincoln's Conservative.* Columbia: University of Missouri Press, 1998.

———. *A History of Missouri.* Vol. 3, *1860–1875.* Columbia: University of Missouri Press, 1971.

———. *Missouri under Radical Rule, 1865–1870.* Columbia: University of Missouri Press, 1965.

Peake, Michael A. *Indiana's German Sons: A History of the 1st German, 32nd Regiment Indiana Volunteer Infantry. Baptism of Fire: Rowlett's Station, 1861.* Indianapolis: Max Kade German-American Center, Indiana University–Purdue University Indianapolis and Indiana German Heritage Society, 1999.

Peterson, Brent O. *Popular Narratives and Ethnic Identity: Literature and Community in* Die Abendschule. Ithaca, NY: Cornell University Press 1991.

Phillips, Christopher. "'The Chrysalis State': Slavery, Confederate Identity, and the Creation of the Border South." In *Inside the Confederate Nation: Essays in Honor of Emory M. Thomas,* edited by John C. Inscoe and Lesley J. Gordon, 147–64. Baton Rouge: Louisiana State University Press, 2005.

———. *Damned Yankee: The Life of General Nathaniel Lyon.* Columbia: University of Missouri Press, 1990.

———. "The Hard-Line War: The Ideological Basis of Irregular Warfare in the Western Border States." In Beilein and Hulbert, *Civil War Guerrilla,* 13–41.

———. *Missouri's Confederate: Claiborne Fox Jackson and the Creation of Southern Identity in the Border West.* Columbia: University of Missouri Press, 2000.

———. *The Rivers Ran Backward: The Civil War and the Remaking of the American Middle Border.* New York: Oxford University Press, 2016.

Pochmann, Henry A. *New England Transcendentalism and St. Louis Hegelianism: Phases in the History of American Idealism.* Philadelphia: Carl Schurz Memorial Foundation, 1948.

Ponce, Peral T. "'The Noise of Democracy': The Lecompton Constitution in Congress and Kansas." In Earle and Burke, *Bleeding Kansas, Bleeding Missouri,* 81–96.

Potter, David Morris, and Don Edward Fehrenbacher. *The Impending Crisis, 1848–1861.* New York: Harper and Row, 1976.

Rattermann, H. A., and Gustav Philipp Körner. *Kentucky's German Pioneers: H. A. Rattermann's History*. Edited by Don Heinrich Tolzmann. Berwyn Heights: Heritage Books, 2001.

Rhodes, Joel P. *A Missouri Railroad Pioneer: The Life of Louis Houck*. Columbia: University of Missouri Press, 2008.

Roediger, David. *Wages of Whiteness: Race and the Making of the American Working Class*. London: Verso, 1991.

Rombauer, Robert J. *The Union Cause in St. Louis in 1861: An Historical Sketch*. St. Louis: Nixon-Jones Printing, 1909.

Roske, Ralph Joseph. *His Own Counsel: The Life and Times of Lyman Trumbull*. Reno: University of Nevada Press, 1979.

Ross, Steven Joseph. *Workers on the Edge: Work, Leisure, and Politics in Industrializing Cincinnati, 1788–1890*. Los Angeles: Figueroa Press, 2003.

Rowan, Steven W., trans. and ed. *Germans for a Free Missouri: Translations from the St. Louis Radical Press, 1857–1862*. Columbia: University of Missouri Press, 1983.

Schafer, Joseph. "Who Elected Lincoln?" In Luebke, *Ethnic Voters and the Election of Lincoln*, 46–61.

Schinnerer, Paul Otto. "Karl Heinzen, Reformer, Poet and Literary Critic." In Goebel, *Jahrbuch*, 84–144.

Sexton, Alexander. *The Rise and Fall of the White Republic: Class Politics and Mass Culture in Nineteenth-Century America*. New York: Verso, 1990.

Sheehan, James. *German Liberalism in the Nineteenth Century*. Chicago: University of Chicago Press, 1978.

Siemann, Wolfram. *The German Revolution of 1848–49*. Translated by Christine Banerji. New York: St. Martin's Press, 1985.

Simeone, James. *Democracy and Slavery in Frontier Illinois: The Bottomland Republic*. DeKalb: Northern Illinois University Press, 2000.

Slap, Andrew. *The Doom of Reconstruction: The Liberal Republicans in the Civil War Era*. New York: Fordham University Press, 2010.

Smith, Donnal V. "The Influence of the Foreign-Born of the Northwest in the Election of 1860." In Luebke, *Ethnic Voters and the Election of Lincoln*, 1–15.

Smith, Edward Conrad. *The Borderland in the Civil War*. New York: MacMillan, 1927.

Sperber, Jonathan. *Rhineland Radicals: The Democratic Movement of the Revolution of 1848–1849*. Princeton, NJ: Princeton University Press, 1991.

Stampp, Kenneth. *Indiana Politics during the Civil War*. Indianapolis: Indiana Historical Bureau, 1949.

Stepenoff, Bonnie. *From French Community to Missouri Town: Ste. Genevieve in the Nineteenth Century*. Columbia: University of Missouri Press, 2006.

Stierlin, Ludwig. *Der Staat Kentucky und die Stadt Louisville, mit besonderer Berücksichtigung des Deutschen Elementes*. Louisville, KY: *Louisville Anzeiger*, 1873.

Stiles, T. J. *Jesse James: Last Rebel of the Civil War*. New York: Alfred Knopf, 2002.

Sutherland, Daniel E. *A Savage Conflict: The Decisive Role of Guerrillas in the American Civil War*. Chapel Hill: University of North Carolina Press, 2009.

Tafel, Gustav. *The Cincinnati Germans in the Civil War*. Translated and edited by Don Heinrich Tolzmann. Milford: Little Miami Publishing, 2010.

Taylor, Nikki M. *Frontiers of Freedom: Cincinnati's Black Community, 1802–1868*. Athens: Ohio University Press, 2005.

Thompson, Henry C. *Sam Hildebrand Rides Again*. Reprint, Marceline, MO: Walsworth, 1992.

Thornbrough, Emma Lou. *Indiana in the Civil War Era, 1830–1880*. Indianapolis: Indiana Historical Society, 1965.

Towers, Frank. *The Urban South and the Coming of the Civil War*. Charlottesville: University of Virginia Press, 2004.

Trefousse, Hans Louis. *Carl Schurz: A Biography*. New York: Fordham University Press, 1998.

Ural, Susannah J., ed. *Civil War Citizens: Race, Ethnicity, and Identity in America's Bloodiest Conflict*. New York: New York University Press, 2010.

Van Minnen, Cornelis A., and Manfred Berg, eds. *The U.S. South and Europe: Transatlantic Relations in the Nineteenth and Twentieth Centuries*. Lexington: University Press of Kentucky, 2013.

Vick, Brian E. *Defining Germany: The 1848 Frankfurt Parliamentarians and National Identity*. Cambridge, MA: Harvard University Press, 2002.

Vierhaus, Rudolf. "'Wir nennen's Gemeinsinn' (We Call It Public Spirit): Republic and Republicanism in the German Political Discussion of the Nineteenth Century." In Heideking and Henretta, *Republicanism and Liberalism*, 21–32.

Voegeli, V. Jacque. *Free but Not Equal: The Midwest and the Negro during the Civil War*. Chicago: University of Chicago Press, 1967.

Vorenberg, Michael. *Final Freedom: The Civil War, the Abolition of Slavery, and the Thirteenth Amendment*. New York: Cambridge University Press, 2001.

Wade, Richard. *The Urban Frontier: The Rise of Western Cities, 1790–1830*. Urbana: University of Illinois Press, 1996.

Weber, Jennifer L. *Copperheads: The Rise and Fall of Lincoln's Opponents in the North.* New York: Oxford University Press, 2006.

Weber, Paul. *America in Imaginative German Literature in the First Half of the Nineteenth Century.* New York: Columbia University Press, 1926.

Whites, LeeAnn. "The Tale of Three Kates: Outlaw Women, Loyalty, and Missouri's Long Civil War." In Berry, *Weirding the War,* 73–94.

Whites, LeeAnn, and Alecia P. Long, eds. *Occupied Women: Gender, Military Occupation, and the American Civil War.* Baton Rouge: Louisiana State University Press, 2009.

Wilentz, Sean. *Chants Democratic: New York and the Rise of the American Working Class, 1788–1850.* New York: Oxford University Press, 1984.

Winter, William C. *The Civil War in St. Louis: A Guided Tour.* St. Louis: Missouri Historical Society Press, 1994.

Wittke, Carl. *Against the Current: The Life of Karl Heinzen, 1809–1880.* Chicago: University of Chicago Press, 1945.

———. *The German-Language Press in America.* Lexington: University of Kentucky Press, 1957.

———. *Refugees of Revolution: The German Forty-Eighters in America.* 1952. Reprint, Westport, CT: Greenwood Press, 1970.

Woellert, Dann. *Cincinnati Turner Societies: The Cradle of an American Movement.* Charleston, SC: History Press, 2012.

Wood, Larry. *The Two Civil War Battles of Newtonia.* Charleston, SC: History Press, 2010.

Wyman, Mark. *Immigrants in the Valley: Irish, Germans, and Americans in the Upper Mississippi Country, 1830–1860.* Chicago: Nelson-Hall, 1984.

Yater, George H. *Two Hundred Years at the Falls of the Ohio: A History of Louisville and Jefferson County.* Louisville: Heritage Corporation, 1979.

ARTICLES

Baldwin, Thomas P. "The Public Image of Germans in Louisville and in Jefferson County, Kentucky, 1840–1872." *Yearbook of German-American Studies* 29 (1994): 83–90.

Barnett, James. "August Willich: Soldier Extraordinary." *Bulletin of the Historical and Philosophical Society of Ohio* 20 (January 1962): 60–74.

———. "Willich's Thirty-Second Indiana Volunteers." *Cincinnati Historical Society Bulletin* 37 (Spring 1979): 48–70.

Bartel, Fred J. "The Institutional Influence of the German Element of the Population in Richmond, Indiana." *Wayne County Historical Society Papers* 1, no. 2 (1905).

Beilein, Joseph M., Jr. "The Guerrilla Shirt: A Labor of Love and the Style of Rebellion in Civil War Missouri." *Civil War History* 58 (June 2012): 151–79.

Bek, William G. "Followers of Duden," Fifth Article. *Missouri Historical Review* 15 (July 1921): 660–99.

———. "Followers of Duden," Eighth Article. *Missouri Historical Review* 16 (April 1922): 343–83.

———. "Followers of Duden," Twelfth Article. *Missouri Historical Review* 17 (July 1923): 479–504.

———. "Followers of Duden," Seventeenth Article. *Missouri Historical Review* 19 (October 1924): 114–29.

Benjaminson, Eric. "A Regiment of Immigrants: The 82nd Illinois Volunteer Infantry and the Letters of Captain Rudolph Mueller." *Journal of the Illinois State Historical Society* 94 (Summer 2001): 137–80.

Bowen, Don R. "Guerrilla War in Western Missouri, 1862–1865: Historical Extensions of the Relative Deprivation Hypothesis." *Comparative Studies in Society and History* 19 (January 1977): 30–51.

Bowman, Shearer Davis. "Antebellum Planters and *Vormärz* Junkers in Comparative Perspective." *American Historical Review* 85 (1980): 779–808.

Brand, Carl F. "History of the Know-Nothing Party in Indiana." *Indiana Magazine of History* 18 (1922): 47–81, 177–206, 266–306.

Cayton, Andrew R. L. "Artery and Border: The Ambiguous Development of the Ohio Valley in the Early Republic." *Ohio Valley History* 1 (Winter 2001): 19–26.

———. "'Going over the River': On the Making and Unmaking of Borders." *Filson* 6 (Winter 2006): 4–7.

Cole, A. C. "President Lincoln and the Illinois Radical Republicans." *Mississippi Valley Historical Review* 4 (March 1918): 417–36.

Dodd, William E. "The Fight for the Northwest, 1860." *American Historical Review* 16 (July 1911): 774–88.

Dunson, A. A. "Notes on the Missouri Germans on Slavery." *Missouri Historical Review* 3 (April 1965): 355–66.

Fellman, Michael. "Emancipation in Missouri." *Missouri Historical Review* 83 (October 1988): 36–56.

Frizzell, Robert. "Killed by Rebels: A Civil War Massacre and Its Aftermath." *Missouri Historical Review* 71 (July 1977): 369–95.

———. "Southern Identity in Nineteenth Century Missouri: Little Dixie's Slave-Majority Areas and the Transition to Midwestern Farming." *Missouri Historical Review* 99 (April 2005): 238–60.

Geiger, Mark. "Indebtedness and the Origins of Guerrilla Violence in Civil War Missouri." *Journal of Southern History* 75 (February 2009): 49–82.

Hansen, Marcus Lee. "The Revolutions of 1848 and the German Emigration." *Journal of Economic and Business History* 2 (August 1930): 630–58.

Herriott, Frank I. "The Conference in the Deutsches Haus, Chicago, May 14–15, 1860." *Transactions of the Illinois State Historical Society* 35 (1928): 101–91.

Hess, Earl J., "The Obscurity of August Mersy: A German-American in the Civil War." *Illinois Historical Journal* 79 (1986): 127–38.

Hofmann, Annette R. "The Turners' Loyalty for Their New Home Country: Their Engagement in the American Civil War." *International Journal of Sport* 12 (December 1995): 153–68.

Hooker, H. D. "George Husmann." *Missouri Historical Review* 23 (1929): 353–60.

Hubbart, Henry C. "'Pro-Southern' Influences in the Free West, 1840–1865." *Mississippi Valley Historical Review* 20 (June 1933): 45–62.

Hulbert, Matthew. "Constructing Guerrilla Memory: John Newman Edwards and Missouri's Irregular Lost Cause." *Journal of the Civil War Era* 2 (March 2012): 58–81.

Hurt, Douglas R. "Seeking Fortune in the Promised Land: Settling the Boon's Lick Country, 1808–1825." *Gateway Heritage* 13 (Summer 1992): 4–19.

Jewett, Thomas O. "Gustave Koerner and the Republican Party." *Journal of St. Clair County History* 32 (2003): 27–36.

Kamphoefner, Walter. "German-Americans and Civil War Politics: A Reconsideration of the Ethnocultural Thesis." *Civil War History* 37 (1991): 232–46.

———. "Immigrant Epistolary and Epistemology: On the Motivators and Mentality of Nineteenth Century German Immigrants." *Journal of American Ethnic History* 3 (Spring 2009): 34–54.

———. "Missouri Germans and the Cause of Union and Freedom." *Missouri Historical Review* 106 (April 2012): 115–36.

———. "St. Louis Germans and the Republican Party, 1848–1860." *Mid-America* 57 (April 1975): 69–88.

———. "Uprooted or Transplanted? Reflections on Patterns of German Immigration to Missouri." *Missouri Historical Review* 103 (January 2009): 71–89.

Keil, Hartmut. "Continuity and Change in the Transfer of Ideologies." Comment on Bruce Levine, "The Migration of Ideology and the Contested Meaning of Freedom: German Americans in the Mid-Nineteenth

Century," 21–24. Occasional Paper No. 7. Washington, DC: German Historical Institute, 1992.

Krause, Bonnie. "German Americans in the St. Louis Region, 1840–1860." *Missouri Historical Review* 83 (1989): 295–310.

Kuppers, James R., Karl M. Gabriel, and John Bidnar. "Beginning Anew: Immigrant Letters from Indiana." *Indiana Magazine of History* 95 (December 1999): 331–49.

Lang, Elfrieda. "Germans in Vanderburgh County, Indiana, before 1848." *Studies in Indiana German-Americana* 1 (1988): 1–13.

———. "The Germans of Dubois County, Their Newspapers, Their Politics, and Their Part in the Civil War." *Indiana Magazine of History* 42 (September 1946): 229–48.

———. "Some Characteristics of German Immigrants in Dubois County, Indiana." *Indiana Magazine of History* 42 (March 1946): 29–46.

LeChien, Jack W. "Lyman Trumbull and Gustave Koerner: Allies for Freedom." *Journal of St. Clair County History* 38 (2012–13): 7–31.

Mauer, Heinrich. "The Earlier German Nationalism in America." *American Journal of Sociology* 4 (January 1917): 521–28.

McCandless, Perry. "The Rise of Thomas H. Benton in Missouri Politics." *Missouri Historical Review* 50 (October 1955): 145–58.

McMurtry, R. Gerald. "Lincoln Visited by a German Delegation of Workingmen in Cincinnati, Ohio, February 12, 1861." *Lincoln Lore* 1575 (May 1969): 1–3.

Merkel, Benjamin C. "The Slavery Issue and the Political Decline of Thomas Hart Benton, 1846–1856." *Missouri Historical Review* 38 (July 1944): 388–407.

Miller, Eugene C. "The Contribution of the German Immigrants to the Union Cause in Kentucky." *Filson Club Historical Quarterly* 64 (October 1990): 466–69.

"Missouri History Not Found in Textbooks." *Missouri Historical Review* 27 (October 1932): 101–2.

Mittlebeeler, Emmet V. "The Aftermath of Louisville's Bloody Monday Election Riot of 1855." *Filson Club History Quarterly* 66 (1992): 197–219.

Morton, John D. "'High Wall and a Deep Ditch': Thomas Hart Benton and the Compromise of 1850. *Missouri Historical Review* 94 (October 1999): 1–24.

———. "'This Magnificent New World': Thomas Hart Benton's Westward Vision Reconsidered." *Missouri Historical Review* 90 (1996): 284–308.

Muehl, Siegmar. "Eduard Mühl, 1800–1854: Missouri Editor, Religious Free-Thinker, and Fighter for Human Rights." *Missouri Historical Review* 1 (October 1986): 18–36.

———. "Hermann's 'Free Men': 1850s German-American Religious Rationalism." *Missouri Historical Review* 4 (July 1991): 361–80.

Niven, Alexander C. "The Role of German Volunteers in St. Louis, 1861." *American-German Review* 28 (February–March 1962): 29–30.

O'Toole, William G., Jr., and Charles E. Aebersold. "Louisville's Bloody Monday Riots from a German Perspective." *Filson Club Quarterly* 70 (October 1996): 419–25.

Phillips, Christopher. "Lincoln's Grasp of War: Hard War and the Politics of Neutrality and Slavery in the Western Border States, 1861–1862." *Journal of the Civil War Era* 3 (June 2013): 184–210.

———. "The Radical Crusade: Blair, Lyon, and the Advent of the Civil War in Missouri." *Gateway Heritage* 10 (Spring 1990): 22–43.

Rattermann, H. A. "Die Pionier-Turngemeinde Amerika's." *Der Deutsche Pionier* 7 (May 1876): 178–82.

Roediger, David R. "'Not Only the Ruling Classes to Overcome, but Also the So-Called Mob': Class, Skill and Community in the St. Louis General Strike of 1877." *Journal of Social History* 19 (Winter 1985): 213–39.

Schneider, John C. "Riot and Reaction in St. Louis, 1854–1856." *Missouri Historical Review* 68 (January 74): 171–85.

Snepp, Daniel W. "Evansville's Channels of Trade and the Secession Movement, 1850–1865." *Indiana Historical Society Publications* 8 (1928): 325–91.

Stephenson, George M. "Nativism in the Forties and Fifties, with Special Reference to the Mississippi Valley." *Mississippi Valley Historical Review* 9 (December 1922): 186–202.

Stevens, Linda Walker. "The Making of a Superior Immigrant: George Husmann, 1837–1854." *Missouri Historical Review* 2 (January 1995): 119–38.

Sutherland, Daniel. "Sideshow No Longer: A Historiographical Review of the Guerrilla War." *Civil War History* 46 (March 2000): 5–23.

Tolzmann, Don Heinrich. "Far West: The Writings of Friedrich Muench." *Der Maibaum* 16 (2008): 5–10.

Zimmermann, Eduard. "Travels into Missouri in October, 1833." Translated by William Bek. *Missouri Historical Review* 1 (October 1914): 33–41.

THESES AND DISSERTATIONS

Anderson, Kristen. "German Americans, African Americans, and the Construction of Racial Identity in Nineteenth Century St. Louis, 1848–1872." PhD diss., University of Iowa, 2009.

Beilein, Joseph M. "Household War: Guerrilla-Men, Rebel Women, and Guerrilla Warfare in Civil War Missouri." PhD diss., University of Missouri, 2012.

Bergquist, James. "The Political Attitudes of the German Immigrant in Illinois, 1848–1860." PhD diss., Northwestern University, 1966.

Elbert, E. Duane. "Southern Indiana Politics on the Eve of the Civil War, 1858–1861." PhD diss., Indiana University, 1967.

Fehrenbacher, Don E. "Illinois Political Attitudes, 1854–61." PhD diss., University of Chicago, 1951.

Hörst, Corinna A., "'More Than Ordinary . . .': The Female Migration Experience of German Immigrant Women in Nineteenth Century Cincinnati," PhD diss., Miami University, 1998.

Kautz, Craig L. "Fodder for Cannon: Immigrant Perceptions of the Civil War—The Old Northwest." PhD diss., University of Nebraska, 1976.

Kellner, George H. "The German Element on the Urban Frontier: St. Louis, 1830–1860." PhD diss., University of Missouri, 1973.

Kelso, Thomas John. "The German-American Vote in the Election of 1860: The Case of Indiana with Supporting Data from Ohio." PhD diss., Ball State University, 1967.

Lammers, Matthew T. "Shaping a True German Identity: Narratives in Herman, Missouri, 1837–1857," PhD diss., University of Missouri, 2008.

McKerley, John. "Citizens and Strangers: The Politics of Race in Missouri from Slavery to the Era of Jim Crow." PhD diss., University of Iowa, 2008.

Mergenthal, Rebekah Myfanwy Kirstin. "Border Lines: The People of the Lower Missouri River Valley and the Expansion of the United States, 1803–1855." PhD diss., University of Chicago, 2008.

Merkel, Benjamin. "The Anti-Slavery Movement in Missouri, 1819–1865." PhD diss., Washington University, 1939.

Padberg, Daniel Lee. "German Ethnic Theatre in Missouri: Cultural Assimilation." PhD diss., Southern Illinois University, 1980.

Price, Charles B., Jr. "The Storm of Disunion over a Border State: Three Editors of Louisville in the Years of Indecision in Kentucky, 1860–1861." Master's thesis, Yale University, 1941.

Rockenbach, Stephen I. "'War upon Our Border': War and Society in Two Ohio Valley Communities." PhD diss., University of Cincinnati, 2005.

Saalberg, Harvey. "The *Westliche Post* of St. Louis: A Daily Newspaper for German-Americans, 1857–1938." PhD diss., University of Missouri, 1967.

Schick, Susanne Martha. "'For God, Mac, and Country': The Political Worlds of Midwestern Germans during the Civil War Era." PhD diss., University of Illinois at Urbana, 1994.

Stanley, Matthew E. "'Between Two Fires': War and Reunion in Middle America, 1860–1899." PhD diss., University of Cincinnati, 2013.

Stanton, Gary Ward. "Brought, Borrowed, or Bought: Sources and Utilization of Patterns of the Material Culture of German Immigrants in Southeastern Indiana, 1833–1860." PhD diss., University of Indiana, 1985.

Taylor, Holly Zumwalt. "Neither North nor South: Sectionalism, St. Louis Politics, and the Coming of the Civil War, 1846–1861." PhD diss., University of Texas, 2004.

Trexler, Harrison Anthony. "Slavery in Missouri, 1804–1865." PhD diss., Johns Hopkins, 1914.

Tucker, Marlin Timothy. "Political Leadership in the Illinois-Missouri German Community, 1836–1872." PhD diss., University of Illinois, 1968.

White, Joseph Michael. "Religion and Community: Cincinnati Germans, 1814–1870." PhD diss., University of Notre Dame, 1980.

INDEX

Page numbers in italics indicate illustrations.

Zachary Stuart Garrison received a PhD in history from the University of Cincinnati. He teaches history at Chaminade College Preparatory School in St. Louis, Missouri.